PERILOUS MOON

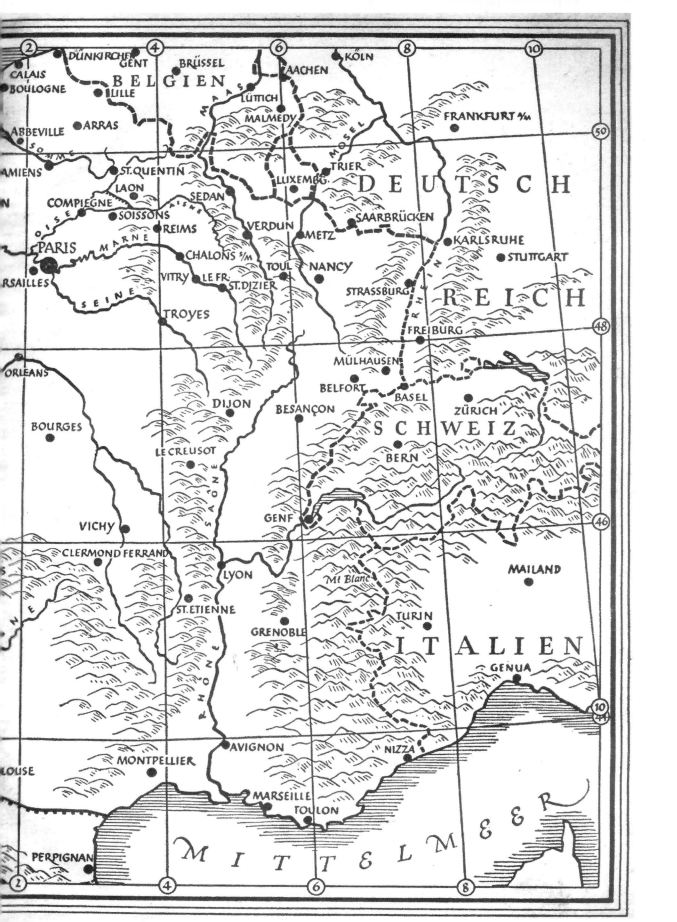

PERILOUS MOON

Occupied France, 1944—The End Game

BASED ON THE UNPUBLISHED MEMORIES OF
RAF BOMBER COMMAND PILOT FLT LT NEIL NIMMO DFC
AND THE ORIGINAL PERSONAL AND 3RD REICH PAPERS RELATING TO
LUFTWAFFE NJG 4 PILOT HPTM HELMUT BERGMANN RK

STUART NIMMO

CASEMATE
OXFORD AND PHILADELPHIA

Published in Great Britain and the United States of America in 2012 by
CASEMATE PUBLISHERS
10 Hythe Bridge Street, Oxford, OX1 2EW
and
908 Darby Road, Havertown, PA 19083

ISBN 978-1-61200-124-1
Digital Edition: ISBN 978-1-61200-136-4

Cataloging-in-publication data is available from the Library of Congress and the
British Library.

10 9 8 7 6 5 4 3 2 1

Printed and bound in the United States of America.

For a complete list of Casemate titles please contact:

CASEMATE PUBLISHERS (UK)
Telephone (01865) 241249, Fax (01865) 794449
E-mail: casemate-uk@casematepublishing.co.uk

CASEMATE PUBLISHERS (US)
Telephone (610) 853-9131, Fax (610) 853-9146
E-mail: casemate@casematepublishing.com

AUTHOR'S NOTE

The author asserts that all military, personal and historical photographs or artwork contained in this book showing emblems of the Third Reich that may emanate from, or reflect, the period between 1933 and 1945 are exclusively included for the reporting of actual historical events, or clarification of actual historical trends during that period in order to actively promote international understanding. They are particularly included for educational and research purposes and are offered in order to further civil enlightenment. Their inclusion is in full agreement with French and German law according to articles R645-186A and 86a and StGB. For the above reasons and for reasons of copyright, any copying or storage in whatever form, be it physical, electronic, or otherwise is strictly forbidden. The purchase, borrowing or loan of this book implies full acceptance of this condition of sale or temporary loan. Any misuse or misrepresentation of any of the material contained within in this book, expressly but not exclusively pertaining to unlawful propaganda or any form of incitement to hatred, will be dealt with accordingly.

COPYRIGHT NOTE

Every reasonable effort has been made to identify the copyright holders of material included in this publication. In case of error or omission, further information relating to rights will be very gratefully received. The publishers will willingly rectify any error in future editions.

All Bergmann images are from original photographs taken by Stuart Nimmo of the original documents at the owner's express invitation in relation to this work.

Enregistrées et protégées par la SCAD (La Société des Auteurs et Compositeurs Dramatiques).
SCAD Services et Conseills aux Auteurs
'Perilous Moon': Numéro d'enregistrement 234690

Cover photograph © Imperial War Museums, Ch 875.

'Every man is a creature of the age in which he lives, and few are able to raise themselves above the ideas of the time.'

Voltaire (1694–1778),
Essai sur les moeurs et l'esprit des nations, 1756

Our two protagonists in all their youth and innocence.
(Nimmo Collection/Bergmann Weitz Nimmo)

Contents

Self-portrait of
Neil Nimmo
taken in 1944
when he was
29 years old.
(Nimmo
Collection)

Dedicated to my father Neil, my French wife Dominique, our extended Anglo-French-American family, the crew of *Q-Queenie* and their families, and all those who resisted, or who still resist, tyranny and oppression.

Acknowledgements

Photograph of anonymous soldier taken in Rotterdam in September 1943. Acknowledgement is given to the many anonymous Axis combatants who unwittingly contributed to this book. Thankfully, they captured events as they unfolded. Whatever their personal leanings, an eye for an intriguing photograph has often proved useful. (3rdR UOPP, Nimmo Collection)

PARTICULAR THANKS AND GRATEFUL acknowledgement are due to Helmut Weitze of Helmut Weitze Military Antiques, Hamburg, Germany for his enthusiasm and generous invitation to make copies of his original Helmut Bergmann Group documents and photographs for publication in this book.

Grateful acknowledgement is also given to the following: Aircrew Association – Ann Sadler; RAF Commands – Joss Leclercq, Deny Alexander, Steve Gater, Floyd Williston, Steve Smith and Dom Howard; Escapelines.com – John Howes and Keith Jones; Axis History Forum – Colin Fraser, Henry L. deZeng IV, Russ Folsom and Bill Murray; 12 O'clock High – Chris Goss; Meteorological Office Records (UK & AXIS charts) – Joan Self; Mairie de Montlhéry – Caroline Bizouerne, Chargée du Patrimoine et de la Culture; In Canada – Dr Stephen Harris, Chief Military Historian, Andrzej Leszczewicz for research into WWII German maps and Jacqueline McDonald for research into WWII Allied maps; In Belgium – Vincent Bourguignon for research into French aircraft identification; In Paris – Alexandre Dupin, Marianne Careme, Joaquim Thomas-Pires and Gisela Moll of ORF France News; In Picardie – Jean-Claude robert; Swiss Embassy in London – Ursula Schneiter; Air Force Museum, Dübendorf, Switzerland – Elisabeth Bengzon and Max Kägi; Public Records Office, Kew; Hans H. Jucker, author of *Beiträge zur Schweizerischen und Deutschen Radargeschichte*; John Murray (Publishers) Ltd. and Ian Ousby for the quotes from his book *Occupation: The ordeal of France 1940–1944*.

For their particular support, I would like to thank my mother and father, Hilary and Neil Nimmo, my ever encouraging family and particularly my brothers Keith and Christian and my sister Kitty, my long-suffering wife Dominique and my children. For their confidence and encouragement, I owe great thanks to Tara Lichterman and Steve Smith at Casemate Publishing and to my indispensable and utterly indefatigable editor Anita Baker and gifted designer Ian Hughes. Others to whom I also owe great thanks are the generous Ian Drury, Paul Maxlow-Tomlinson, Torcuil Crichton, Noëlle Namia, Sandra Hewett, Arnie Wilson, Anthony Gustav Morris, Roger Rushton (English-proofreading.com) Gaston Dabronne, Philippe Welsh and to Isabelle Monod-Fontaine and Ambroise Monod, for their generous and open trust with their family history, including that of Maximilien Vox. Finally, I would like to thank Manfred, a good German friend who reminded me that 'it's much easier to be a hero in a democracy'. How true that was – and still is.

Introduction

WHEN FIRST 'HELPING' MY father Neil Nimmo to write this account of his unplanned stay in France, it was simply the case of a son pestering his 'old man' to write down an exciting, extraordinary tale. Neil had told it so well to us three sons – but just once. We'd been enthralled by such adventure, such danger; it beat Biggles or Dan Dare any day and the story stayed with us. However, I was too young to have appreciated how traumatic that period had actually been. I simply thought it was a great adventure story and didn't understand why it remained unwritten.

A highly detailed 3rd Reich Map published in 1940 prior to the invasion of France. (Veilhagen & Klasing, Nimmo Collection)

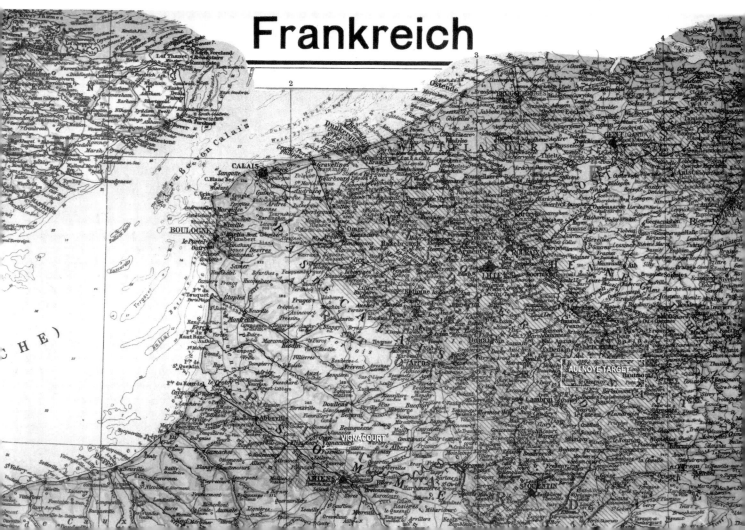

Frankreich

Years later I asked about writing it down again, more diplomatically I do hope. My father didn't say 'no', but again the idea seemed to just hang around. When my father eventually fell ill, we were to find out that in fact he had made fitful attempts to write, and yes, it really was on the backs of envelopes and so on. Despite considerable gaps, the core was there but he had become stuck on one episode – the attack on his Lancaster and the crash. He had written that chapter time and time again and clearly each time it had proven highly traumatic.

Neil asked my brother Keith to accompany him to France to revisit his trek south, and he became keen to try writing again. However, his illness (Parkinson's Disease) had really taken hold, and writing was impossible. Therefore, it seemed a very good project for us to tackle together – and so it was. Twenty years ago, just before he died, I thought we had finished and, as World War II's surviving actors dwindled and that period wafted into history, I simply compiled the account as an important piece of family history.

Once in a while, as new information appeared, I added a note or two. Then in December 2004, many years after my father's death, the beginnings of an intriguing parallel story began to unfold answering long abandoned questions. As it unravelled, the two accounts inevitably dovetailed making the tale all the more powerful, and the wider story cried out to be written. My father had been a much admired professional photographer and so I wanted to use that medium to help tell his story. The photographs I tracked down, and how and where I found them, led on to even more research and some great surprises. Some of the photographs I discovered are from Helmut Bergmann's own albums but many were privately taken by Axis combatants, and have only recently come to light.[1]

The canvas was now huge and as many historians have written so well on all aspects of the two world wars, it seemed a folly and a conceit to attempt the same. That fully admitted I've nevertheless been keen to put the wider story into context. For instance, I personally find it hard to imagine that in December 1903, just 40 years before the events covered in this book, the bicycle makers Orville and Wilbur Wright successfully flew the first airplane. It is also tragic to think that, in that belligerent period, someone immediately thought that this wonderful invention could be used to drop bombs on people.

By 1908, revolution and war were in the air and as empires flexed their young men's muscles, Dublin-born Alfred Harmsworth (Lord Northcliffe), founder and owner of *The Daily Mail* and owner of *The Times*, looked at the rundown British Navy and Army and at how aeroplanes were developing and he fretted. On 11 May 1908 he wrote to his friend Winston Churchill: 'We must be careful about aviation because Britain is no longer an island.'

Northcliffe saw to it that *The Daily Mail* was patriotic to a point. His popular paper stood, he said, 'For the Power, the Supremacy and the Greatness of the British Empire'. This struck a popular nationalist chord, although some accused him of warmongering.

Launching *The Daily Mail* race to be the first aviator to cross the English Channel, Northcliffe offered a massive £500 prize. Then, thinking again about the urgency – and doubtless his circulation figures – he made the prize a staggering £1,000. Ostensibly a sporting event, the race was also politically motivated. It appealed to the population as taking part would call for steely nerves, not to say certain recklessness as in those early days of primitive aviation a pilot could expect to fly for a total of 20 minutes before having a fatal crash.

Automobile headlamp manufacturer, Louis Blériot, flying his delicate, instrument, rudder, aileron and flap-free Blériot Eleven 'string bag' was the unlikely winner. Blériot had actually expected a fellow Frenchman (chain-smoking Hubert

Louis Blériot at Northfall Meadow just before he crash landed. (Bettmann/Corbis)

Latham) to win and seemed almost caught out when, on take-off, Latham's engine coughed and died marooning him on the Channel shoreline. Thus, Louis Blériot became a serious, if rather alarmed, contender for the £1,000 prize. As he drifted out across the Channel into history, Blériot was indeed brave. He had no concept of navigation and couldn't swim. Lost for a while, it was by luck rather than judgement that he spluttered down close to Dover Castle. As he ploughed the turf at Northfall Meadow it was already clear that navigation was key to successful flying.

Lord Northcliffe blazed Blériot's triumph across newspaper-selling headlines and the feat mesmerised the British public and the War Office. The clarion calls for more battleships died off. Aeroplanes were now 'the thing' and rapidly became war machines. Then Archduke Franz Ferdinand was shot. On Christmas Eve 1914, 12 years after The Wright brother's first flight and just six years after Blériot's historic Channel crossing, German pilot Lt Johannes (Hans) von Prondzynski dropped the first bomb on Britain. Like Blériot he only just missed Dover castle.

By October 1917 the Russian Revolution and the subsequent interest in communism that fired across Europe terrified and ignited the crumbling imperial powers. By 1918 World War I may have been over but the ensuing dangers, which should surely have been foreseen, were not. The rise of Communism across Germany and France, Germany's relentless humiliation

Louis Blériot. (Hulton-Deutsch Collection/Corbis)

by the Allies, the rise of fascism, the corrupt Weimar Republic, the 1929 Stock Market Crash and Germany's ruin were almost bound to lead to someone like Hitler being hailed as a saviour. As far as he was concerned World War I hadn't ended, it was simply halftime. Warning signs were little heeded and the Allies appeared to lose their foresight.[2] Many appear to have been so blinded by the depth of the Great Depression, by the political and military infighting or by general lethargy, that they couldn't gauge the urgency of the even greater storm building beyond their own frontiers.

In no time, by using various deceptions, Herman Göring (once the squadron leader of Von Richtofen's 'Flying Circus', who in the meantime had been working as a pilot for a Swedish airline) was now a senior Nazi and close to Hitler. Defying the ban on German rearmament, he was constructing what became the world's finest air force. This new Luftwaffe was to play a fearsome role during the early days of World War II.

As war machines, aeroplanes were a success. Bombs became bigger and ever more destructive and air forces became a strategic necessity of war. It says something about humanity's rapid progress that Orville Wright was alive to witness both jet-powered fighters and the atomic bombs being dropped on Japan at the end of World War II. In fact, on 28 August 1945 he wrote to Major Lester D. Gardner:

I once thought the airplane would end wars. I now wonder whether the airplanes and the Atomic bomb can do it. It seems that ambitious rulers will sacrifice the lives and property of all their people to gain a little personal fame.

This book is offered as the personal story of the pilots of two such war machines during a short period when their lives briefly crossed. While I've tried to remain open-minded and to understand how one of them became what he was, this may not make for comfortable reading at times. I've consulted expert and keen amateur historians, crosschecked and liberally drawn on information that I hope helps to put the following story into context (please see the Bibliography for further reference). I'm in awe of what it has been possible to discover and if anything I have written is incorrect, the fault will doubtless be mine.

Stuart Nimmo, Paris, August 2012

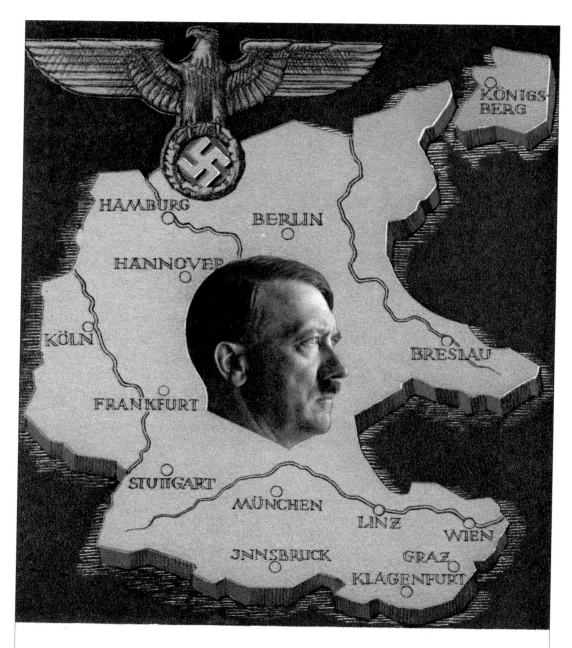

KÖNIGS-
BERG

HAMBURG

BERLIN

HANNOVER

KÖLN

BRESLAU

FRANKFURT

STUTTGART

MÜNCHEN

LINZ

WIEN

INNSBRUCK

GRAZ

KLAGENFURT

13·MÄRZ·1938
EIN VOLK EIN REICH
EIN FÜHRER

1 April 1944 – A Telegram for Breakfast

BY APRIL 1944, THE tide of war had, at last, turned against Germany. Hitler's armies had been driven from North Africa, were fighting a desperate rearguard action in Italy and, on the Eastern Front, were retreating along a line that stretched all the way from the Baltic to the Caspian Sea. In northern France and the Low Countries it was the lull before the storm. Here they waited for *Le grand débarquement* (the great assault), which they knew must come soon as combined Allied forces were poised to launch a great invasion from across the Channel. However, to aircrew of RAF Bomber Command, the picture looked very different. In the long and bitter winter of 1943/44 they had taken the most fearful hammering. For them it was a simple matter of survival.

The Grand Strategy had been to bring Germany to its knees by wiping out their main cities. However, it seemed to us that this had been a total failure. Not only had the RAF failed to destroy German morale, but they had lost more bombers than they could replace despite the Herculean efforts of the factories to produce more. The RAF was coming out of winter not only with fewer aircraft, but also with almost totally inexperienced aircrews.

During that icy winter of 1943/44, Berlin had been the main target. However, on those bitter, cold nights when the weather was clear enough for accurate bombing, headwinds blew from the east putting the German capital beyond range of RAF Lancasters and attention had been switched to targets nearer home.

Eight hundred or more Lancaster, Halifax and Stirling bombers would drag their loads of bombs across the dark skies and dump them on whichever German city (Essen, Mannheim, Bochum, Frankfurt, Hanover or Kassel) had been chosen for the full treatment that night.

The RAF casualties were horrendous. On the 16 raids on Berlin alone that winter, approximately 750 aircraft and 5,000 aircrew had failed to return. On raids nearer home, when the Luftwaffe night-fighters had less time to hunt down their prey, the loss rate was lower. However, over that winter as a whole, such were the losses that the total heavy bomber force of 1,000 aircraft was effectively wiped out. By mid-March 1944, there were few of the original aircrew left and none of the original aircraft.

As the nights grew shorter, the season for long-range raids drew to a

Original NSDAP party election propaganda from 1938. By March 1938 any self-respecting intelligence service knew exactly what was coming and in this election card Hitler spelled it out clearly. The large bite out of Germany is Czechoslovakia – Sudetenland, Bohemia and Slovakia. By 10 October 1938 Sudetenland was taken, Slovakia then broke away, and by March 1939 the remaining Czech lands had been captured. Poland would be the next target in the sights of this seemingly unstoppable juggernaut. (Nimmo Collection)

close. However, on the night of the 30/31 March 1944 one last, punitive attack was made on Nuremberg. It was the RAF's greatest disaster of the war. Of the 795 aircraft that set out, 94 failed to return, 12 crashed in England and a further 59 were seriously damaged. Such losses were unsustainable. The attacks on the German cities were abandoned and instead strikes were carried out against oil and rail targets in northern France in preparation for the coming Allied invasion. In the dark days that followed the Nuremberg raid, there was feverish activity throughout Bomber Command. Replacement aircraft were somehow cobbled together and flown to the depleted airfields – often by women pilots of the Air Transport Auxiliary. Hundreds of telegrams were despatched to the four corners of the British Isles summoning replacement aircrew to join their allotted squadrons.

Having spent the first years of the war as an RAF flying instructor in Calgary just east of the Canadian Rockies, I was recalled to Britain in early 1944 and was soon in the thick of it. I was on leave at home in Dulwich when one of those telegrams landed beside my breakfast plate. It was Saturday 1 April, April Fool's Day, and the very day when, to their horror, the Americans bombed Schaffhausen in neutral Switzerland, causing a shocking loss of life. With that and the Nuremberg raid, it had been a pretty desperate week for the Allies.

Regrettably, the telegram was no hoax and 48 hours later, as dawn broke over 101 Squadron Ludford Magna, I climbed shivering and stiff-jointed from under a damp and grubby blanket, in a damp and grubby Nissen Hut, on a cold and windswept airfield in a remote corner of Lincolnshire. I was just back in Europe and it was clear that battle experience was to come rather sooner than expected.

This is an account of a period of my life that began with the telegram and eventually ended just over a year later on VE Day (8 May 1945). Like all those on flying duties in the RAF who survived the war, I had much more than my share of luck. Had events not gone my way on very many occasions I would not have lived to tell this tale, nor would I have left children and grandchildren to tell it to. It is for you lot that I am recounting this so that you can see for yourselves how very nearly you never existed.

Neil Nimmo, Hove, 1992

Flying instructors Neil Nimmo (left) and Brian Blennerhassett in Calgary, Canada, in 1942. (Nimmo Collection)

CHAPTER 1
The Reluctant Hippopotamus

The Raid on Aulnoye-Aymeries 10/11 April 1944

I AWOKE THAT FIRST MORNING at Ludford Magna to the mournful screeches and bangs of wind battering through gaps in the corrugated Nissen hut. Over the next six days stormy spring weather settled in across northern Europe and all operations were 'scrubbed'. However, the urgency of the situation was palpable and, as was the tradition, we new members of 101 Squadron met, formed ourselves into crews and generally got things organised.

The moment the skies cleared, we flew two long night training sorties and then our first 101 operation to Villeneuve-St-Georges, just south of Paris (near what is now Orly Airport). It went without a hitch but we arrived back at Ludford Magna drained and exhausted.

We had not expected to fly the following night. However, by lunchtime on 10 April I knew that we were 'on the list' but we were too tired to care and knew that other crew felt much the same.

By mid-morning on 10 April, the ground crew were working flat out repairing the Lancasters, checking the replacement aircraft that had trickled in and loading and arming the aircraft. By 15:00 we were switching on, warming up and checking radio and radar sets.

That night there were to be three targets with 100 bombers on each and we were scheduled to be in the last wave to leave. Our battle-worn, but nevertheless magnificent, Lancaster III was SR-Q, or *Q-Queenie*, and was to prove a game bird in all senses. She wasn't old but she did not have that factory fresh smell to her and rather draped herself across the sky.

Q-Queenie had been delivered from the Woodford Manchester assembly line in October 1943 registered as DV288 'SR-D' and fitted with American (Detroit) Packard-built Rolls Royce Merlin engines. She'd already bombed Berlin several times, had been knocked about a bit and for some reason had been re-registered as 'SR-Q'.

Eleven nights previously *Q-Queenie* only just survived the desperate Nuremberg raid and spent much of the intervening time being swarmed over and patched up by ground crew. Roy Chadwick's Avro Lancasters were usually wonderfully responsive, solid and reliable aircraft that one felt somehow 'as one' with. However, *Q-Queenie* had been damaged and I suspect that something wasn't quite right with her airframe as she was not as responsive as she might have been. However, she was still a dependable Lancaster and needs must, so she was to go.

Five of *Q-Queenie*'s crew on that fateful night were on their first tour and they were: Flt Lt Neil D. Nimmo (pilot); FO Ernest Berchell (navigator); Sgt 'Jock' Alexander (flight engineer); Sgt Jim A. Tooley (wireless operator) and FO Peter Johnson (air bomber). The other two crew members, Sgt Eric J. Munslow (mid-upper gunner) and Sgt Geoff Stansfield (rear gunner), were both on their 35th operation.[1]

At the briefing we learned that our target would be the Aulnoye-Aymeries rail marshalling yards close to the Franco-Belgian frontier. It seemed to be nothing special – in the parlance of the day, 'a piece of cake'. Due to take off at 20:00, we donned copious layers of clothing as protection against the bitter cold found at altitude. We were eventually delayed until 22:00, by which time we were awash with saccharine, condensed milk, Benzedrine and caffeine – anything to stay awake.

We finally fired up the four Merlins and taxied to take-off. The shadowy, black shapes of other aircraft and a multitude of red, green and white navigation lights surrounded us. Then, all of a sudden, I saw an enormous vivid orange flash and felt, rather than heard, a bone-rattling thud. A Lancaster had swung on take-off and its fuel tanks had blown-up. We were instantly alert; death was quite literally waiting in the wings, 2,000 gallons of it.

Finally airborne by 23:20, we climbed to 1,000ft, where we slipped through the last layer of cloud to find that the moon had just risen and that we were in the midst of a brilliant, starlit night and a sea of other aircraft. The first part of the trip proved quite uneventful. We flew south, leaving the Sussex coast behind at Selsey Bill. As we crossed

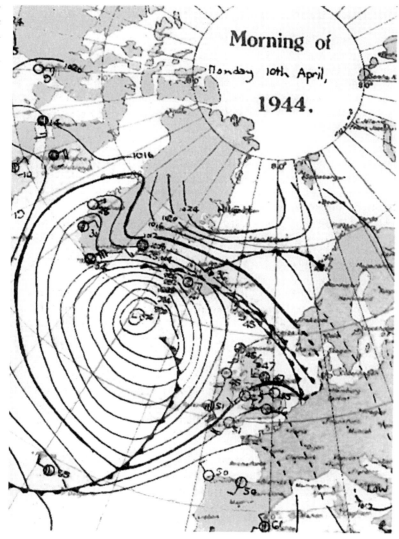

Met Office forecast for 10 April – extrapolated over occupied Europe. (Met Office)

Morning of Monday 10th April, 1944.

the channel, the cloud cover disappeared altogether – the visibility was perfect but our cover had completely gone. I kept on track and at around 01:20 crossed the French coast, keeping well clear of the German defences and trouble, or so I hoped. After about three hour's flying time my Canadian navigator, Ernest Berchell, announced that we were 15 minutes from the target. 'George' (the autopilot) was unplugged and the bombsight was connected, then time dragged. I flew on for what seemed to be an age before Berchell gave me the final approach co-ordinates and I swung north. 'One minute to go', said Berchell, and just as he said it the green target indicators cascaded down directly in front of us. Peter Johnson, the Australian bomb-aimer, called, 'Bomb doors open!' and then it all went wrong.

There were two leading Pathfinder Mosquito 'master-bombers' that night. I could hear them as they were dropping their marker flares and chatting on the radio: 'How's that one old man?' . . . 'Looks bloody miles away to me', came the reply. I cursed inwardly. We were right on course and within a minute would over-shoot the target. However, Peter said he could cope and to go for it anyway. If we were not given the final OK, I would have to orbit and come in again. However, the master-bomber rather reluctantly confirmed the run but it really wasn't our night. Peter triggered the bomb release but I didn't feel the expected upward lift as *Q-Queenie* shed her explosive weight. It didn't feel right and, sure enough, the bombs had failed to release. They were still all ours.

I decided to make another orbit, prompting groans from all except Peter, for whom I had much respect – we had flown together several times. He was a great chap, particularly good at his job. We were both determined to get a good photograph of our work that night. Bomber Command were increasingly keen on this as photographic analysis was key to judging the success of a raid.

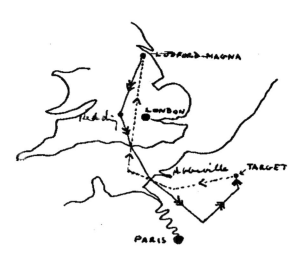

Flt Lt Neil Nimmo's diagram of his Ludford Magna to Aulnoye-Aymeries flight path. (Nimmo Collection)

While the second run went well enough, it put us too far behind the main stream for safety. Flying at just under 7,000ft, battle-scarred *Q-Queenie* wasn't crisp and seemed rather slow. It was a bit like flying a soggy pancake. Thus, the scene was set for disaster.

As the bomb doors closed, I rammed the Lancaster's throttles forward as far as the gate and swung into a steep left-hand turn onto a westerly heading. It was about 02:30 as we left the target and, with the four engines at maximum cruising revs, I set course for home.

We were heading for the narrow gap between the flak batteries around Amiens and those at Abbeville. At the pre-flight briefing the advice had been to 'avoid Abbeville, the gunners there are really hot stuff, and don't forget to watch out for night-fighters. We might as well have been told, 'and when you swim the Nile, don't forget the crocodiles!'

We were lagging behind and had little hope of overhauling the mainstream of bombers, now some 5 miles ahead of us. I knew that, as stragglers, we were extremely vulnerable. However, it did not occur to me that there was anything to be done other than to stick to the flight plan, fly accurately, and keep my eyes skinned for enemy fighters. A year later, when I was vastly more experienced, I think I would have stuffed the nose down and, at the highest permissible airspeed and the lowest possible altitude, got the hell out of there by the shortest route available.

However, if one had to fly straight and level, there couldn't have been a more beautiful night for it. The moon, full or nearly full, was high on the port side and shone out of a cloudless sky. A slight haze, of the kind that might be expected on the second night of an anticyclone, seemed to intensify the moon's brilliance and fill the air with light so that only the brightest stars were visible.

A mile below us lay the landscape of occupied France, drained of all colour except shades of indigo. I could make out the dark mosaic of woods and fields and, following a parallel path to our own, there were sharp stabs of light as, for an instant, the moon was mirrored in a stream or pond.

For safety's sake, we had made it a rule between us to keep the chat on the intercom to the minimum. The navigator and wireless operator, who were curtained off in their separate, lightproof cubbyholes, passed changes of course and the occasional weather report on to me. However, for long periods we flew in alert silence. Those of us with a view of the sky kept watch for enemy fighters, although we all knew that when an attack came it would most likely be from beneath, where our blind spot lay.[2] In all probability, the first I would know of it would be the desperate call of 'CORKSCREW!' from one or other of the gunners.

I rehearsed in my mind, as I had done over and over again, what my immediate and instinctive actions must be: full port (or starboard) aileron (wing-flap) and at the same instant a fierce, full opposite rudder, straight into a violent side-slip; forward with the control column (always turn towards the attacking aircraft) and then as the plane tried to go over on her back, reverse everything – full starboard aileron, full opposite rudder, the stick right back into my guts, then over to port again, always skidding, side-slipping in a way that would mean instant grounding at any flying school.

I would have to watch the airspeed, for we couldn't afford to stall and if exceeding 300mph we might not be able to pull out of a dive below 5,000ft. It was very hard work indeed, a bit like leading a reluctant hippopotamus into a tango. I only hoped that I could keep it up until we had lost the fighter or the pilot had gone for easier prey. In the event, it didn't happen like that at all. We had been flying for about 20 minutes, with no more than another ten to go before we would cross the coast.

I was beginning to wonder when, if ever, the action would begin when Jock, the flight engineer, touched my arm and pointed upwards. Way above us a cat's cradle of con-trails were drifting across the moon, which could only mean one thing – there were night-fighters up there waiting to be called into action. The crocodiles were sliding down the mud banks and into the water. It was truly chilling! My immediate thought (and to this day I can think of no other explanation) was that the enemy fighters had been orbiting. The navigator's voice called for a change of course to 285°: 'Just seven minutes 'till we cross the coast.'

Straight ahead of us two new planets had appeared in the sky. A bit larger than Jupiter, they hung, seemingly motionless, while to starboard lines of tracer shells streaked upwards in fast moving dotted lines converging at points peppered with sharp little flashes. It was the first time that I had seen tracer fire and flak.

My eyes came back to the two lights shining ahead. They puzzled me because we did not seem to be getting any closer to them. Surely, if they were magnesium flares, they would be whiter and brighter and grow bigger as we approached them? Then one swung slowly to the left, arched over and plummeted towards the ground, where it exploded in a ball of flame. I called to the navigator to make a note of the time the Lancaster, which had been about eight miles ahead of us, had hit the ground and then waited for the second one to go.[3]

The firework display from the Abbeville batteries was spectacular. It was not aimed at us yet but, if the cones of tracer fire meant anything, one or two unseen aircraft were taking a pasting. The sheer concentration of German light and firepower seemed limitless. It was a daunting, dreadful sight. Tearing my gaze away and looking up, the con-trails were no longer in the path of the moon but I didn't know whether that was good or bad news. The second Lancaster followed the first. 'Oh hell,' I thought, 'this is it. Anything can happen.' At least three more Lancasters were in trouble over Abbeville and to the north-east, where the German flak batteries were having a field day, it was a fearsome display.

By now we were approaching the area where the remains of the two Lancasters were burning on the ground, each making a scattered ring of fires. From above it looked like glowing ashes from a pipe that has been knocked out on the hearth. Suddenly, we all but flew into a parachute. For a moment the silk canopy was brightly lit in the moonlight and looked enormous. I quite clearly saw the airman swinging from its harness and as I instinctively banked to starboard it shot out of sight under our port wing. I called out to the navigator to log it and was checking the time with him when the mid-upper gunner interrupted shouting, 'Shut-up!' There was urgency in his voice, which clearly spelt danger and at that very moment I felt a thump through the controls – a 'bump' as if we had hit another aircraft's slipstream. Looking back at the starboard wing, I could see that the inner engine was on fire.

It was quite a small fire at first but it had to be extinguished quickly, otherwise it would attract the night-fighters, as blood attracts sharks. As I cut the engine I called the flight engineer to feather the prop and operate the Graviner button (fire extinguisher). I remember thinking, 'He is already doing it. We are coming up to the channel coast and if the fire doesn't go out we are in big trouble. What the hell do we do?'

'Better get the front hatch open Peter,' I called, 'just in case.' I called to Berchell for our position and estimated time of arrival at the coast. For some reason the fire wasn't going out and seemed to be spreading. The windmilling prop was making it hard to hold the aircraft straight and we were slowly yawing to starboard. 'We'll have to jump', I thought. First things first, I needed to get the aircraft to fly 'hands off'. I throttled back the other engines and wound the rudder-trim until the pressure on my left leg went and we were flying straight. At the same time, I trimmed back a shade until she held level flight. However, now we were heading directly towards the flak and the coastline. There were enemy fighters about and we were disastrously coned by searchlights – lit up like a Christmas tree.

Peter Johnson's voice came shakily over the intercom, 'I can't get the hatch open!' I heard a voice yell, 'Well *get* the bugger open!' It was mine. At that the navigator catapulted himself out of his compartment and tried to crash his way past Jock, the flight engineer, towards the escape hatch. A fight started and suddenly the whole thing was out of hand. As the navigator broke his way through and disappeared down the steps into the nose of the aircraft there was a breathless call from Peter – he had got the hatch open! I heard my voice call, 'Let's get the hell out of here', but the Canadian had already gone and I never did get my navigational fix.[4]

I called to the gunners and the wireless operator. There was no reply. Jock dived behind my seat and came up with my chest parachute and with great coolness he clipped it onto my harness. He then attached his own parachute, put his hand on mine and slithered down the steps and out of my life. I kept calling to the others at the back but there was no answer. How long I stayed there calling I can't begin to guess, it seemed like forever.

By now the flames had spread along the wing and were streaming back towards the tailplane. The cockpit was lit up like day. I felt incredibly lonely. All I could think was that the others must have gone. I undid my seat belt, disconnected my oxygen hose, yanked out the intercom jack plug and clambered out of the seat and down the steps. Then a nightmare situation developed – a real nightmare that I still have over and over again. I should have taken off my helmet with its oxygen hose and intercom lead before clipping on the parachute. The oxygen hose caught up in the internal structure and tied me to the aircraft. I couldn't free myself. I tore at it feverishly and for a dreadful timeless moment I thought I'd had it.

Q-Queenie began to go over on her back and the reverse 'G' forced me up against the roof of the compartment. I was floating, doubled up and tearing at the oxygen tube with all my strength. Suddenly, it broke free but I still couldn't get down to the gaping hole of the escape hatch. In my efforts to find handholds to force myself down, I turned right round so that I was facing the tail of the aircraft, and there at the entrance to the rear was Jim Tooley, the wireless operator. He too was forced up against the roof so that his head was bent over at a grotesque angle. Brightly lit by the flames, his face was drained of all colour. He was staring at me uncomprehendingly![5] Then, suddenly, like a champagne cork popping from the bottle, my feet were caught by the slipstream and with great force I was sucked out into the night.

When I opened my eyes I saw that I was very close to the ground, 500ft up at a guess, and falling towards a vast ploughed field. A road, like a narrow white ribbon, stretched hedgeless towards a cluster of farm buildings in the middle distance, and I could see their rooftops shining in the moonlight. I had the strangest sensation that the earth was rushing up towards me with ever-increasing velocity and then – wham! – it slammed against me, knocking the breath out of me, rattling every bone in my body. All the same, I had been so very lucky. There I was flat on my face in what turned out to be the softest bed of freshly ploughed earth. I lay quite still for a minute or two, hugging the ground, listening for the approach of a Panzer Division, which would surely have been detailed to pick me up. However, except for the distant sound of a dog barking and the barely audible rumble of the retreating bomber force, there was absolute silence.

As soon as I was sure that I was not in imminent danger of being captured and that it was safe to move, I cautiously looked and saw at once that I must get rid of my parachute. The white silk canopy shone in the moonlight like plastic teeth in a discotheque. I was in luck again as only 30 yards from me there was a neatly built mound of mangel-wurzels. I hauled in the parachute, to which I was still attached and, as I made my way over to the mound, bundled it up into my arms. I must have landed badly, for I found that one ankle (I've long forgotten which) was painful when I put my weight on it. However, I reckoned it wasn't too bad and that the pain would wear off before long.

The mound was ideal for hiding my parachute and, choosing the side farthest from the road, I laid the huge white silk canopy in a shallow trough which ran round the base of the heap. I found that it folded down to virtually nothing so that all I had to do was drag earth over it with my hands. It could not have been easier.

I ripped off my RAF wings and my flying officer epaulettes and removed my black tie and detachable collar (studs back and front). I put the wings in my pocket and buried the rest, together with my flying helmet and oxygen mask, beside the parachute. Then, sitting back on the sloping pile of turnips, I thought about my next move. It never occurred to me, either then or later, that I should give myself up. My one thought was to get back to England – but how?

In the inside pocket of my RAF battledress was a flat perspex box containing the escape kit with which all aircrew were issued before a flight over enemy territory. The contents would vary slightly depending on the country or countries over which we happened to be flying. I knew without looking that mine would contain, printed on either side of a silk square, maps of France and the Low Countries. There would be French and Belgian Francs in notes; chocolate; a slab of Kendal Mint Cake; 4 Benzedrine tablets; some water purifying tablets; a flat rubber water bottle and needles and thread, but no ticket home.

I knew that I was not far from the Channel coast and that the whole area around and to the north of me would be bristling with enemy troops awaiting the now inevitable Allied invasion of Europe. I could not be far from where *Q-Queenie* must have come down and at least three more Lancasters had crashed in the immediate vicinity. When daylight came the area would be crawling with Germans. My overriding priority must be to get the hell out of there.

Paris lay about 80 miles directly to my south and I thought that the best thing that I could do would be to set off in that direction and try to make contact with the Resistance if the opportunity presented itself. Having made that decision, there was no point in hanging about. The visibility was already beginning to drop as the moon sank in the sky, and I was concerned that by dawn the mist I had seen forming in the valleys would very probably become widespread fog.

I could make out the Plough and the Pole Star so, taking my bearings and a deep breath, I crossed my fingers and set out towards the dark horizon. My ankle seemed to improve with use, but it was slow going over the ploughed furrows. The fields seemed to go on forever over gently undulating ground. I have no recollection of coming across either a ditch or

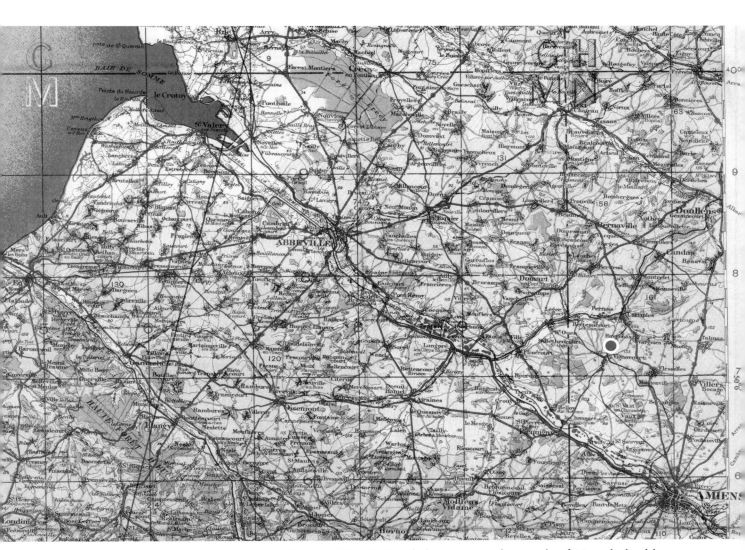

Original 1943 Allied military map (ref: 4042, 2nd edition) showing the Somme Estuary. The added red target indicates *Q-Queenie*'s crash site. (Nimmo Collection)

a hedge but then, unlike the English countryside, much of Picardy had been blasted and levelled during World War I.

I had just been through a deadly experience and while such an event was statistically very likely, the shock of it actually happening was profound and time seemed to become completely dislocated. That said, it was probably too early for the inevitable reaction to set in. I think I was probably on my own version of auto-pilot with my whole attention concentrated on getting away. I felt wide-awake, particularly clear headed and absolutely determined to get back to England. I knew would have to be very careful. One false move and I would have had my chips especially as my battledress and flying boots were far too conspicuous.

An hour or so went by and the air became appreciably colder and, sure enough, mists and fog began to form in the hollows. I kept moving south and after a while I found myself climbing a long gentle incline where, at the top, a shroud of mist had started to turn a rather odd, warmer colour. I couldn't think what this was, at first I thought it might be my imagination. However, as I climbed closer to the top of the rise, I began to see that this diffused, swirling flickering wasn't just mist but smoke too and was in fact coming from a heavy red glow in what must be a dip beyond the rise. At this point I was becoming very wary indeed. Even so, I still had no idea what this light could be. Eventually, crouching low I looked down over the edge of the rise and found myself staring into hell itself. It was a dreadful scene of utter devastation. Spread across a circle some 150 yards in diameter were the shattered, torn and twisted remains of a Lancaster bomber.

Fires flickered all over the place and the appalling stench of hot metal, charred remains and of rubber nearly choked me and made my eyes stream. Nobody could have survived that impact or the explosion that had clearly

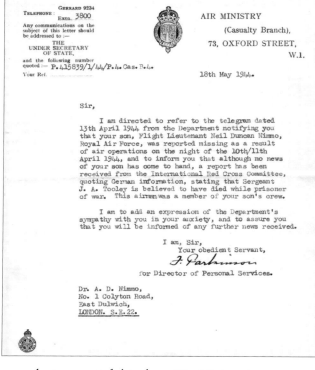

War Ministry letter informing Neil's father that Neil was missing. (Nimmo Collection)

followed. It was a sickening sight and one that I was only too grateful to be able to turn away from. Ultimately, though, you don't escape scenes like that, they re-visit you again and again, they are yours for life. Looking back on it there was an unthinkable thought so, out of some sort of self-protection maybe, I simply didn't think it. It now seems all too obvious that this dreadful sight had to be all that remained of *Q-Queenie*.

I backed off and made a wide detour around the wreckage before heading south again. After a while the terrain changed, eventually becoming woodland. By then the moon had all but set and eventually, as the daylight slowly crept up, the mist thickened into a deep, increasingly disorientating fog leaving me groping rather too vaguely forward. All my senses seemed on hold and for a time I made virtually no progress.

CHAPTER 2
The Night Hunter

A Crocodile and a Wild Boar

Eighty miles to Neil's south-east, a three-crew Messerschmitt night-fighter glided through the last of the moonlight to land at Juvincourt, just north of Reims. Its pilot, 23-year-old Hauptman Helmut Bergmann, was elated but utterly drained by the night's efforts.

As he touched down, ghostly wisps of fog spiralled out as vortex from the plane's wingtips and, with a brief scorch of rubber, Bergmann taxied to the stand. As the crew shut down and clambered out a battered crew truck arrived. Bergmann slumped in and dropped instantly asleep.

Contemplating the comatose pilot and rummaging through the usual debris in his pockets, the radio operator Gunter Hauthal carefully fished out the most promising cigarette end and lit up.

'I don't know how he does it Willi', he coughed.

'Anything to avoid your frightful *Zigarettenstummel*', groaned Gunner Schopp.

Hauthal sighed as the Renault rattled off, 'Ja, Ja, Willi OK!'

Windswept, battle-scarred Juvincourt, the Nachtjagdgeschwader 4 (NJG 4) base on the Picardie-Ardennes border, was loveless and hardly home. It had the dubious distinction of sitting right on the front line during World War I and the RAF had then used it as a forward base until France had fallen. The airstrip had then become a Luftwaffe fighter base, part of their web of airstrips along the Franco-Belgian border.

Bergmann was too tired to care about his surroundings and relief tinged his crew's excitement. Their Bf 110 4G's fuel gauges had fluttered near empty and they'd been running on vapour during that final approach. But who cared? '*Der Blonde Helm*'[1] had hit top C and it wasn't over yet. It might be dawn but their rapacious mess would want every last detail. Amazingly, the result of the night's work was seven down, without receiving so much as a scratch!

Bergmann grabbed a sandwich when they arrived at the mess and, easing onto a chair, sipped an atrocious acorn coffee. He let Willie and Gunter entertain the mess and lost himself in the night's remarkable events – he had few real friends at Juvincourt. By 11 April 1944, Bergmann was a decorated, experienced (i.e. still alive) night-fighter pilot. A dedicated Nazi,

he was now sated. However, just two hours earlier he had been a very hungry hunter indeed . . .

Early the previous day the turbulent late March and April weather had finally blown on eastwards and the rainstorms had cleared. After a blustery day the evening's NJG 4's meteorological briefing had promised a fine, cloudless sky and as the full moon was then just 24 hours old his reaction had been, 'a bright night then, an April Moon, ripe for bombing but maybe even better for night-fighters?'. He had been right.

As dusk had fallen, NJG 4 Operations Centre had flashed 'Fasan'[2] putting the airfield on immediate standby and Bergmann had felt the atmosphere tense. There had been a time when he'd have had to fight a velvety black fear but he had grown to like these moments. While some crew crept off to be sick Bergmann felt an adrenalin rush; it gave him a real buzz.

The war had become one of diabolical inventions and vacillating electronic supremacy. The Allies would have been alarmed to know that since late 1940 Luftflotte 3 had been monitoring the distant crackle of radio disturbance as enemy ground crew throughout the length of eastern England checked and prepared aircraft for the coming night's raids. Analysing that giveaway radio interference, Luftwaffe Intelligence could reasonably predict the number of Allied aircraft being prepared, and even the airfields they would come from. They could, therefore, anticipate the severity of the night's planned raids on occupied Europe. Further intelligence would also be anxiously awaited from the many listening posts and Luftwaffe observation posts scattered along the Channel coastline and deep into occupied Europe. There were many concentrated along the Calais straights where, on a clear, blustery day, the chalk cliffs of England's coastline were actually visible.

These Luftwaffe outposts were camouflaged and often underground making up a veritable rabbit warren of ingeniously constructed, makeshift hides and bunkers, making them as hidden as possible from the gaze of dangerous lone, RAF aerial recognisance aircraft. To the casual eye, the hides that were exposed looked like peasant's shacks or shoreline flotsam. Some were just holes in the ground, some quite grand in their way; several showed marked signs of humour and some looked like 'Hans Und Gretel' houses. However, the truth was that, as with Hansel and Gretel, the deeper and wider Hitler spread out across Europe and began to fail, so the lonelier these vital outposts were becoming.

On the other side of the Channel, shortly before take-off, Allied aircrews switched on their on-board radar and the added radio disturbance confirmed Luftwaffe suspicions. Consequently, the Germans had a good idea of the intensity of that night's raids, including the one to Aulnoye-Aymeries, long before the bombers had taken off.

Opposite: Unteroffizier Helmut Bergmann on his way up! (Bergmann Weitz Nimmo)

A photograph from Helmut Bergmann's own collection showing an earlier Messerschmitt Bf 110 3C + FS. (Bergmann Weitz Nimmo)

A German observation post, which is well camouflaged from prying RAF eyes. (3rdR UOPP, Nimmo Collection)

Luftwaffe observation crew using polarizing glasses. When communication lines from the outlying visual observers started to buzz, the operations centres would have a much clearer idea of what the night's targets would be. (3rdR UOPP, Nimmo Collection)

A Luftwaffe 'villa', or underground bunker, near Calais. (3rdR UOPP, Nimmo Collection)

'Villa Hugo' lurking somewhere deep in eastern occupied Europe. (3rdR UOPP, Nimmo Collection)

A very small forward observation post, or a very large man. (3rdR UOPP, Nimmo Collection)

A Kriegsmarine patrol observing and mine-laying off the French coast in liaison with the fighter control vessel *NJL Togo* in the German Bight. (3rdR UOPP, Nimmo Collection)

Kanal Wache (Channel watch) keep watch for the night hunters' prey. (3rdR UOPP, Nimmo Collection)

Adjusting the night's local Luftwaffe defences. (3rdR UOPP, Nimmo Collection)

At the fringe of occupied Europe ran a string of radar posts, anti-aircraft flak positions, observers, patrolling ships and Luftwaffe aircraft, all of which contributed to the rather inflexible *Kammhuber* defence. On that night in April, they would have been on alert and awaiting reports of first sightings. Nachtjagdgeschwader (night-fighter squadron) operations centres from Norway to the Spanish border pooled and collated information, projecting the results onto large, frosted glass screens. They could generally predict what was coming but where it was coming to was another matter entirely. The night's targets could be city centres, armaments or steel factories, or maybe the supply networks again.

Nazi Germany and her occupied territories were now a massive target to defend and, as always, this sort of rapid, aggressive empire building relied heavily on plunder in order to avoid shortages of supplies as the troops ran the risk of outrunning the supply chain.

Q-Queenie's crew was one of many to brave Germany's colossal firepower. To sustain this firepower, the armaments had to come from somewhere. Germany couldn't possibly supply it all, and so relied to a great extent on the spoils of war. The German forces pillaged and captured whatever they wanted. What they couldn't use was transported home by rail to the Ruhr to be smelted down, often using forced labour.

The Luftwaffe commanded batteries of heavy flak cannon and searchlights, which were often rail-mounted. Specialist *Luftflak* units would use German-made armaments but had also mastered the art of hunting in dark barns, and corners, routing out, capturing, filching and recycling whatever could be found. The 3rd Reich had managed to keep their forces supplied using spoils from the massively expensive, incomplete and totally useless Maginot Line, (which the Germans simply bypassed and stripped of heavy weapons) and early World War II battles. Captured spoils were often antique and included WWI Renaults (everything from cars to traction units); British- and French-made cannon, old World War I Hotchkiss macine guns, tanks captured or abandoned at Dunkirk and re-bored Russian armaments from the early successful weeks of Operation *Barbarossa* on the Eastern Front. All this vital booty was gathered at depots – Luftwaffe-run front line *Zweigparks* which fed on to main *Beuteparks*. By 1944, this part of Herman Göring's empire had become the Luftwaffen-Berge-Bataillon. Crashed aircraft, vehicles and weaponry – all the detritus of war – had become crucial and it was very probably the way the bulk of *Q-Queenie*'s remains went. They were most probably smelted down and turned into Messerschmitts.

The disaster of abandoned Allied transport on the roads to Dunkirk. Many of these vehicles would have been destined for German smelting plants to be turned into weapons for the Reich. (3rdR UOPP, Nimmo Collection)

Dunkirk shoreline as the Germans saw it once the dust settled. More booty for the victors. (3rdR UOPP, Nimmo Collection)

It sounds efficient enough but by April 1944 a great deal was wrong. The disastrous, bloody Eastern Front, the fighting in North Africa and the shambolic Italian retreat had taken their toll. Reichsmarschall Göring had proved hopeless at keeping the Luftwaffe adequately supplied and, while technical advances and intelligence were remarkable, the Reich's night-fighter force was battered and out of date. The air superiority of the early years and the success of the Blitzkrieg had been thrown away.

Endless raids on the Ruhr, the Reich's industrial heartland, had cut coal and steel production causing delays which slowed the arrival of the Luftwaffe's urgently needed supplies and spares. For weeks Allied bombers had concentrated on wrecking the Reich's industries. Krupps at Essen had been pummelled; raw materials were drying up; aeroplane and part manufacturers were no longer keeping pace with the Luftwaffe's losses and, most importantly, key aircraft types were out of date.

Designed in the 1930s, the Messerschmitt Bf 110's basic airframe was old. Despite sporadic improvements and new engines in full battle configuration, with a crew of three, it was a slow beast and offered a short range. Additional under-wing fuel tanks were often fitted but these too added to the weight and also caused drag which, of course, burnt up an important part of the extra fuel.

A captured French ambulance being repaired and repainted. (3rdR UOPP, Nimmo Collection)

Helmut Bergmann's own photograph of crew openly studying 'Der Dicke' (Göring) and his ever-expanding paunch. The Reichsmarschall would not have appreciated this photograph – his official photographs were usually heavily retouched. In fact, they were so retouched that they made him look like a Roman bust. (Bergmann Weitz Nimmo)

Intriguing and exciting prototype aircraft, including a top-secret jet-engined fighter, had already landed at Juvincourt. However, the jet had quietly disappeared, to who knows where.

Göring rumbled on, now reining over an enormous, crumbling war empire. On a visit to the Reims bases, he had come as a bit of a shock to Luftwaffe personnel. Amid all the pomp, the increasingly hungry pilots had lined up and had waited. When he came, all had noticed that the Reichsmarschall was even larger than expected and was positively bursting out of his grand uniform. They were surprised, partly by the size of his girth

and also because Göring did not resemble his official, grotesquely flattering portraits at all and even those photographs made him look as if some over ambitious mortician had been at work. In short, *Der Dicke* ('fatso' – Göring's nickname) was huge. He was clearly too well fed, which was rather offensive when many were on such short rations.

These were very tense times for the Luftwaffe as losses mounted and units were constantly regrouping and Bergmann had lost far too many colleagues. Although these losses had been frightening and painful at first

Prior to the Blitzkreig and Occupation, French Air Force Chief of Staff General Vuillemin had been shown the Reich's might – and what already lay in store. (3rdR UOPP, Nimmo Collection)

Some '*Beute*' weapons were positively antique. With these captured French World War I Renault 'FU' traction units and renovated cannon are a German Luftflak unit who were using the Loire valley town as cover. (3rdR UOPP, Nimmo Collection)

The *Zweigpark* at Soissons, Picardy, was one of many scattered around northern France. It looked for all the world like a dodgy Luftwaffe-run used car lot. This one is offering all they could want to fire back at the manufacturers – everything from cannon to the well-camouflaged, American-made French (3 Escadrille) Curtiss Hawk 75A-1 fighter. Dunkirk and the fall of France had been catastrophic, resulting in allied-made weapons now being turned on the Allies. (3rdR UOPP, Nimmo Collection)

he had learned to cope. He felt that he generally had a grip on things and he was no longer afraid of death. In fact, that possibility had by now become a probability. He had already been injured and could expect and accept that possibility too, with one exception – being trapped in a fire – death by fire terrified him.

As expected on the night of 10 April, the main Luftwaffe meteorological staff had produced forecasts covering both enemy and Luftwaffe bases, and as usual they'd been used to try to predict the night's probable targets. Fuelled, armed and ready to scramble, night-fighters and their crews waited. As usual the crews ate their increasingly meagre *abendbrot* and chatted, wrote home or had a quiet smoke.

At 01:55 further signals arrived warning NJG 4 that a large incoming wave of RAF bombers was banking south-east over the French coast, heading behind the mobile anti-aircraft batteries and turning up towards Belgium. Possible targets included the rail marshalling yards to the north-east of Laon. Gunter Hauthal, who had taken to most things French, groped for his pack of yellow Gitanes Maïs, lit up a *clope*, shot a glance at Willi Schopp and took a deep lungful. 'Here we go again', he thought.

Aulnoye-Aymeries was a key goods-train marshalling yard connecting

Above: Flak guns came from various sources. These are two of many Vickers 94mm AA guns abandoned by the BEF which ended up in German hands. (3rdR UOPP, Nimmo Collection)

Right: A German police regiment train on captured French/American Hotchkiss machine guns manufactured back in 1941. (3rdR UOPP, Nimmo Collection)

Germany and the Low Countries with occupied France and was a prime target. Much of the Reich's military supplies destined for forward positions in occupied France were routed through Aulnoye. In fact, NJG 4's own dwindling supplies came that way and these marshalling yards were definitely on NJG 4's 'patch'.

After a foul, wet winter the bright week at the end of February had proved particularly devastating. With those cold days had come American daylight

Another of the many weapons that captured war booty was turned into, flak range, radar and guidance systems became very elaborate. (3rdR UOPP, Nimmo Collection)

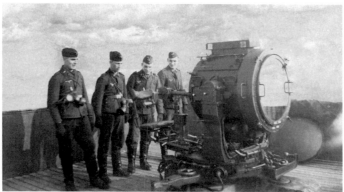

One of very many Luftflak carbon arc searchlight units. They were often train-mounted on *Scheinwerferwagen*. (3rdR UOPP, Nimmo Collection)

A German view of searchlights and flak over Calais. (3rdR UOPP, Nimmo Collection)

Fifty miles east by north-east along the channel coastline, the RAF run the gauntlet during a particularly violent night over Ostend. (3rdR UOPP, Nimmo Collection)

North-east of Abbeville at Boulogne-sur-Mer, the RAF 'taking a pasting'. This is what all aircrews flying night missions over France had come to dread. (3rdR UOPP, Nimmo Collection)

German Costal flak, shell bursts and, to the far right, a rare photograph of what looks to be a burning four-engined aircraft. (3rdR UOPP, Nimmo Collection)

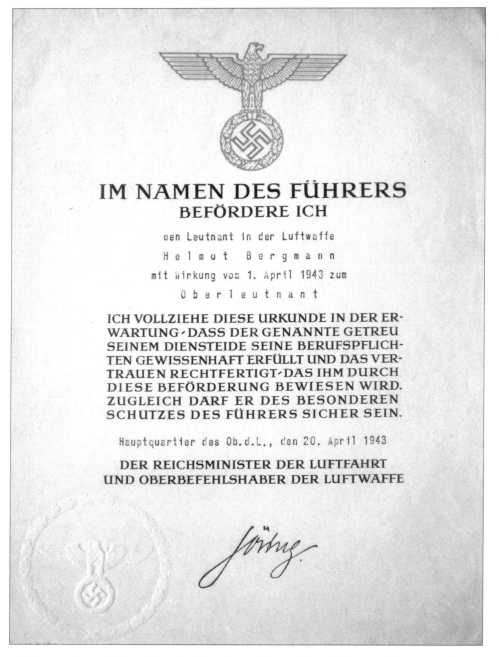

Helmut Bergman's letter of promotion. (Bergmann Weitz Nimmo)

raids on aircraft factories the length and breadth of the Reich: Regensburg, Gotha, Oschersleben, Brunswick and others had been mercilessly bombed. It hadn't ended there, great swathes of the Reich's medieval cities, with their twisting lanes and tightly packed timber-framed buildings had been firebombed. All that history was simply burnt to the ground along with the inhabitants, all gone forever. It had seemed utterly remorseless and horrific.

Helmut Bergmann took the night of 12/13 June 1943 very personally as

Above: Family friends perished in the flames. (Bergmann Weitz Nimmo)

Above right: Winding back lanes and ancient timber-framed houses such as these were obliterated in Sir Arthur Harris' Bomber Command's firestorm raids. The idea was to crush front line troop moral by putting their homes and family in great danger. (3rdR UOPP, Nimmo Collection)

his home city of Bochum had been bombed and thoroughly gutted. Despite near total cloud cover, using a type of ground profiling radar, the Allies had somehow seen right through that cloud. That night the RAF had probably targeted Robert Mauser's coke and *benzol* fuel plant, but as usual they didn't care that they had torched the 'old town' – even the medieval Pauluskirche and St Marienkirche were destroyed. It was shocking and, if anything, that ghastly night, followed a month later by the atrocious Hamburg firestorm, had given Bergmann a purpose. He loathed Allied *terrorfliegers* (terror flyers) for everything they stood for and above all for what he and his family had lost.

Many thousands of good town's people were killed during that raid, people he and his family had known and loved, including his father's friends who had been blown-up or burnt alive. The Bergmanns certainly knew who their enemies were.

In the weeks peceding 10 April, Bergmann had noticed a change in the fortunes of the Allies – during their huge raid on Nuremberg they had been severely mauled. High winds had blown the bombers off course to the north-east and the raid had gone very badly for them. A God-sent weather front had built over the Nuremberg target and the few remaining enemy bombers that had made it were mostly lured off course by badly placed marker flares and by local diversionary fires – a clever tactic that had worked well. The Allies had mainly bombed open country miles from Nuremberg and although a few country towns had suffered, the old centre of Nuremberg had been saved, this time.

It seemed that the RAF hadn't yet realised that their 'Monica' tail warning radar system was a death trap. Almost as soon as it was in service, a set had been found in Holland in a crashed Wellington and passive receivers were rapidly designed to pick up its pulses. For months these new receivers had secretly used 'Monica' as a homing beacon. It was a great success and made Bergmann's life much easier – or rather, it should have, but he had personally found 'kills' frustratingly elusive.

Better still though, the Luftwaffe's top-secret SN2 radar seemed immune to 'Window'[3], the British radar-deceiving foil. Had Telefunken produced these new sets in reliable quantities things would be very different. Günter Hauthal had heard that during late 1943 and early 1944 Telefunken had in fact produced more SN2 sets than expected. However, of the 300 or so delivered, only 49 had been fitted and just 12 were actually working. This hopeless state of affairs made the RLM (the Reich's Air Ministry) look even more incompetent.

On the night of the Nuremberg raid Luftwaffe Command had very successfully predicted the RAF's course. All over Axis-held Europe night-fighter squadrons had scrambled to key beacon points and were waiting to clean up – and they certainly had. Obviously shaken by their losses, the Allies now appeared to be switching their attention away from the Reich's beleaguered cities and to German logistics and supplies.[4]

This was a logical move as it would be hard to overstate the importance of German-controlled rail networks. At some stage during an advance most things took to the tracks. Ingenious, but often unstable, convertible rail/road trucks and other vehicles – everything from bicycles to tanks – were devised and given rail wheels.[5] As the Blitzkrieg called for top secrecy, shock, high-speed and, importantly, sustained momentum, the invading Germans relied heavily on existing rail networks. Therefore, as the Allies retreated their armies blew-up what they could of the rail infrastructure. However, incoming Wehrmacht and Pioneer Corps rapidly repaired it. [6]

By all accounts, it was the American commander General Eisenhower who best understood the implications of Axis-controlled Belgian and Vichy French rail networks, and that they would become crucial to the movement of German troops and supplies during the build-up to the anticipated Allied invasion of German-held Europe. Regardless of collateral damage these networks had become prime targets and the retargeting that had taken place since the beginning of April was ominous – much German effort and speculation was now going into predicting actual Allied invasion points.

As war battered on into the spring of 1944, so the allied attacks on Reich-controlled rail networks increased. With their powerful fighter-bombers and with partisans working within the SNCF leaking more and more information, attacks on individual trains increased. These trains were not without armaments of course. While on the move, during dawn and daylight hours, they relied on flak cannon mounted on specially constructed carriages. Four-barrelled (*vierling*) flak cannon were highly effective against incoming fighter aircraft or ground targets as far off as a thousand yards and by 1944 these flak wagons were an integral part of troop trains. Even

Left: Luxembourg marshalling yard – the next yard? Aulnoye. (3rdR UOPP, Nimmo Collection)

Centre left: This was by no means the heaviest cannon to be positioned by rail. A temporary branch line curved off to offer the chosen coordinates and to enable targeting of the shells (shown in the photograph to the right) in large quantities. It also allowed the canon to be hauled off before the RAF or USAF arrived. (3rdR UOPP, Nimmo Collection)

Below: Rigged as a rail locomotive, a Büssing-NAG truck is rapidly laying track. (3rdR UOPP, Nimmo Collection)

The 3rd Reich relied heavily on rail transport. Marshalling yards, which were key to troop movements, were heavily guarded by gunners and the Gestapo. (3rdR UOPP, Nimmo Collection)

Nevertheless, the most bizarre accidents and raids kept happening such as here at Nancy station. (3rdR UOPP, Nimmo Collection)

Some were the work of the French Resistance, often involving SNCF *cheminots* who, if caught, were shot or sent to concentration camps. (3rdR UOPP, Nimmo Collection)

By 1944, the Allies were seriously damaging the Nazi rail networks. (3rdR UOPP, Nimmo Collection)

A burnt-out supply train. However, it was well away from the Normandy coast, not far from Dijon. (3rdR UOPP, Nimmo Collection)

1944 photograph of a 2cm *Flakvierling* 38 Flak Abt. 224 unit on a purpose-built carriage. (3rdR UOPP, Nimmo Collection)

Missing rail spikes could bring things to a halt. (3rdR UOPP, Nimmo Collection)

France, spring 1944, and yet another night attack on the rail infrastructure. (3rdR UOPP, Nimmo Collection)

As they multiplied, these attacks almost seemed random. They weren't of course. (3rdR UOPP, Nimmo Collection)

Hitler's personal Führersonderzug (command train) had one.

However, the *vierling* flak cannon were less effective against the higher-altitude RAF night-bombers that were now attacking key junctions and marshalling yards. It was during these attacks that NJG 4 and sister Luftwaffe night-fighter units took over and pursued the attackers with a vengeance. Larger Luftwaffe Luftflak units with much heavier cannon protected strategic targets. 'What' had wondered Bergmann on that full-mooned April night, 'will it be tonight? Laon, Aulnoye, Ghent maybe?'[7]

He had some catching-up to do. In previous weeks NJG 4 had seen success – five pilots had logged kills and one Lt Hromadnik had destroyed no fewer than three Halifax bombers in one night. Despite other setbacks,

Arterial crossings were now prime targets and kept under close observation, nothing as tempting as these were safe now. (3rdR UOPP, Nimmo Collection)

Allies, partisans and *résistants* all across occupied Europe seemed hell-bent on quite literally stopping the 3rd Reich in its tracks. (3rdR UOPP, Nimmo Collection)

this part of the air war seemed to have swung the Reich's way a bit.

Since going operational in 1942, Bergmann had scored 16 kills, which was not bad. However, since November 1943 he'd had no success at all. He still savoured that one November night over Maastricht when he'd managed to shot down a Halifax and a Sterling. However, since then there had been nothing. No kills in four months. It felt mediocre to him, depressingly mediocre, and he felt that he really must do better.

It had been a bitter winter with late snows during which the ground engineers had made heroic efforts to keep every serviceable aircraft flying. However, during the dank, gloomy months, the increasing lack of spares and the need to cannibalise unserviceable machines had led Bergmann to ponder a bit. Thinking back, nothing was really going as planned. Father had said that National Socialism would rapidly bring a better more ordered world. He had urged him forward, but in truth, by April 1944 Bergmann was no longer quite so sure as to which way 'forward' was. These thought were fuelled by the fact that despite the near fatal hammering meted out to the British *terrorfliegers* over the past weeks, the 'murderous Tommies'[8] just kept coming. Somehow, their Air Ministry was still producing heavy bombers and crewing them with aircrew from an alarming number of different countries (this was demonstrated by the diverse nationalities of captured aircrew). Meanwhile, the Luftwaffe had no heavy bombers and crewing of existing aircraft was becoming a nightmare. Word was that RAF crew flew a number of missions and then were rested or trained new pilots. It wasn't like that in the Luftwaffe. Once posted, NJG pilots kept going on sortie after sortie, often several in 24 hours. Battle-experienced pilots were not teaching new pilots old tricks which Bergmann felt was a missed opportunity.

One careful owner – for restoration or body parts. (3rdR UOPP, Nimmo Collection)

Juvincourt, February 1944 – Bf 110 Nº 52 out in the snow being fitted with a replacement engine. It's a rare sight as '52' was still equipped with the new but unsuccessful rocket launchers. Their weight and drag proved a serious handicap and apparently they were soon removed. (3rdR UOPP, Nimmo Collection)

As casualties mounted at Juvincourt, experienced crew were becoming rare. In fact, many new pilots were rank beginners, often new to night flying, let alone night fighting. With little or no blind-flying training, many concentrated solely on surviving what was clearly a terrifying experience. If these pilots were courageous enough to attempt to do battle, it often proved to be their last attempt at anything. 'Very tough' thought 23-year-old Bergmann as to him most new pilots were only kids.

As a night-fighter, the Bf 110 G4 was an OK aircraft but the result of just too many improvements. The aircrew all felt that the Junkers Ju 88 was a much better aircraft as it was better equipped and roomier with better communication between the crew. However, the G4 was a big improvement over earlier Bf 110 versions as it was not bad to fly, responsive to controls and offered great visibility. It was slow but with a night-fighter that didn't matter much as RAF bombers were slower. Bergmann felt that it was a bit like flying Father's over stocked glasshouse but as he wasn't tall it suited him well enough. However, an engine were lost the Bf 110 G4 was all but unflyable. Holding full rudder was an immense strain due to the weight of three aircrew, a mass of Liechtenstein Fug202 radar equipment[9], guns, ammunition, exhaust flame dampers, extra fuel tanks, rockets, etc. Every kilo burnt fuel and cut the range that could be flown. The main hope now was that new aeroplanes would at least be delivered complete, but such were the shortages that this was often not the case – parts (for the radar, for example) were either missing or not working.

The new upward-firing 'Schräge Musik'[10] cannons were a winner though – if you could get them. Mounted obliquely through the canopy, they usually made an attack from under the enemy successful. The official Schräge Musik was copied from a homemade design by Paul Mahle – one of the more talented Luftwaffe gunners and a remarkable natural engineer.

However, again official production figures were hopeless. Some ground crew made bootleg copies of the officially copied gun, but they were a bit '*windig*', a bit dodgy and as they were so short of materials only the 'Aces' would get even these.

All in all, the Juvincourt mess was increasingly depressed with crew beginning to talk openly. To them the problem seemed to be Luftwaffe High Command. Herman Göring may have been a World War I fighter Ace, but he'd not been popular even then – not invited to reunions, that sort of thing. Now he was seen as a danger, an embarrassment and a considerable dead weight. Seriously over confident of an early victory, since the awful defeat at Stalingrad he seemed to have given up. There were also rumours that following an earlier accident he had become seriously addicted to morphine.

By April 1944, many Luftwaffe airfields had been heavily bombed – Juvincourt, Laon and nearby Courcy had all taken a plastering. All airfields were known to enemy intelligence – with so many flights and radio traffic that was inevitable – and Allied reconnaissance from high-altitude Spitfires and Mosquitoes added to their information about airfield movements. Also, French terrorist cells had long been known to be at work around Juvincourt. Back in August 1942, one had been caught red-handed. Édouard Charlot, a Reims Gendarme who had infiltrated the Herman

Bf 110 NJG air and ground crew make a final check before take-off. (Bundesarchiv, 1011-658-6360))

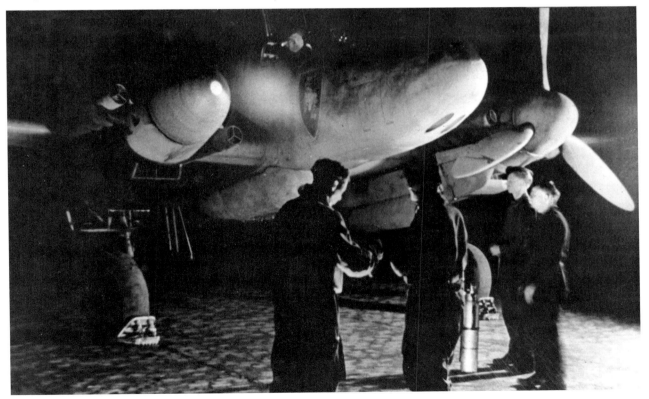

Göring Gendarme Barracks, had turned out to be 'Dadart', the head of a small Resistance cell code-named 'Uranus'. All five members[11] were caught and shipped east to labour camps where they were to survive. Gendarme Charlot had not been so lucky. He had lasted a full three months in Gestapo hands before being guillotined at Frankfurt.

By now Allied spies would certainly know all about NJG 4. However, despite this, Juvincourt was still up and running and just before 02:00 on 11 April, the squadron was scrambled. Hauthal flicked the glowing end off yet another cigarette and pocketed the stub before rushing off to the waiting planes. As they were finally cleared for take-off, Bergmann's twin Daimler-Benz V-12 engines sucked fuel and roared. He, Günther Hauthal and Wilhelm Schopp lifted off, their cramped, heavily armed fighter clawing through the low ground-mist and up into clear, bright moonlight.

Fully aware of what was now required of them, and above all of him, Bergmann adjusted his hold on the *steuerknüppel*.[12] He was determined to make his mark and to defend the Reich, which by all accounts needed defending. At Juvincourt there was now open talk that an Allied invasion had to be coming soon and *latrinenparole* gossip had it that an attack would arrive just to the north, along the Nord-Pas-de-Calais coastline.

It was a fact that during the last few days the Allies and their *Terrorfliegers* had been targeting key logistics in a wide area roughly inland of Dunkirk, where four years earlier the British had been so soundly thrashed. Just the night before, Canadian flyers had bombed Ghent. However, it seemed that they had drifted off target and, getting it badly wrong, bombed a largely residential area and killing a great many civilians. 'That won't do them much good with the locals' thought Bergmann. He tightened his grip, 'there are too many of these *Terrorfliegers* about, we will have to do something about that'.

The general opinion at Juvincourt was that any soldier worthy of the task would want to avenge a defeat like Dunkirk and that it was obvious that the Allies would want to invade and counter-attack that way to try to rub the Germans' noses in it. Bergmann wasn't so sure about any of this. He felt that the Calais and Dunkirk coastline was a bit obvious and that it could be a ruse as the British were so devious. Bergmann knew all too well that something was up. He felt that in his bones and it wasn't a good feeling at all – more a sense of a deep dread. He would concentrate harder than ever and get this operation right. With that thought, he focused on the immediate task at hand. At 02:12 Hauthal's Liechtenstein radar latched onto the Lancasters' tail radars, and south-east of St Quentin, on an instruction from ops, they banked north-east to corner the bomber stream. As they did so, the horizon started to explode – first green, then red, and then all hell itself broke out.

Seriously motivated, Helmut Bergmann gained altitude. The already

North-east France: The RAF Target, Bergmann's flight and his victims. Paris – Bottom left. Reims – higher, far right. Juvincourt – A. Laon – B. Bergman banks north-east C for RAF Target – D. Lancaster victims 1–7 (*Q Queenie* #6). Neil makes contact with Monsieur Lyon and the resistance – X. (*Andrée's Allgemeiner Handatlas*, Veilhagen & Klasing, Nimmo Collection)

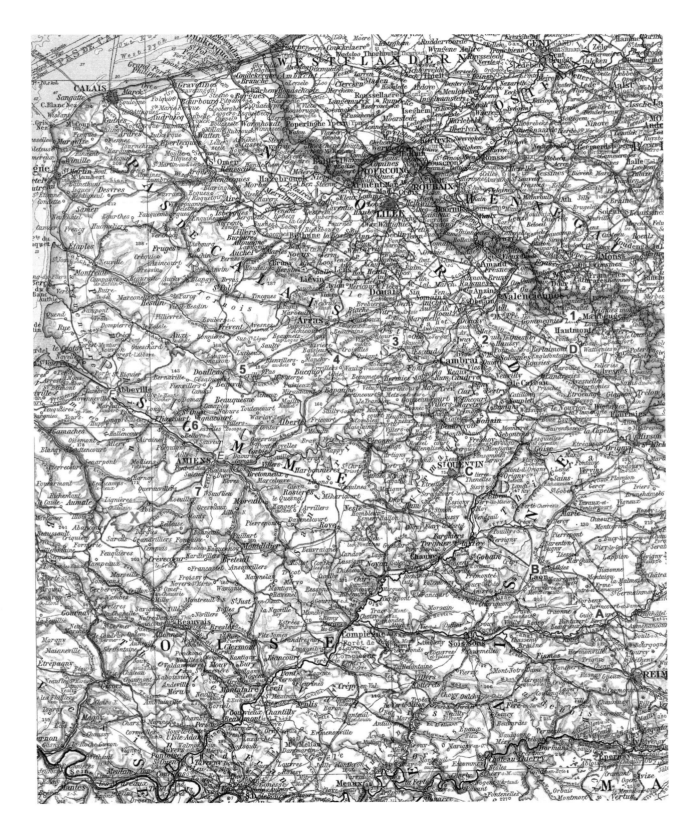

blazing target was just six minutes off. It was the Aulnoye marshalling yards. A couple more minutes and . . . Hold it . . . There they were . . . Yes . . . And there! There was a glint of moonlight off polished perspex, fleeting silhouettes against the fire, and then another glint. Got them! Bergmann dived away from the blazing marshalling yards and, while losing height, checked with Günther Hauthal and positioned the Messerschmitt neatly ahead of the Lancaster tail-enders as they dropped their markers and explosives on the rail yard before gratefully banking off on their homeward leg.

At 02:08 Gunter Hauthal picked a potential victim behind their Messerschmitt. Just to the north of the blaze Bergman banked back, repositioned and synchronised his speed while sliding below the Lancaster. At the right moment he opened the throttles, hauled back on his joystick and . . . UP!

At 02:20 Bergmann struck with his twin nose cannon, raking the Lancaster from 100 metres away and the first Lancaster of the night was destroyed. It crashed at Vieux Mesnil just five and a half kilometres due north of the Aulnoye yard. ND 586 AR-B was from 460 Sqn RAAF Binbrook. FO Arthur Probert, the 25-year-old pilot, and all but one of his six crew were Australians. They had an average age of 21. Mid-upper gunner Flt Sgt Bill Hogg was just 19. There were no survivors; all would be buried at Maubeuge close by the Belgian border.

With a pumping heart, and Schopp and Hauthal whooping it up behind him, Bergmann 'got stuck in'. Banking away west-south-west, they could clearly see the returning stream and were in hot pursuit. Just to the north of Solesmes, 23.87 kilometres further on, Bergmann struck again, shooting down LL 830 UL-R2, a Lancaster I from Elsham Wolds. On board were the pilot Flt Lt F. Barnsdale and his six crew. Again, all were killed and would be buried in the communal cemetery at Solesmes.

A further 23.18 kilometres west, just south-east of Sailly and north of Cambrai, Bergmann and his crew claimed their third kill, a Lancaster III ND 844 PH-M. Its pilot, PO F. Richards, and his crew were from 12 Sqn RAF Wickenby. This time there was one survivor, Sgt K. C. Kent, who was captured. The other crewmembers were also destined for Solesmes communal cemetery.

At 02:43, 33.92 kilometres still further west, and only a few hundred metres north of the centre of the little commune of Achiet Le Petit, Bergmann claimed his fourth victim. He left no survivors. Flt Lt R. W. Picton DFC and other crewmembers were already heroes, now they would all be interred in the tiny cemetery at Achiet le Petit.

Seven minutes later and a further 24.52 kilometres westward, Helmut Bergmann spotted victims five and six. He hit the fifth over the hamlet of Beauquesne and, leaving it crippled, fired a marker flare and went after victim six. Lancaster III JB 732 PM-S eventually crashed at Meharicourt 32 kilometres east-south-east of Amiens. The pilot, New Zealander PO J. W.

Armstrong, battled to keep *S-Sugar* airborne just long enough for those crew who could to bail out. However, he seems to have had little control over his direction. He, and two other crewmen, died and are buried at Meharicourt. Two more were captured and two evaded capture.

Meanwhile, Bergmann, Hauthal and Schopp had moved on to Lancaster six, leaving their last target to perish. They had peeled off and again lost height just over Villers Bocage where, banking low and to the north, they caught up with their target and again approached stealthily from below and behind. They clearly saw the massive Lancaster, a black silhouette against the clear night sky, and as they drew closer they saw the eight tell-tale blue exhaust flames. This was *Q-Queenie* in the last few moments of her short, and very violent, existence.

Aboard the Lancaster, Flt Lt Neil Nimmo had just watched the seemingly hopeless sight of searchlights coning two, possibly three, other Lancasters over Abbeville and seen them downed. He was appalled by what was happening ahead of *Q-Queenie*, but could only guess at what was happening right behind them and what was about to take place.

Then came the sudden shock of the silk parachute as they so nearly flew into the canopy suspended airman. As Neil Nimmo instinctively banked to avoid him, Helmut Bergmann noted Neil's move, but did not see the parachute, or the airman. Aboard the night-fighter there was an almost frozen pause, followed by an easing into position, and then . . . UP! Hanging on the props, close to stalling, Thud! Thud! Thud! One hundred metres directly beneath *Q-Queenie* Helmut Bergmann let rip, thundering loudly into their starboard wing. Nobody inside could have heard much and some of those aft of the cockpit suffered the result of this attack a great deal more acutely than Neil Nimmo. As Bergmann says:

> I saw the Lancaster . . . The pilot was taking evasive action, weaving about, maybe avoiding searchlights. I started firing at 02:52 a.m. from about 100m below and into the fuselage and the right wing, which promptly caught fire. The burning Lancaster [was] trapped by the searchlights. At 02:54 I saw it burning on the ground.

His deadly roller-coaster attack had finally ended. He had destroyed a remarkable six RAF Lancasters and their crews and, having given them a taste of hell itself, Helmut Bergmann was now low on fuel and would have to call it a night. Elated, Bergmann, Schopp and Hauthal headed off for Juvincourt. What they now longed for were their beds. As the fun seemed to be over, Gunter Hauthal stretched his back and switched off his passive radar. It had been a very satisfactory sortie indeed; six down, six fewer bombers, what a stir that would cause. However, their night was not yet over.

Q-Queenie was not the last Lancaster to be heading for the Channel coast that night. Others, on RAF raids on Ghent, Laon (Juvincourt's sister airfield) and Tours, down on the Loire, were also straggling homeward, willing their aircraft north to the channel, every mile a precious step towards Britain and safety.

Just five minutes later, Schopp sat up rigid and stared out beyond his cannon. Had he seen it? He gazed south-east into the night. Hauthal noticed and rapidly flicked on the radar receiver. There it was, a blip, and then the clear glint of a moonstruck perspex canopy, followed fleetingly by the silhouette of a Lancaster against bright water. 'Another Tommy,' yelled Schopp, 'to the south, over there!'

'Ja, ja,' said Hauthal, 'it's on its own.'

'Dear God,' muttered Bergman, 'we're almost out of *benzin* . . . OK *Sie zwei Jäger*[13] . . . have we had enough?'

'*Nein*!' said Schopp. '*Sie scherzen Herr Hauptmann? Fügen Sie sie in den Beutel*,'[14] muttered Hauthal.

Moments later, at 03:06 to be exact, they destroyed a seventh victim. Lancaster III MD 636 CF-O, *O-Orange*, from 625 Sqn, RAF Kelstern, was piloted by another New Zealander, Flt Sgt W. J. Green RNZAF. Only one airman would survive – Sgt E. Finlay who was captured. The other six now rest in the Saint Pierre Great War Cemetery at Amiens.

There were few survivors of those hectic 46 minutes that fatal Easter Monday night – only one airman survived Bergmann's first four attacks. According to Bergmann, time aboard stricken *Q-Queenie* must indeed have stood still. Their seemingly endless agony had in fact lasted just two minutes. Helmut Bergmann's flight log states:

02.54 a.m. near Vignacourt, British Lancaster, shelling by night fighter, 15km NW Amiens, and engagement at 1000m, position 100m from the individual target.

Shortly before they were targeted, Neil Nimmo and *Q-Queenie*'s crew had spotted an enemy fighter's contrails as it flew backlit against the moon. Luftwaffe night-fighters usually attacked from below and from behind. However, the Lancasters were brightly moonlit from above and backlit from below. A well-placed, high-altitude pilot could plan an attack as the Lancasters' camouflage wouldn't save them from a full moon – they were simply lumbering targets. Helmut Bergmann had timed his attack to perfection. His 'kill report', (item 23 '*Führungsverfahren*') contains two words that tell us a great deal: '*Wilde Sau*' (Wild Boar), was the code name for a tactic introduced to counteract 'Window'.[15] *Wilde Sau* accounts for the high altitude contrails. Introduced by Major 'Hajo' Herrmann, an experienced Luftwaffe bomber pilot, the idea was to free-up the more successful pilots in otherwise redundant single-engined day fighters from the over rigid radar-dependent Kammhuber line 'box' defence system.

By circling at altitude, independent of any 'Window'-swamped radar, the idea was that they would spot Allied bombers backlit by their own blazing targets or searchlights and go in for the kill. The main drawback was the single-engined fighters' very limited range. They couldn't take off until the target had been identified, and so needed the target to be well alight in order to get there and find the silhouetted bombers quickly. However, the tactic worked although any single-engined *Wilde Sau* fighter pilot was in mortal danger as they were often attacked by 'friendly flack' and known to crash into each other when, on their last gasp of fuel, they made emergency landings at the nearest possible airstrip. Twin-engined night-fighters such as the Bf 110 G4 with their greater (though still very short) range began using the same *Wilde Sau* method. Bergmann's report notes that he did use the *Wilde Sau* technique and had used the dreaded and technically out-dated, 'Von Hinten Unten' approach. However, all this extreme manoeuvring burnt up large quantities of precious fuel.

Bergmann's kills were confirmed. Seven Lancasters were wrecked and 38 crewmen were killed. Bergmann gave the credit to Schopp for spotting the victims. His own skills were rewarded when later on 11 April he was promoted and had the great satisfaction of filling out his flight papers as a new hero and the new *Staffelkapitän* of 8./NJG 4.

Like a good many of the German military, Bergman liked photography and was meticulous about record keeping. However, one of his less salubrious habits was that of visiting his victims' crash sites where colleagues would photograph him clambering over the destroyed aircraft and even

Helmut Bergmann liked to visit his victim's crash sites and dance on the remains of the aircraft. (Bergmann Weitz Nimmo)

doing war dances on the wreckage. Some of these photographs were gruesome, but even so Bergmann would add them to his albums, which must give a good indication of his frame of mind.

Overnight Helmut Bergmann became a star and he was on a roll. He was blond, young, and handsome in a very Germanic way; a bit short maybe, but above all a good, solid Nazi flyer. He was immediately put to use by the Reich's relentless propaganda machine. One suspects that he had also finally won his right to fit *Schräge Musik* cannon as two weeks later he shot down three more Lancasters in just three minutes, which was simply too rapid for the already deadly Von Hinten Unten technique. Transferred to 6./NJG 4 on 4 May, that same evening he shot down a further five bombers within the space of 30 minutes, and now he was becoming an 'Ace'. On 26 May he celebrated his 24th birthday in style. Just days later, on 9 June, he was decorated again, this time with the Ritterkreuz

A composite image: Stielers Handatlas 1939 map #33 overlaid by Helmut Bergmann's original flight plan showing his seven 'kills'. (Justus Perthes/ Gotha/Bergmann Weitz Nimmo)

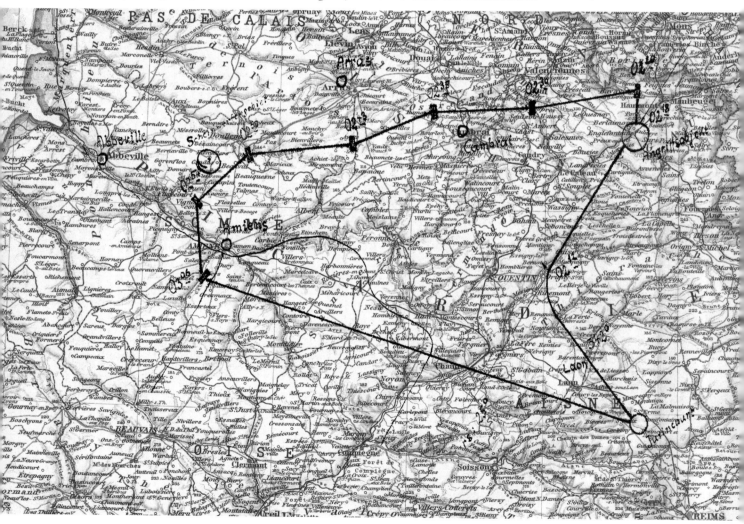

(the coveted Knight's Cross of the Iron Cross). This timing was unusual as such honours were almost always saved up for Hitler's birthday on 20 April each year, as he liked to award the Knight's Cross himself.

However, these were far from usual times and Bergmann's success needed to be seriously lauded. After all, cynically speaking, baubles cost nothing but military men would come close to dying for them. With each presentation of a Knight's Cross, the ensuing propaganda was of priceless value as it raised morale both in the field and at home, and morale boosters were crucial in an increasingly beleaguered Fatherland.

Helmut Bergmann had become a true danger to the Allies.

Bergman sleeps it off. 'Faithful "Stoltz" stands guard'. In fact, Bergmann's paperwork confirms suspicions about his neatly combed hair and freshly pressed pyjamas. This is another Luftwaffe propaganda photograph, 'Faithful. Stoltz' was probably borrowed from the guardhouse. (Bergmann Weitz Nimmo)

Helmut Bergmann. (Bergmann Weitz Nimmo)

Feldwebel Bergmann, who was very soon to become Hauptman Bergmann and then a *Staffelkapitän*. (Bergmann Weitz Nimmo)

B e r g m a n n , Hauptmann,   Im Felde, 11.4. 1944
8./Nachtjagdgeschwader 4
════════════════════════════════════

                        G e f e c h t s b e r i c h t

        zu den Abschußmeldungen vom 11.4. 1944, 02,20 Uhr, 02,30 Uhr,
        02,35 Uhr, 02,43 Uhr, 02,50 Uhr, 02,54 Uhr und 03,06 Uhr

        In der Nacht vom 10./11.4. 1944 startete ich um 02,04 Uhr zum
        Einsatz und flog mit Kurs 342° in 1500 m Höhe nach "Krebs".

        Nach etwa 8 Minuten meldete mir mein Bordwart, daß etwa 1500 m höhe
        und hinter uns ein Flugzeug sei. Nach seinen Angaben machte ich
        Kursverbesserungen und sichtete bald den Gegner, der in ca. 3000 m
        Höhe mit Kurs etwa 25° flog. Kurz vor uns waren in Bodennähe einige
        grüne Kaskaden, die das Angriffsziel (Aulnoye, 18 km SW Maubeuge)
        kennzeichneten. Über dem Objekt beschoß ich den als "Lancaster" er-
        kannten Gegner von unten aus 100 m Entfernung. Mit starkem Brand in
        Rumpf und Flächen stürzte N des Objektes ab und schlug um 02,20 Uhr
        brennend auf. Aufschlagort: bei Vieux Mesnil, 10 km SW Maubeuge.

        Gleichzeitig sichteten wir in gleicher Höhe mehrere andere Flugzeug
        die vom Angriffsziel mit etwa Westkurs abflogen. Um 02,28 Uhr schoß
        ich aus ca. 100 m Entfernung von senkrecht unten zwischen die rech-
        ten Motoren einer "Lancaster". Sie brannte dort sofort und schlug
        um 02,30 Uhr brennend auf. Aufschlagort: 6 km N Soleames, 20 km O
        Cambrai.
        Wir sahen laufend weitere Ziele und beschossen um 02,33 Uhr, noch
        mit Westkurs fliegend, in ca. 3000 m Höhe aus 100 m Entfernung wie-
        derum eine "Lancaster". Angriff von hinten unten. Starker Brand in
        Rumpf und rechter Fläche. Das Flugzeug stürzte steil ab und schlug
        um 02,35 Uhr 1 km SO Sailly, 3 km NW Cambrai, brennend auf.

        Um 02,42 Uhr griffen wir als 4.Gegner wieder eine "Lancaster" aus
        ca. 100 m Entfernung von hinten unten an. Rumpf und rechter Flächen
        ansatz brannten sofort mit heller Flamme. Wir erkannten die Kenn-
        zeichen: BD Kokarde ER. Um 02,43 Uhr brennender Aufschlag 1,5 km
        NNW Achiet la petit, 8 km NW Bapaume, 20 km S Arras.

        Den 5. und 6.Gegner erkannten wir in SO Richtung eines Scheinwerfer
        gebietes. Ich setzte mich bei ersterem darunter und schoß um 02,48
        Uhr aus ca. 80 m Entfernung in die rechte Fläche. Dort sofort star-
        ker Brand. Das brennende Flugzeug wurde von Scheinwerfern erfaßt
        und bis zum Aufschlag um 02,50 Uhr von Scheinwerfern angeleuchtet.
        Mein Bordwart gab nach dem Beschuß Erkennungsignal Nr. 4. Aufschlag
        ort: bei Beauquouesne, 9 km SSO Doullens, 30 km ONO Abbeville.

        Den 6.Gegner, ebenfalls eine "Lancaster", sah ich wenige Augenblicke
        später. Sie schien den Scheinwerfern auszuweichen. Flughöhe etwa
        3000 m, Westkurs. Ich schoß um 02,52 Uhr aus 100 m Entfernung von
        hinten unten in den Rumpf und die rechte Fläche. Dort sofort Brand
        mit heller Flamme. Das brennende Flugzeug wurde wieder von Schein-
        werfern angeleuchtet. Um 02,54 Uhr bemerkte ich den Aufschlagbrand.
        Wir schossen auch hier ES 4. Ort des Aufschlages: SSW des Schein-
        werfergebietes bei Vignacourt, 15 km NW Amiens.

        Von diesem Aufschlag flogen wir in weiter Linkskurve nach Osten.
        Mein Bordwart sah bald ein Flugzeug mit Westkurs uns entgegenkommen
        Wir erkannten wieder eine "Lancaster" und schossen um 03,04 Uhr aus
        80 m Entfernung von hinten unten in den Rumpf. Der Gegner brannte
        sofort. Um 03,06 Uhr bemerkte ich den brennenden Aufschlag. Ich
        erkannte im Feuerschein, daß die Aufschlagstelle W eines Flusses
        war. Aufschlagort: Guignemicourt, 7 km SW Amiens.

                                                    Bergmann

Bergmann's flight report – *Q-Queenie* is at 'Den 6'. (Bergmann Weitz Nimmo)

22

8./Nachtjagdgeschwader 4   Im Felde, 11.4.1944......
==============================

A b s c h u ß m e l d u n g.

1.) Zeit (Tag, Stunde, Minute) und Ort   11.4.1944, 02,43 Uhr, 1,5 km
    des Absturzes mit kurzer Gelände-   NNW Achiet,la petit, 8 km NW
    beschreibung,   Bapaume, 20 km S Arras

2.) Durch wen ist der Abschuß erfolgt: Hptm. B e r g m a n n

3.) Typ des abgeschossenen Flugzeuges   " L a n c a s t e r "

4.) Staatsangehörigkeit des Gegners: " E n g l a n d "

5.) Art der Vernichtung: Beschuß durch Nachtjäger

6.) Art des Aufschlages: Brennend aufgeschlagen

7.) Schicksal der Insassen: 7 Tote

8.) Gefechtsbericht des Schützen: Ist in der Anlage beigefügt

9.) Zeugen   a) Luft   Fw. Hauthal, Fw. Schopp
                    b) Erde   Uffz. Kißler, Flt. Grevillers

1o.) Anzahl der Angriffe, die auf das   1
     feindliche Flugzeug gemacht wurden:

11.) Richtung, aus der die einzelnen   Von unten
     Angriffe erfolgten:

12.) Höhe, in der der Abschuß erfolgte.   3ooo m

13.) Entfernung, aus der der Abschuß   1oo m
     erfolgte:

14.) Taktische Position, aus der der   Von hinten unten
     Abschuß angesetzt wurde:

15.) Ist einer der feindlichen Bord-   Nicht beobachtet
     schützen kampfunfähig gemacht
     worden:

16.) Verwandte Munitionsarten: 2 cm M-Gesch.Patr. O.L.

17.) Munitionsverbrauch: M.G. FF: 18 Schuß

18.) Art und Anzahl der Waffen, die bei   2 M.G. FF
     dem Abschuß gebraucht wurden:

19.) Typ des eigenen Flugzeuges: Bf 110 G-4

2o.) Weiteres taktisch und technisch   Kennzeichen des Feindflugzeuges:
     Bemerkenswertes: BD Kokarde ER

21.) Treffer im eigenen Flugzeug: ./.

22.) Beteiligung weiterer Einheiten: ./.

23.) Führungsverfahren: "Wilde Sau"

24.) Hat der Gegner bei "Li-Erfassung"   Dunkel, ohne Li und SN 2
     Abwehrbewegungen gemacht:

                                          Hptm. und Staffelkapitän

Bergmann's report on shooting down *Q-Queenie*. (Bergmann Weitz Nimmo)

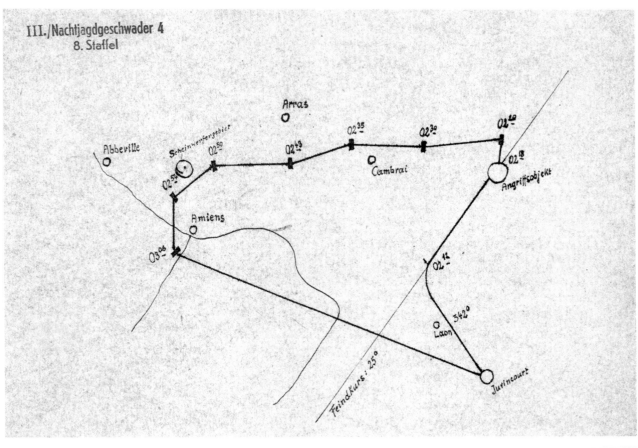

Helmut Bergmann's
original flight plan and
kills on 10/11 April.
(Bergmann Weitz Nimmo)

Der Reichsminister der Luftfahrt
und Oberbefehlshaber der Luftwaffe
Luftwaffenpersonalamt
Az. 29 Nr.   281   /44 ((A) 5, V)

Berlin, den 6.7.44.

An 8./N.J.G. 4

Der   8./N.J.G. 4

wird der Abschuß eines britischen Kampfflugzeuges vom Typ

   Avro "Lancaster"   am 11.4.44. 02,54 Uhr

durch Hptm. B e r g m a n n

als   zwölfter (12)   Luftsieg der Staffel anerkannt.

I. A.

B 5221- 5. 44. S.

Berlin confirms Bergmann's
Q-Queenie claimed kill.
(Bergmann Weitz Nimmo)

Left to right: Wilhelm Schopp, Helmut Bergmann and Günther Hauthal. The three are celebrating new-found fame after shooting down seven Lancasters in 46 minutes. (Bergmann Weitz Nimmo)

Helmut Bergmann with an unknown woman – possibly his girlfriend as it was unlikely that he married – taken just weeks before he was killed. (Bergmann Weitz Nimmo)

Göring personally signed this photograph in red for Bergmann. (Pohn Bergmann Weitz Nimmo)

Another shot of Bergmann with the unknown lady. (Bergmann Weitz Nimmo)

CHAPTER 3
Day One

On the Run

DAWN CAME AT LAST so I could make better progress. However, the fog persisted and visibility was still down to about ten yards. Following a track down a wooded hill, I heard voices approaching and the swish of bicycle tyres on a tarmac road. I dropped to my hands and knees as, just a short way ahead of me, the cyclists went past. I could hear their every move but mercifully the fog hid me. It was a sharp reminder that fog was a mixed blessing as I had all but stumbled onto a main road. Hurriedly retracing my footsteps through the damp grass, I headed back up the track to where I had noticed a path branching off, and found it again. It was well used, winding its way between oak trees and across a carpet of woodland flowers including primroses, celandine, wood anemones and, despite the cold, wet spring, early bluebell shoots. As I limped along I noticed how good it all smelled. Seeing the same wild plants as we had at home was somehow reassuring. After the night's horrors my senses were heightened and I appreciated these small things. Feeling more at ease, I looked for somewhere to rest until the fog cleared.

Suddenly, looming out of the damp air, I saw that the path led straight to the back door of a small, shabby, redbrick house standing alone amongst the trees. There was no garden or fence, but a clothesline full of family washing was strung across to the nearest tree. As I looked at the house I realised that all my values had changed again. Nothing in the world mattered to me except who lived there. I could not afford to make a mistake and so watched intently while the hours went by.

As the fog fitfully cleared, the sun broke

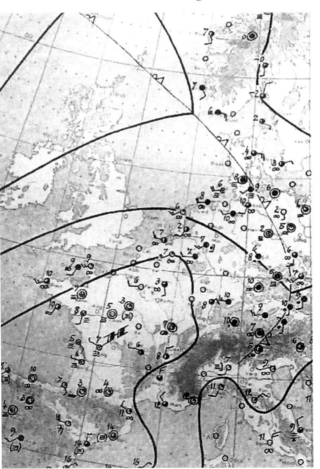

The Luftwaffe weather forecast chart for 10/11 April 1944. (Met Office)

through and two children appeared at the back door. I ducked down as they began playing. Then a man charged out of the house shouting and flailing his arms like a mad man; I had no idea what he was doing as it was too early in the year for wasps. Eventually, like the children, I took no notice and as the sun grew hotter I inevitably fell asleep. On waking, it was clear that quite some time had passed. The sky was darker and the place appeared deserted. Then I heard the children running up the path behind me. They were getting close. There was no time to do anything so I just waited for the awful moment when I would be discovered.

However, they stampeded past, almost grazing my left ear with their feet in their headlong rush into the house. They hadn't noticed me. Bad ankle or no bad ankle, I decided to move on and scurried away like a startled pheasant down across the wood and out of sight.

When I had put a quarter of a mile or so between the house and me, I collapsed against a tree waiting for the sounds of hot pursuit. However, all I could hear was bird song and the breeze in the branches above me. I gave myself a good talking to and vowed not to run again, a valuable lesson that would soon be put to the test.

Cumulus clouds were building up and by early afternoon they had obscured the sun. As I trudged on, the day became uncomfortably close and sultry. Every so often I thought I heard the sound of traffic in the distance. It was very faint at first but it grew louder and before long I realised that I was approaching the edge of the wood. Stopping at a good vantage point I spied out what lay ahead.

The wood bordered a large, ploughed field and, about 50 yards away on the far side of the furrows, there was a tree-lined road running roughly north–south[1]. To the north, about half a mile away and partly hidden behind trees, were two factory chimneys. To the left, a long way off, two peasants were working the land. As I watched, from the direction of the factories air-raid sirens started to wail and I heard the sound of aircraft approaching fast from the south. Two Mustangs came into sight. They were in loose formation, flying at no more than 200ft, twisting and weaving with their engines screaming at full throttle as if the hounds of hell were after them.

They passed over me and out of sight, heading north. With a growing sense of desolation and loneliness, I listened to the sound of their engines fading into the distance. In half an hour, I thought, those lucky devils would be having tea and hot buttered toast – crumpets even – at Douglas Bader's squadron at Tangmere near Chichester, on the Sussex coast.

From time to time camouflaged lorries rumbled by and less often what looked like German staff cars raced past. 'Bastards', I thought as I watched them disappear into the distance and turned my attention to the peasants away to the left. The situation looked promising so I went off in that direction, while still keeping hidden at the edge of the wood. They worked with their shirtsleeves rolled up, both wearing black trousers and cloth caps. They were bent over weeding, working very slowly along a furrow. Each time they moved forward it brought them closer to the edge of the wood. I could see that if I confined my movements to when they were over by the road, I would eventually be able to reach a position where I would be hidden from view but still able to see what they were doing. When I drew level with them I crawled nearer to the edge of the wood and curled myself up behind a small hawthorn bush and watched.

The two moved slowly and in silence. They looked like father and son – both were stocky and moved in the same way when they stood up to take a break. I decided to attract their attention when they were close enough. I felt that if they were related – and I felt pretty sure they were – then it was safe to approach them together. At any rate, it would be as safe as anything could be under the circumstances. However, things didn't go exactly to plan.

When they were about 40 yards away from me the boy stood up, stretched his back and found himself looking straight at me. I knew he had seen me. For a long, long moment we just stared at each other, not moving a muscle. Then, without giving any hint of a sign, he bent back to his work. He was about 15 years old, with fair hair and dark skin. Very slowly he worked his way across to the older man's side and, without stopping work or looking up, they began to converse. I could see their lips moving but they didn't even glance at each other. I knew they were talking about me.

They continued to work in silence until the older man stood up and, with his back to me, faced in the direction of the road. He was obviously looking to see if there was anybody else in sight. When he was satisfied that there was not, he turned and looked towards me for a moment. His movements were very slow and deliberate. The two of them were not far off now and soon covered the 20 yards to the wood. However, instead of walking directly towards me they stood and unhitched their shoulder bags while chatting normally to each other. This was to be a lunch break. They moved further into the wood and stopped some little way in.

They had given up pretending that they hadn't seen me so rather self-consciously I turned to watch them and the older man beckoned to me to follow them deeper into the wood. I crawled over to where they were sitting and took my RAF wings badge from my pocket to show them, making signs with the other hand to indicate an aircraft crashing. They nodded and pointed to the sky and seemed friendly. I tried some very halting French. I managed to make myself understood but couldn't fully understand them. I guess they spoke a pretty heavy patois.[2] I wondered if the old man had fought alongside the British in World War I. He said '*soldat*', pointing to himself and something about 'Tommy', so clearly he had.

He opened his knapsack and lifted out a bottle half full of white wine and a chunk of bread, which he broke in two, handing me the larger half. I was very hungry and almost frantic with thirst. I had not had anything to drink for nearly 24 hours.

I don't know why, but as I took the bottle I began to say '*Dankeschön*' and turned to ice as I heard my voice choking the word off mid-syllable – but the damage was done. They were both staring at me in disbelief. I really did see death itself looking straight at me and I was transfixed.

Gradually, the deadly look died and a blessed air of understanding calmed the old man's face. '*Ah oui!* Tanks', he said. 'Tanks', and then quickly added something to the boy. I heard the word 'Tommy' again. I have no doubt that had the old man not been of a generation that had fought in the World War I, I would have been strangled and buried in the wood that night. I would probably never have been heard of again. However, the old man clearly wanted me to be what I was. He was pleased, I think, with his knowledge of the English idiom.

There were smiles now and I lifted the bottle to toast them before drinking. The wine was pretty rough but I could have happily have drunk the lot and passed out at their feet. However, I was careful to take only a

Amiens, in the front line again. (3rdR UOPP, Nimmo Collection)

The great escape! (3rdR UOPP, Nimmo Collection)

little and show the appropriate pleasure and gratitude that I truly felt. Using great gestures and much whispering the old farmer managed to convey to me that I was right to head south. It seemed that Amiens was crawling with '*les boches, les nazis execrable!*' Apparently Amiens had been wrecked yet again quite recently as for some reason the RAF had bombed the town station and the local prison.[3]

The bread and wine sharpened up my senses and soon, using signs and pidgin French, the two of them told me that two RAF aircraft had come down the night before, and that one *aviateur*, a sergeant, had died that afternoon. His parachute had burnt as he fell. What an awful end, so close to escape too. I wondered if it was our wireless operator, Jim Tooley. I hoped not.

That's all I remember. I must simply have passed out and slept for two or three hours. I was wakened with a start by the cracking of a twig and lay absolutely still listening to the soft sound of someone approaching from behind me. Eventually, I turned over to face whoever it was and, to my great relief, found that it was the boy. He was carrying his knapsack and a black jacket bundled over his arm. Motioning me to keep down, he came and sat beside me. Opening the knapsack, he took out another bottle of white wine and, pulling the cork out with his teeth, he handed the bottle to me.

Thanking him, I took a long swig. Again, the wine was thin and sharp – I had to make a conscious effort not to cough. It seems amazing now, but that day was the first time I had ever tasted wine and it had come as quite a shock! He gave me bread and a good, coarse white goat's cheese. Once I'd eaten he gestured that I should try on the coat. It was a bit tight across the shoulders and the sleeves were an inch and a half short, but I was extremely grateful for it and did my best to show it. He pulled a rusty-black cloth cap, with a button on the top, from out of his jacket front and handed it to me. This excellent titfer fitted. With a battered pair of old hobnail boots thrown in as well, for all the world I felt like the cartoon character Andy Capp!

Feeling rather furtive in my new outfit, we sat down as I laced the boots, which fitted reasonably well, and I listened carefully as he gave me instructions. These were conveyed in his patois and were accompanied by numerous hand gestures – it's funny how well these linguistic moments do actually work. He indicated that he would lead me to safety and pointed to a distant lane. I was to stay well behind him, just keeping him in sight. When we reached a village he would leave me and I was to make my way to the church in the square where, he said, I would find *un ami*. He repeated that on no account must I get nearer to him than '*trois cents metres*' (300m). In any case he could see from my limp that I would be unable to walk fast. I knew the enormous risk that he was taking. If we were disguised as civilians and captured after contact with the Resistance we were technically spies and there would be no protection from the Geneva Convention, as it stood. Members of the Resistance ran hideous risks. If caught they would certainly be tortured until they betrayed their fellow workers and then they would be shot anyway.[4]

For this reason a Resistance worker who passed aircrew 'down the line' on their way to Switzerland or Spain would only know the workers on each side of him or her. That way, if anyone were caught, the few other members whom he or she knew could be whisked into hiding and the line would be broken until they were replaced. That was the theory but it did not always work out that way.

Before we set out on the journey, the boy scraped a shallow trench with his bare hands, folded my battledress jacket into it and covered it with dead leaves. I clean forgot to remove my pilot's wings from the pocket, so I was now an 'unidentified flying object', which would of course be very dangerous if I were caught.

The boy set out and, crossing the field and road, disappeared down the lane. I gave him a three-minute head start and, as I followed across the field, the setting sun appeared from behind a bank of clouds. From this I could tell we were heading south-west. To begin with all went well, though after a while I lost sight of the boy. It was a long, long way and night was falling, so it was with great relief that I found myself entering a village and saw the outline of a church steeple against the darkening sky.

As in wartime Britain, from dusk until dawn the whole of Europe lived in total blackout with not a light shining anywhere (this avoided giving landmarks to bombers). The houses on each side of me appeared like black shapes cut from cardboard. They seemed tiny and crowded in on all sides, but in the darkness they had no more form or substance than the silhouettes of cut out stage scenery before the lights go up.

A few furtive steps took me into a small square which, I was startled to find, was crowded. I couldn't see anyone but I could hear people chattering and laughing all around me. After the fear and loneliness of the past hours it was overwhelming and claustrophobic. I was suddenly surrounded by invisible people, or so it seemed. I had the horrible feeling that they could see and were discussing me, and this threw me. Not knowing why this was, or what to expect, in total bewilderment I made my way as quickly and as quietly as I could to the safety of the church, which loomed up on the far side of the square.

One of the large wooden doors stood ajar and that mustiness often present in churches seeped out to me. Edging sideways through the gap, I entered the pitch black beyond. Cautiously slipping off my new tackety-boots, I stood listening. To say that I was alert would be a gross understatement. I was deeply on edge, and not at all sure that I liked this game. The church was as dark as a tomb and at first it seemed empty. However, I gradually became aware that somebody was creeping about in the belfry above me. Eventually, it seemed that whoever it was up there was aware of my arrival. However, even though I was really expecting it, as he broke the silence and spoke I jumped out of my skin. My nerves were at breaking point!

Clearly, the owner of this unseen voice had heard me enter. He was certainly talking to me as there was no one else there. However, I couldn't understand a word he said and he couldn't understand my execrable French. '*Je suis un aviateur anglais.*' No reply. I might have been the man from M.A.R.S. for all the voice cared.

The more we, or rather I, tried to converse, the angrier this man seemed to become and eventually I decided that it wasn't safe, and that I should cut my losses and leave fairly promptly. I slipped my boots back on and, a bit like the pantomime dame, tiptoed back out.

I left the church and the village as quietly as possible and continued south. Thinking back on the afternoon, and what the old farm worker had told me, I felt reassured that, despite this disappointment, at least I had made the right decision to head south. Given the news about the recent Amiens raid it had been the best choice as it was very likely to be the safest direction in which to head.

Crossing the river Somme, I found that the bridge wasn't guarded and that I can't explain. I was just lucky. It didn't seem odd at the time, but then I didn't know which river it was or even that the name of the village had been Hangest-sur-Somme.[5] At that point it was a river of absolutely no importance at all.

I walked all night, navigating south by the stars, and then before dawn, with the ground already damp with dew, I tried to sleep in a haystack, which I would not recommend as it was exceedingly uncomfortable. With first light – just a lightening of the darkness – I moved on and soon found myself in the beginnings of an orchard, where I had a very strange experience. I found myself facing a soldier in medieval French dress. I am quite sure that it was a hallucination, but that's what dreams are. I was beyond fatigue and I suppose in no rational state. I imagine it was a little like the effect of smoking pot. However, I don't completely discount what I

The area around the Somme was indeed 'crawling with Germans'. (3rdR UOPP, Nimmo Collection)

saw. As far as I'm concerned I really did see this and can still vividly recall it. The figure was dressed all in grey with velvet breeches and a gun of sorts over his shoulder. I was riveted to the spot and then, as something drew my attention, I looked away for a moment. When I looked back, he had simply disappeared. It could have been a configuration of the branches in an apple tree I suppose, but what I saw, in close detail, was a musketeer from the mid-17th century. Whatever it was, or whatever caused the experience, I believe that I saw a ghost.

The bright light of day never seemed to come. High cirrus cloud backlit by the moon cast a very soft, dim light. I wasn't going anywhere for the moment, so I simply waited. The orchard was attached, or belonged to, a biggish French farmhouse and had a row of cottages and a track that led off somewhere. As I took this in a man pulling a bicycle backed out of one of the cottages. He, like my apparition, was dressed in grey and he was carrying something over his shoulder. I realised that this was a rifle and that he was a German soldier! He was the first I'd seen at close quarters and it was quite a jolt. He got on his bike and cycled off to the left, which was the direction I wanted to take. As he disappeared out of sight, I continued to walk south and the light gradually increased.

I must have covered a lot of ground. At first it was just fields and woodland but then, through the early mist at about 6 a.m., I came to the outskirts of an ancient village or hamlet of incredibly primitive houses[6] and the nearest thing to a road I had seen for a day. I was fascinated because this place too was from another era and at first seemed so unspoiled. As I walked into the village, a child carrying a bucket of water came and joined me. She just walked alongside, glancing at me. Ahead of us and a little to the left, another church loomed up and out stepped a man in a long grey coat. Again I was shocked to see that this was a German Officer. There was nothing I could do but keep walking.

I believe the child had come from the cottages on my right where several women looked at us from their doorways. I thought at the time that it was because I was a stranger but what I now believe is that, alerted to my presence and aware that I was walking into a trap, these villagers had sent the child to attract me away from what I was to find at the end of the street.

The road bent to the right and as I turned the corner I saw that I was walking straight into a German breakfast parade. They were assembling, facing what seemed to be their commanding officer. He was busy mustering and snapping at them. I kept walking towards them as it was the only option. The one thing I had learned the day before was don't run, don't draw attention to yourself, simply keep going, keep plodding along.

The cottages ahead of me were freshly wrecked, with camouflaged tanks and armoured cars driven right through the walls and parked in the ground floors. The 'peaceful, unspoiled hamlet' was actually crawling with SS panzer troops. I walked straight between the sergeant-major type and the front rank of his men. They didn't take a blind bit of notice of me. By this time the child had disappeared off the face of the earth. I didn't see her go, and I'm glad of that because I might have been drawn into doing something dangerous. I just kept walking with the raucous sound of a drill going on behind me – it was the same kind of thing you get in every army: 'ATTTteennnn . . . WAIT for it you 'orrible little man . . . AttennnTION! . . . Get yer hair cut! . . . What do you think this is? Bognor *bloody Regis*?' All in German of course. Not knowing whether to laugh or scream, and with the hairs on the back of my neck prickling up, I plodded on while expecting a bullet to sing through me at any moment. However, these Germans were otherwise occupied.

Coming out onto a tree-lined main road, or what passed for one in those parts, I trudged south all morning and eventually saw the spire of what looked to me like a Romanesque church. This time it turned out to be at the top left-hand corner of a village square. It was square and squat and the bell was ringing. Remembering the advice we had been given about priests often sympathising with the Allies, I walked up the stone steps and into the well of the church.

There was one other person in there about four rows in front of me – a woman dressed in black. Shortly a priest came in and started to give the service for his congregation of two – her and me. I didn't understand a word. It was in probably in Latin, which was not a subject I had excelled in at school.

This priest was short and unkempt. He hadn't shaved and looked a bit grubby. However, I was also aware of the pungent rabbitty smells coming from my own borrowed jacket and also that I was unshaven and had slept in a hedge. As I thought he might be prepared to help me, I sat, listened and waited. When eventually he moved towards the altar the woman followed him. It appeared that he was giving communion – or were they whispering to each other? As I didn't join them he finally came over to me and without saying anything he knelt. To my surprise the elderly woman came as well and this time sat in the row right behind me. They were really quite close and as we were the only people in the church this seemed a bit intimate, and very odd.

I needed to think fast, so I closed my eyes as if praying. Nothing happened and nobody said a thing. There was absolute silence. Why had the woman moved behind me? Was it normal to do what she had done? Could I place my trust in either of them? With my head tilted forward, I kept one eye firmly shut in the hope that I looked pious. Actually, I did pray hard, and thought even harder. Again, it was only for moments but in my mind it seemed to drag on. I sized up the situation. The priest might well be a good, man – why not? Possibly the woman was as well, but possibly not. She was simply too close, suspiciously close, as if she wanted to hear what I said to this Catholic priest.

I had been told not to approach anyone unless they were alone. I had already broken that rule once and got away with it. I felt that if I spoke to the priest he might or might not want to help, but with the woman right behind me listening – as I was now sure she was – I would incriminate the priest as well as myself. It was a risk I would not take. That decided, I finished praying, stood up and, nodding my thanks to the curious priest, walked to the door, turned and genuflected as best an Anglican non-church goer can. Then I simply walked out and that was the end of that. I walked south out of the village feeling a great sense of disappointment.

There were almost no people to be seen as most men were away at war, leaving just women, children, the elderly and priests and there were almost none of those. Therefore, I was well aware that in that church at best I had been an unwashed and unshaved curiosity. In fact, I would have been a curiosity anywhere and I must have been sticking out like the proverbial 'sore thumb'.

Eventually, I came to a track leading up a bank, which seemed a convenient spot to turn off the road. At the top of the bank an endless vista of hedgeless farmland stretched way off to the south. It was empty and utterly soulless and for the first time I broke down and sobbed bitterly. I suppose it was bound to happen at some stage. Admittedly, I felt abandoned and very alone, so given the circumstances it was inevitable. Shock and fatigue had arrived with a rush but I was deeply angry too, which in a way helped me in this tricky situation.

Just a generation ago, very close to this empty landscape, the Battle of the Somme had claimed hundreds of thousands of lives. Many families, on both sides, lost an entire generation of young men – very many were barely out of their teens, and had little or no understanding of why they were fighting. Some families would never recover. They would simply die out. I was thinking of the Gordon Highlanders and the Cabrach plateau below the Pictish Tap O'Noth.[7] The whole area was now abandoned, a village with shops, streets, homes and outlying black houses and a kirk – all killed off by the 'war to end all wars'! Like so many others, my own family had known its tragedies. My Perthshire-born mother's maiden name was 'Love', my aunt Chris (splendidly baptised 'Christian Love') lost the man she was to have married and, as with many women of her generation, she would never find another to replace him.

World War I, what sort of folly was that anyway? Here we were 25, years later, at it again. So many good souls perishing in an attempt to stop some bloody tyrant. What was wrong with a society that so many people seemed to blindly follow an ogre like Hitler, or that strutting peacock Mussolini? Why did they do that? What force did these dreadful types hold over ordinary, decent human beings? I felt that this trait wasn't in my culture – I hoped not. Maybe we were just lucky. Then maybe not. I feared the worst for most of my crew and many others. I was lucky, very lucky, but here I was standing alone in the vastness of old battlefields. I found it all very hard to understand.

It took me a while to realise how unproductive these bleak thoughts were and as I spied ahead, over what seemed a vastly hostile plain, I gathered my wits and, in a more practical frame of mind, set out, skirting to the south-south-west as close to cover as possible. For some reason that seemed to be the most promising route. As I went, I remembered something that made me smile. It was a quote from a thoroughly amusing anti-war book, *The Good Soldier Svejk* by Jaroslav Hasek, which was one of those new paperback books that I had treated myself to. Hasek said 'Wars are great aren't they? They are always glorious, always honourable, always the fight for justice, and always the other fellow's fault. That's maybe why we have so many of them. . . .' How hopelessly true.

CHAPTER 4

Die Dreißiger und die großen Hoffnungen

The Corruption of German Youth

BORN INTO A MILITARY family in Bochum, Westphalia, on 26 May 1920, Bergmann was very likely to join the Nazi party. By 1935, when he'd reached the age of 15, he was obliged to join the Hitlerjugend (Hitler Youth). While not officially obliged to join the Nazi party it would probably be expected that a Luftwaffe major's son would. His red and white swastika armband confirms that he did as was expected as any wearer would have been in the Nazi Party youth division. National Socialism was something he'd almost certainly embraced while going through '53 Straubing Donau' boot camp and while at Eger in the Sudetenland, both of which were on the Bavarian-Czech frontier (his flying school, Schülerkompanie AB, was also near Eger). The training had been hard but they had been heady, promising days. Flying was Bergmann's passion, and for him there was no better way of doing it than by fighting for the expanding fatherland, helping the Führer to rebuild the Reich. Bergmann became a true Nazi and they were not that common among Luftwaffe pilots.

During Bergmann's youth, Germany had slumped into a political shambles and was deeply restless. At first, the Nationalsozialistische Deutsche Arbeiterpartei (NSDAP or Nazis) offered ostensibly radical ideas of shaping-up, giving their youth a sense of pride, reconstructing the infrastructure and shaking off the general sense of oppression. With the depth of the depression this had not only greatly appealed to many German families but to many others as well including, it should be remembered, a fair number of British families and organisations. However, at the politico/military Hitlerjugend camps, Germany's young were indoctrinated, flattered and battered into knowing that they were the best, an order-following 'master race'. Failure to grasp that was simply not on the agenda.

Hitlerjugend propaganda. Hitler set about indoctrinating Germany's youth and in this bizarre propaganda photomontage, der Führer (or possibly just his head on someone else's body) and an unfortunate child in Hitlerjugend uniform pose against a stock image of an enthusiastic public. (Nimmo Collection)

Helmut Bergmann 'at the awkward stage' in 1932. Clearly self-conscious, he doubtless craved a pair of long trousers. (Bergmann Weitz Nimmo)

Bergmann (3rd from left) at Straubing Donau 'boot camp'. Early military training was tough and competitive. The 'hard case' at the left appears to be an army *Feldwebel* (Sergeant) and a decorated marksman. Becoming a fighter pilot had always been Bergmann's aim. His father Heinrich (himself a Luftwaffe major) was clearly expecting a good deal of his son, and Helmut would not let him down. (Bergmann Weitz Nimmo)

Bergmann (far left) at Straubing Donau 'boot camp'. (Bergmann Weitz Nimmo)

Although a bit retiring at first, Helmut Bergmann could produce a radiant smile when he liked, which wasn't often. The shyness was soon knocked out of him at Straubing Donau and Magdeburg, where on Kristallnacht (Night of Broken Glass), the Hitlerjugend went on the rampage. It wasn't long before he too was sporting the fashionably 'Old Prussian Warrior' hand on hip stance of Hitler's brainwashed youth. The Führer, his Reichsjugendführer, Baldur von Schirach, and their unsavoury bullies moulded this generation so that many became the 3rd Reich's unquestioning and arrogant 'unintelligencia'.

As a youngster, Helmut Bergmann had always shown a passion for aircraft and flying. He was born to it, and his passion would come at the just right age, when a whole new generation of young pilots was needed. By March 1933, Göring had founded the RLM and, contrary to (and because of) the Treaty of Versailles, which banned German re-armament, all air clubs became part of the German Flying Sports Association (DVLA). This was the thinly disguised and rapidly growing new Luftwaffe. Thus, Bergmann would get his wish to become a pilot, a course which also drew him into the Nazi party.

He started his training as a Luftwaffe pilot at Eger (known as Cheb in Czech),in Bohemian Sudetenland, a bastion of German National Socialism since way back in 1895). Bergmann's father Heinrich would visit him there when he could. Eger proved an exciting place and Hitler himself paid several rapid day visits to the Reichsgau. As Eger was so historical important to the NSDAP, it was here, with the town largely cleared of Jews and the market *Hauptplatz* festooned with Swastika flags and re-named Adolf Hitler Platz, that the Führer delivered speeches to his mesmerised public.[1]

As Germany took control of Bohemia and then the whole of Czechoslovakia, Jewish-owned property was abandoned and businesses were sold for the price of an exit visa, and so the Nazi party became even more popular among the remaining Sudetendeutsche. Just 52 kilometres north-east of Bayreuth (home to Hitler's favourite Wagnerian opera house) and to the south-west of magnificent Dresden, Sudetenland was overwhelmingly loyal to the Führer.

Heinkel had a factory and airfield at Eger where it produced the He 117, a plane nicknamed *'Der Luftwaffenfeuerzeug'* (The Flying Coffin) – clearly it was not a great success.[2]

Father Heinrich's photograph of 'Oma' and Helmut, who was by now being formed by the Hitler Youth and already a member of the Nazi youth section. (Bergmann Weitz Nimmo)

Helmut Bergmann – now completely moulded by the Hitler Youth and the Nazi party. Unless you were a serious Nazi, being photographed in uniform quite so often as Bergmann was, was very rare. Bergmann's photo albums tell us rather a lot about him, and it isn't good. (Bergmann Weitz Nimmo)

Helmut Bergmann with
D-ETIS, a Focke Wulf
named 'Rote Erde'.
(Bergmann Weitz
Nimmo)

Adolf Hitler Platz with flags.

Major Heinrich Bergmann and Helmut Bergmann. This and other more faded photographs, suggest a rather 'stiff' relationship between Helmut Bergmann and his military father. Major Heinrich Bergmann only ever appears in his Luftwaffe uniform, even on family walks and picnics! The white cap cover was usually reserved for weddings, formal occasions and so on, yet Major Bergmann seemed to live in it. He was at best a proud man, and may have proved an intimidating father. (Bergmann Weitz Nimmo)

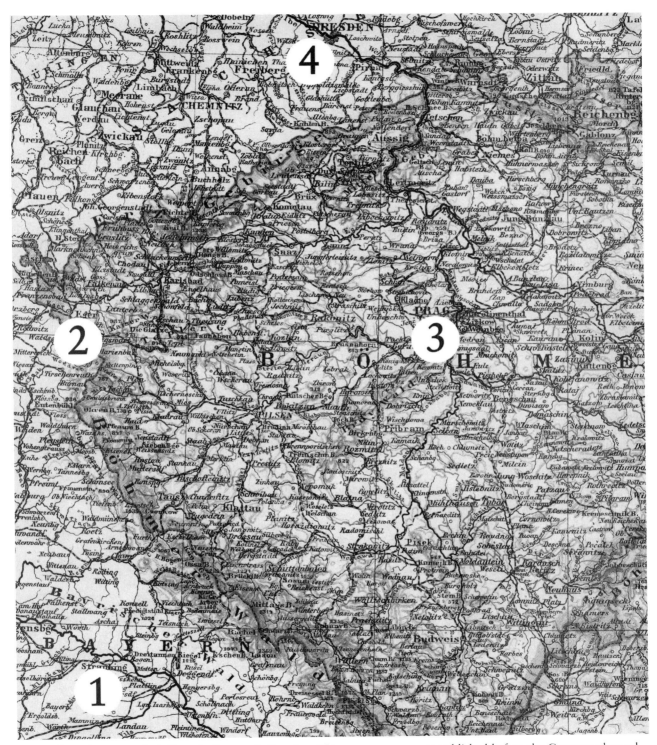

1. Straubing 'boot camp'; 2. Eger; 3. Prague; 4. Dresden. This pre-war map was published before the Germans charged east across the frontier annexing Sudetenland and Böhemia and then occupying the whole of Czechoslovakia. (Nimmo Collection)

Adolf Hitler Platz at Eger, Sudetenland. (Nimmo Collection)

Below: A German soldier's photograph of people waiting at Schweissing (two stops down the line from Eger) for the next train out. Just days after the September 1938 Sudetendeutsche revolt, the Germans moved east across the frontier. Sudetenland was no place to be if you were Jewish. (3rdR UOPP, Nimmo Collection)

3rd Reich postcard showing the intimidating Kirchensteige perched above the river Eger (or Ohfie). (Nimmo Collection)

Eger – Kirchenstiege

Luftwaffe accommodation at Eger was very basic. When the winter winds blew snow in from Poland and Russia in the north-east, the barracks were bitterly, deeply cold, and Helmut Bergmann felt it. (3rdR UOPP, Nimmo Collection)

A great many young Luftwaffe fighter pilots trained here. They were an exuberant lot and nothing much stopped the fun. In winter 1940/41, the Reich looked unstoppable and the Luftwaffe a force to be proud of. The crushing defeat at Starlingrad, with some 147,000 German dead and 91,000 taken prisoner, had yet to happen. (Bergmann Weitz Nimmo)

A night out with 'der Freundeskreis' at the Regina Bar, Munich. Helmut Bergmann is on the right. (Bergmann Weitz Nimmo)

Another of Helmut Bergmann's photographs of friends at Eger. The central pilot seems likely to be the future Ace Heinz-Wolfgang Schnaufer. (Bergmann Weitz Nimmo)

The Bergmann family. Helmut (left) is shown with his father Heinrich, mother Edith and younger brother. (Bergmann Weitz Nimmo)

Helmut Bergmann found the next Eger project more inspired. The Heinkel He 219 'Uhu' night-fighter was produced at Eger and was the first aeroplane in the world to be fitted with ejector seats. Heinkel, it seemed, had begun to listen to pilots.

Bergmann was also impressed by Albert Speer's plan to form squadrons of jet-powered fighters with pilots recruited from the Hitlerjugend. However, while the idea was approved, events moved so quickly that it wasn't to happen. It was an exhilarating time for the Eger trainees as Poland was invaded, France and Britain declared war, the Blitzkrieg swamped the Low Countries, the Allies were driven into the sea, and France and the Channel Islands were occupied.

Bergmann couldn't wait to get involved. Proving a capable pupil, he was

Charging into France via the Ardennes, foot soldiers, cavalry and horse-drawn transport proved as necessary and as adaptable as ever. (3rdR UOPP, Nimmo Collection)

The 3rd Reich invaded their neighbour the way the French and Germans usually did, largely on foot or on horseback. Bicycles had proved useful since the Boer War and so they did again during the Nazi version of the 1940 Tour de France. (3rdR UOPP, Nimmo Collection)

Raising the dust under a leaden sky, Army Group A in the Ardennes forest. Von Rundstedt bypassed the Maginot Line and these German soldiers are a visual reminder of the historic and strategic importance of the Ardennes. Foraging and marching west, they could almost be a Roman cohort. From Christmas 1944 to the end of January 1945 – during the desperate Battle of the Bulge – von Rundstedt re-attempted the Ardennes route into France, and failed. (3rdR UOPP, Nimmo Collection)

selected to train as a night-fighter pilot and posted to Schwäbisch Hall 'Blindflugschule'[3], where he learned to fly on instruments in '*Der Paula*' an adapted Junkers Ju 86. The Luftwaffe Ace-to-be Heinz-Wolfgang Schnaufer[4] was there too. All this drew Bergmann out of his shell and he made some friends, though his politics left others cold. Leave could be spent out on the tiles in Munich or, if possible, at home. He worried greatly about the increasingly bombed Ruhr. His home town of Bochum, Westphalia, was built on iron ore and coal. Coalmines, synthetic fuel plants and steel mills worked round the clock to supply the Ruhr industries, and for that reason became an important Allied target. He was relieved that his mother Edith and the family lived in the comparative safety of Haudorf bei Münster, not so far from Westerholt. Nevertheless, still he fretted. At Haudorf his family lived too close to the railway junction for comfort. By 1941 Helmut Bergmann would be doing his bit to defend the Reich, and his family, as part of the night-fighter shield in the airfields of north-eastern Occupied France. With the Allied bombing intensifying and the Luftwaffe lagging badly, night-fighter units were much needed and at Juvincourt Helmut Bergman found himself to be on the front line.

The Battle of France was rapid and ruthless. While Paris was left largely unscathed, many other towns and cities were wrecked. (3rdR UOPP, Nimmo Collection)

Yet more devastation in north-east France. (3rdR UOPP, Nimmo Collection)

16 June 1940. Lieutenant General Kurt von Briesen taking the salute at the rapidly organised Avenue Foche Nazi victory parade, opposite what would soon became Gestapo Paris HQ. (Nimmo Collection)

Liebe Eltern!   7.4.42. /8./10.

Für Eure Post aus Kissingen vielen Dank. Ich glaube ich habe
alles erhalten. Es freut mich sehr, dass es Euch so gut dort
gefallen hat und, dass es Vati wieder besser geht.

    Hier hat sich nichts allzubesonderes ereignet.Einige Tommies
wurden abgeschossen,aber auch einige Kameraden mussten dran
glauben.

    Ich habe die Bitte ,dass Ihr mir folgende Sachen schicken
möchtet :

        I) mein Feahrrad,bitte so,dass nichts geklaut wierd.
        2.) das Hemd,Kragen,die ich in Handorf liegen liess.

    Für heute viele grüsse

Above: 'Dear parents'. News about shooting down 'Tommies'. (Bergmann Weitz Nimmo)

Left: Helmut Bergmann in his own cockpit. (Bergmann Weitz Nimmo)

Below: Bergmann's cockpit. (Bergmann Weitz Nimmo)

Bergmann ready to protect the 3rd Reich. This is probably a staged propaganda shot. (Bergmann Weitz Nimmo)

CHAPTER 5

Trapped

The Corruption of German Youth

CLIMBING UP A LONG valley, I saw that I was approaching a cottage where an elderly woman was weeding her vegetable garden. She heard me coming and, propping herself up on her hoe, scrutinized my arrival in a distrustful way. I begged a cup of water and asked her if she would please fill my water bottle. Not knowing what to make of me she seemed scared stiff. It was clear that she was quite alone there and terrified, poor old thing – maybe she thought she was going to be raped. I do hope not. Despite her obvious fear, she was good enough to give me the water. I thanked her as best I could and walked on, leaving her to her vegetable patch and what seemed to be her own vast solitude.

Trudging on through the day, I eventually found myself in another orchard and there, in the middle distance, beyond the pear trees, was the roof of a house with a barnyard in front. It looked promising or, at the very least, worth investigating. Thus, I found myself slipping into the barn. I searched out a reasonably comfortable spot in a shadowy corner where, on a stack of empty jute sacks, I could rest and continue to gather my thoughts. As twilight began to fall and the birdsong died away other, more sinister, sounds came from the far, dark corners of this barn – small scratchings and scufflings and what seemed to my heightened imagination to be chuckling and whispering. Suddenly, something scurried along a ledge not two feet behind me. If I'd had hair it would doubtless have stood on end and I came to the rapid conclusion that this really wasn't for me. Clutching my precious water bottle and escape kit I shot outside and leaned against a wall, sucking in lungfuls of fresh evening air. I was on edge and becoming over twitchy.

It was still light enough to see the shapes and some of the details of the buildings around me. The barn backed onto a small, but substantial, brick-built house in the classical French style. This was guarded by a wall about two metres high which made up the left-hand side of the cobbled yard that I found myself standing in. Against this wall were two or three rows of raised rabbit hutches beside a brick lean-to and a tool shed, or maybe it was an outside loo. I felt that if I climbed the hutches and onto the slanting roof, I would have a much better view of the house and garden.

Above: The Farmhouse, still just as it was, with the rabbit hutches and wall. (Nimmo Collection)

Above right: In the background, the barn in which Neil Nimmo rested, waiting for dusk. (Nimmo Collection)

I stretched up and placed my escape kit and water bottle on top of the lean-to roof. Then, as silently as possible I shinned up the rabbit hutches and heaved myself onto the tin roof. However, in doing so I nudged my water bottle, which promptly fell into the garden that lay ahead on the other side of the wall. Without a second thought, I swung my legs over the wall and dropped down the other side. It was a bad mistake, the kind of thing one does when over-tired. Retrieving the bottle I turned to climb back and found that the ground was considerably lower on the garden side and that there were, of course, no rabbit hutches to give me a lift. I looked around for a way out.

A pair of tall, closed iron gates lay at the far end of the garden beyond the house, which had its windows shuttered for the night. A small chink of light was showing through the left ground floor shutter. I tiptoed over to where I could see through this gap and into the room. There was a child of about ten and someone who, from the kind of dress she was wearing, looked to be the child's governess. They were seated at a polished table reading a very large book, possibly an atlas.

I took a deep breath and tapped on the shutter, causing them both to jump up and, as they huddled together, they gazed in terror in my direction. This made me think they must be alone in the house, as they would surely be shouting for help if help were at hand. I tapped again and after a moment's pause they both moved quickly beyond my limited vision – towards a door I guessed. I don't know what I expected them to do but I thought that I had blown it. However, after a pause there was the scraping of an upper window shutter being opened and the woman's head appeared.

Grabbing the initiative, in a stage whisper I blurted out, '*Parlez-vous anglais?* . . . err . . . RAF.'

'*Et alors!*' – 'So what?' – came the blunt reply, adding, '*Allez vous en monsieur!*' – 'Get out of here'. I didn't recognise the words but her tone of voice said it all. Stretching my French to the limit I hissed '*La résistance?*'

'*C'est quoi la résistance?*' – 'Never heard of it!', she answered, and then a little more kindly, and in English, 'You'll really have to go please *monsieur*'. She pointed to the gates behind me.

I could see that I was onto a loser and decided to make as dignified an exit as possible. I blew her a two-handed kiss and bowed low. I felt it was the sort of graceful gesture that Charles Boyer would have made when playing Napoleon and it was just a pity that in the dusk she may have missed the finer points of my performance. As I retreated to the gates I heard the window bang shut. However, on turning the squeaky handle it seemed the gates were locked. I swallowed my pride, and on knocking again, she saw the point and let me out. We parted fairly amicably – maybe she had seen my first gallant exit after all!

I set off into the gathering gloom and, as best I could, continued southwards towards Paris for some hours. I was moving very, very slowly, as I couldn't see well, even in the starlight. It was now about three nights after the full moon and the moon wasn't up. I suppose, at best, I was moving at about half a mile an hour down a road I could hardly see even using my peripheral vision. I was reminded of a fellow pilot who was as good as blind in one eye. Wanting badly to be a pilot, during his medical eye test he had covered his left eye with his left hand and read the chart with his right eye – 20/20. He then raised his right hand and covered his left eye, reading again with his right eye. He still had 20/20 vision and was passed medically fit!

After a great deal of time, in the early hours of the morning I heard a familiar sound, which to begin with didn't mean much. Then I caught the faint but familiar whiff of coal smoke and steam and thought, 'Good God . . . a train! Wake up Nimmo!' From then on this distant sound and the occasional smell on the breeze held real significance. Here was something one reads about, or sees at the cinema – jumping a train! However, the reality is very different from the image portrayed. I took my bearing from the stars and orientated myself to face west. From where I now faced what sounded like a goods train was coming very, very slowly from my left-hand side and so must be heading north-east towards Amiens. From the steam engine's labouring effort it sounded very heavily loaded. After a bit it stopped, more or less in front of me now but still a little way off. 'Well,' I thought as I picked up pace, 'here's a chance.' I tried to reason it out. It seemed to me that this was probably an ammunition train that was heading up to the coast at the Pas-de-Calais, some 20 miles to the north of me on the other side of Abbeville. I knew just about enough of the layout of northern France to have an idea of the geography involved. I thought it wouldn't be too difficult to climb up onto the train as it appeared to be travelling at an exceedingly slow speed. After all, this was similar to something I did most days when travelling from Dulwich to central London.

In those days before the wa, we would line up in Barry Road and as the buses came around the corner we would start running at somewhere near the speed of the bus, grab the upright pole on the back platform and, as the driver accelerated, our legs swung up into the air and we floated along for a blissful ten yards like a flag in the breeze. Then, as the driver put his brakes on, we floated down onto the platform with a penny (which was all the fare cost) ready to drop into the conductor's hand. Having seen this performance every day for the past five years the bus conductor would never react; he wasn't going to be drawn into expressing any admiration.

It was a very different matter when it came to dealing with a night train. Nothing was similar and all and the odds were stacked against me. It may have looked as though it was travelling at walking speed, but in reality it was travelling at a good 20 miles an hour. I could only see by the light from the firebox of the first of what turned out to be two separate trains, and instead of pavement there were ballast and sleepers which got dangerously in the way.

The second train halted long enough for me to attempt to get on. The problem was that once away from a platform goods trains are way off the ground. They come about chin high, which makes it very difficult to get on. I didn't know where this train was really going but it seemed to me that to catch it would be to be making progress of some sort. However, I was so worn-out by now that I simply couldn't manage it, which was fortunate, as in any case things took a very much better course.

When the second train had left I could see that the reason for them coming to a halt was a level crossing. On the opposite side of the track there was a small hut. It looked like a signalman's box, but was smaller than they usually are in Britain. I could see a chink of light coming from under the door. This was quite exciting and it could be that help was at hand at last. We had been told that there was a large communist element amongst French railway workers and that they were very anti-German, particularly since the invasion of Russia.

Crossing the track, I gently knocked. There was a sound of rustling – something was going on inside. I knocked again and a man opened the door. He was blocking what little light there was – so we were almost in pitch darkness. '*Oui? Que fais-vous ici monsieur? . . . Comme même vous ne devriez pas se promener sur les rails comme ça!'* Basically, what did I want and what was I doing on his railway track? Or that's what I took him to be asking. Stepping aside, without waiting for a reply, he motioned me to enter.

Inside, by the oil lamp, I saw a look of real fear in his eyes. *'Je suis un aviateur anglais,'* I said. 'RAF. *Aidez-moi!'* I had rehearsed it a bit by this point.

'Dis donc! Qu'est-ce que j'ai avoir avec ça moi?'

I got the general idea. However, despite his fear he remained remarkably calm. He showed absolute neutrality and seemed non-committal. He did not seem prepared to help, but he didn't show me the door either so I had to do something and kept pressing the point that he must know somebody who could help me. After about 20 minutes I felt a draught and was sure that someone was standing right there behind me. It then dawned on me that while I had been pleading, he had manoeuvred us so that I had my back to a curtained-off wall. I was terrified. Was it the Gestapo? Had I walked into a trap? I was definitely 'pimming'.[1] I slowly turned and saw a woman. She was carrying a pistol, which she pointed away, and simply asked, 'Are you English or American?' The man (who had been speaking French all the time) told her in English what I had said, and quite well enough to show that the situation was not at all as I had feared. He had been carefully testing me and, thank God, he was satisfied. Subsequent conversations revealed that this remarkable man was a leading Resistance worker in the area. He had already helped some 12 or 15 airmen on along the Resistance chain. My prayers had been answered. I couldn't have been luckier.

Monsieur Lyon[2] was the station master at this small country halt and was only referred to as 'Monsieur Lyon de St Segrée'. I was taken to his incredibly sparse house. It was, to my eyes, poverty stricken with no carpet, no covers, no pictures or anything that could be considered a luxury. However, the whole place was spotlessly clean in the way that French homes are – even the bottoms of their chair legs are polished! I was given some very welcome soup, a hunk of dry bread and a serious cheese and was told that as daylight was coming I would have to go and lie up in the woods while they were getting things organised. They said that at dusk the following day Monsieur Lyon would come to the woods and whistle.

Back in the woods, utterly exhausted but believing that I had found help, I gave in and dropped into a fitful sleep. I had a vivid dream about China, our Dachshund.[3] In this dream China was chasing sheep and I was trying to stop him; someone was whistling. This, of course, turned out to be Monsieur Lyon. It was a lovely evening, the air was warm and at last seemed peaceful. However, putting his finger to the side of his nose, as the French sometimes do, Monsieur Lyon motioned me to be very cautious. *'Tout le monde et sa femme est la.'* The world and his wife were about. 'The

A 'draisne' rail car. (3rdR UOPP, Nimmo Collection)

area to the east is being searched, and there are *draisne* [rail patrols] out on the tracks.'

Monsieur Lyon confirmed what the farm workers had told me, saying that the area around Amiens and north-east towards the Belgian border was deadly at the moment. News a few days ago of a Resistance attack on a German troop train near Lille had proven true. Unfortunately, he said, it had led to particularly vicious reprisals. Some 80 souls had been taken out and slowly butchered in front of the village women and children.[4] Monsieur Lyon added that for all our sakes I was not to be seen arriving at the hamlet we were heading for and that for the time being I would be kept comfortable but I would simply disappear. This, he said, had all been arranged. It sounded very wise to me.

Following this blessed *cheminot*, I picked my way back through the woods skirting fallen trees and a large clump of last year's surprisingly noisy bracken. Shortly, we joined a path that led us to a point where, while avoiding the signal box, we could cross the tracks. I could just see that on the opposite side of the rails the path continued off into the trees. Monsieur Lyon stopped inside the edge of the wood and looked and listened, not a word was said. He eventually decided it was clear and quietly explained that there were German rail patrols and Gestapo in the area. He was being extremely cautious, but it was obvious that while we were actually crossing the tracks we had no cover at all.

I was taken to his home again and introduced to two women. One was buxom, in fact very buxom, with a most elaborate hat. The other was tall, thin and 'spiky' and missing her two front teeth. She too had an elaborate hat. I was to find that it was typical of the Resistance workers to wear highly fashionable clothes as if going to a special event. By this time it was getting quite dark and we set off from the level crossing to Souplicourt, a simple little village a mile or two away.

I was going to stay at Jeanne Marguery's home – she was the spiky one. The buxom woman was Mme Duvray. Miss Marguery's house was a very basic single-storey peasant's place, with just one bedroom and one broom cupboard, which was to be my bedroom. There was also one tin *cabinet*, or loo. It was explained to me at length that if I was to stay in Jeanne Marguery's humble abode, they would have to lock me in.

It was back to basics. I was a prisoner with a straw bed, locked in this little house for the best part of three weeks and with good reason – it was to keep us all safe. My new home was really little more than a cubbyhole

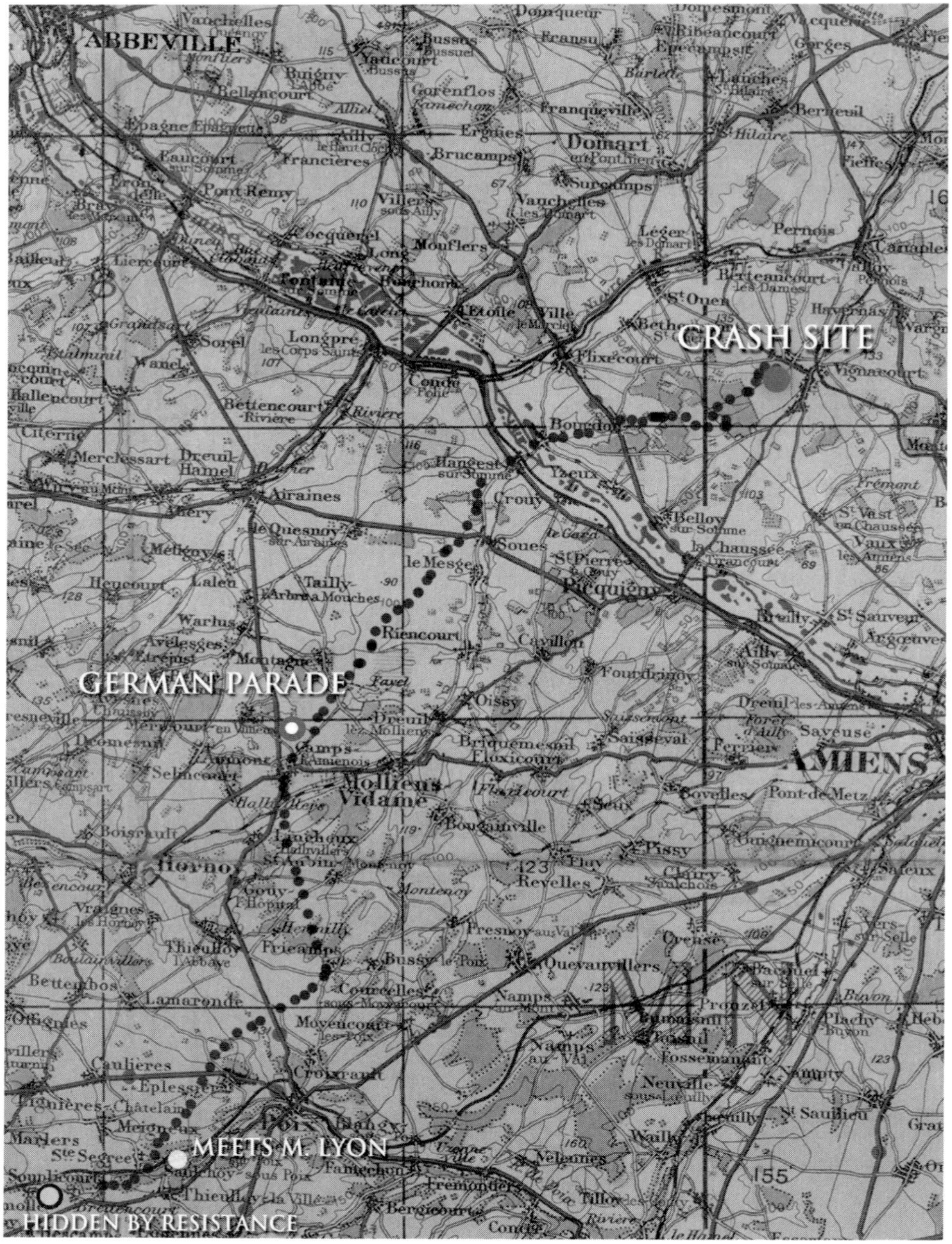

SOUPLICOURT is at
49^0 44'48.72"N,
1^{0}53'51.68"E

for the usual 'under the stairs' sort of things; doubtless they would have gone under the stairs had Jean Marguery had any. We cleared out a sort of cosy nest for me, carefully scattering objects in other corners of her home as if they had always been there, while others were gathered ready to be thrown out. Jean was clearly a hoarder of 'useful things' (that would never to be used). I'm sure that this was simply a sign of the thrift required by a simple circumscribed existence. In any case, I was from a Scottish family and I was used to such behaviour. While my father had been a General

This Souplicourt cottage still looks very much the same as Jeanne Marguery's home would have done in 1944. Her own house has been rebuilt and is no longer recognisable. (Nimmo Collection)

Practitioner, he had the same inability to throw things away, which was a very Scottish attitude. It was not meanness, 'thrift' is the right word and in poorer communities it seemed that thrift was rightly ingrained.

Jeanne Marguery went to work early each morning. At first light I would hear her doing her toilet – no holds barred – in the next room. A real clatterer and banger, she would then make toast and coffee and busy herself sweeping and tidying up to her satisfaction. Poor Jeanne, she was definitely a spinster and I think very embarrassed to have a strange man invading her home. She was a lady of habit and this ceremony was repeated every day, always with the same admonishment in a French spoken so rapidly that I never did quite manage to make out what she was saying. Her missing front teeth and her very strong local accent did not make it any easier to understand. Considering the risks she was taking for me our lack of communication was a pity. However, she spoke no English at all and although my French was improving daily, there was really no conversation. Another problem was that Jeanne really only wanted to talk herself anyway.

She would chatter fervently while she burnt toast on a toasting fork, which she then waved around an inch away from my face, always remarking: '*Mais vous amez ca bien cuit, n'est pas?*' Everything else she said was political. Whatever else she was, Jeanne Marguery was a die-hard communist. At that stage I didn't really understand why she was helping the Resistance as I had thought that communists usually kept themselves to themselves.[5] Before she left for work she would bang on my door and without waiting for a response, thrust it open, dump the tin cabinet on the stone floor and beside it, a small pile of newspaper torn into handy-sized squares. Minutes later she would slam the front door and turn the key noisily in the lock. During this time they took all my clothes and gave me things that were quite untraceable. I tried to help by giving them the money from my escape kit but they simply wouldn't hear of it. She would drop in at lunchtime just to see what was going on and then come back at about four or five in the afternoon. She worked as an agricultural labourer.

I suppose I must have been bored on my own all day but I have no memories of being so. For a start, after the days of insecurity it was a great luxury and an enormous relief to have a roof over my head and to be comparatively safe. After the grim experience of the past few days, this 'back to the womb existence' at Souplicourt was, I think, exactly what I needed. A few days of total peace and almost monastic silence gave me time to think things through, come to terms with the horror of the crash and the very probable deaths of some of my crew. To a great extent war had hardened RAF squadrons to such losses. By 1944, crews would disappear forever on a nightly basis, and while one suspected the worst, and certainly did miss friendly faces, somehow one just got on with it – quite frankly, it was the only way to survive. However, the old truism was there – when the worst happens to you and *your* crew it was quite another matter. It did become shocking and, yes, it did hurt,

I knew all too well that all of my crew had been in the greatest danger and were likely to have been wounded or to have lost their lives. I found it best, and more productive, to wonder how the others, those who I knew had bailed out, were getting on? What had their luck had been? I tried to visualise them on their own treks to safety, were they together or apart? For some reason I could always see Jock and Peter doing well – I hoped so anyway.

I found that I wasn't alone in my cupboard. By the dusty gloom of a small rippled glass skylight I found that a large, hairy and painfully thin spider was already in residence and seemed to be eyeing me up. I found her outlook on life interesting, particularly when, rather optimistically I thought, she started to spin a large web from under a shelf stacked with tins of odd screws, rusty washers and so on, across to the doorframe. It was beautifully done and I admired her considerable dexterity. Once she'd finished it and fussed about a bit, she just sat in a corner under the shelf and waited, watching me. We stared each other out for hours on end. Once in a while, she would ease out a leg and give her trap a silent twang, plucking it so that it shimmered invitingly. I could almost hear her smacking her lips. As there was no other obvious prey about I guessed that the invitation to dinner was for me, or possibly Jean Marguery of course!

This web set me thinking about the contrails we'd spotted drifting across the moon, and how that web too had clearly been the beginning of our trap. Like this spider, the Luftwaffe had taken note of their prey, plotted our course home and positioned their web of fighters across our path, navigating to bring themselves below and behind us.

The more I thought about this and the Luftwaffe's dreadful successes in recent weeks, the more I wondered at how they were achieving such success? They weren't in that good a shape, so it had to be due to more than navigation and positioning. It was as if we were flying giant magnets, each drawing in enemy fighters. I wondered about that. I had been careful about radio silence and probably a bit boring about stopping the chatter on board. Other pilots weren't so careful and I wondered just what the Germans were listening to? Could they be homing in on that in some sophisticated way? However, they'd got us and we didn't chatter. Had the Luftwaffe come up with some new sort of powerful radar device? Whatever it was I was sure there was something going on but couldn't work out quite what it might be. Whatever it was, it was working far too well.

Apart from my increasingly hungry spider and Jean Marguery and her incinerated offerings, I was visited every two or three days by two middle-aged Frenchmen who spoke fair English. They would come, I guess, to check that I wasn't cracking up. They had an air of authority about them and at first quizzed me about my background and family so that, they said, they could pass a radio message back to Britain saying that I was safe and well.

MI9 and the Resistance had developed a technique for handling those of us in my situation. I was never allowed to feel that I was forgotten or neglected and so was not tempted to escape and get on the move again. Having shown themselves as *résistants*, that was the last thing they wanted. Once an evader had been picked up he was potentially a very great danger to the Resistance. Should I have gone off on the loose again and fallen into the hands of the Germans, dressed as I was they would know that I had been helped. I would have been interrogated and tortured until I told them everything I knew. Of all those who fell into the hands of the Gestapo, only three or four were so incredibly brave that they were able to resist betraying those who had helped them. The Gestapo were ruthless, sadistic thugs and many died under interrogation, so I was hot property to be guarded carefully until I could be passed down the line on my way to Spain or Switzerland, or flown home in a covert mission.

One Saturday, about a week after I moved into her cupboard, Jeanne returned at lunchtime in a highly agitated mood. She had what turned out to be news of a heavy air raid on Paris. 'Why would the Germans want to bomb Paris?' I asked. '*Les allemandes? Non, non, monsieur*, it was your friends *les anglais*, and the Americans, they have made a big mistake.' Apparently, Monsieur Lyon had heard about this and was sure that the target had actually been the Porte de La Chapelle rail marshalling yards but that the RAF had gone wrong and bombed a residential area just to the south-west – something to do with the Sacré Coeur. 'Montmartre was badly damaged', she said. '*Beaucoup de morts et de blessés . . . nos amis. . . .*' She was very upset. Something had clearly gone wrong as, apart from the Renault works on an island in the Seine at Boulogne-Billiancourt and military targets in the deep suburbs, Paris hadn't yet really been targeted. If it was true it sounded as if there had been a pretty dire blunder of some sort.

The two Frenchmen returned two or three days later and told me that they had passed the message to the Air Ministry in London who would tell my family. They confirmed the RAF disaster at Montmartre and that German and Vichy propaganda were making the most of it.[6] Two more days passed and the English speaking pair were back again. This time with a very convincing tale of how my family had been contacted and had sent a message back to reassure me that everything was all right at home and so on. In fact, sadly, that wasn't true. I was also told that they were expecting a Lysander within the next few days – when the moon had waned – and they would probably be able to arrange for me to be picked up and flown home. I could be in London by the end of the week.

It was common knowledge that Lysander aircraft undertook those sorts of missions – they came from 100 Squadron and flew out of RAF Temple, near Sandy in Bedfordshire – so I believed what I was told. I was strung along this way for about three weeks. However, it turned out to be wishful thinking. I discovered later in England that none of this happened. They were simply keeping my spirits up, and it worked.

There were other things to keep me interested. Several times I was taken over to the farmhouse where the overblown Madam Duvray lived with her diminutive husband. She was as good a cook as Jeanne was awful. Her husband was a tiny, wizened, little old farmer with missing teeth. He kept a cloth cap on at all times. I guessed that he slept with it on. He would cut his food with a penknife, which he had honed to unbelievable sharpness first. It only had to touch meat and the meat fell apart. During one memorable meal, one of several courses was a great bowl of hard-boiled eggs (there seemed to be about 50 of them) bathed in homemade mayonnaise, cream and butter. Imagine that in the middle of war! He complained about how greedy the Germans were while, like a crab's claw,

Foraging parties would raid farms of everything useful: food, livestock, utensils and in fact anything else they fancied. (3rdR UOPP, Nimmo Collection)

his hand would come round and scoop a fourth and then fifth egg onto his plate!

I was not told about these suppers in advance. Jeanne would wait until it was quite dark and I was beginning to wonder when she would start cooking something, and then she would suddenly announce that we were eating out. The oil lamp would be extinguished, the door would creak open and we would edge, hand-in-hand, out into the night. We would go along a path, across a road or track and up a hill until, by the smell of straw and cow dung and the sound of restless chickens, I knew we were in a farmyard. The house would loom black against the sky. Somehow, Jeanne would find the door and gently tap. We would wait in silence and then, still in pitch darkness, the door would open and a heavy curtain would be pulled aside just long enough for us to slip inside.

The entrance opened into a big room with an oil lamp suspended from a beam over a large round table set for six. There was a huge primitive iron stove on the right fuelled by burning logs. However, neither the flames nor the yellow beams from the oil lamp were sufficient to light up the corners of the room, which fell into deep shadow.

The first time I went, as on other occasions, there was reassuring warmth from the fire and the most deliciously appetising smell of melted butter and garlic. I was so hungry that I could have eaten a horse, which was just as well as for all I knew I was about to do just that.[7] Whatever it was it smelled wonderful and was most definitely appreciated. Steaming in front of the hot stove were two large, faintly alarming, damp smelling dogs. They sniffed at me suspiciously. I stared back and offered the back of my hand to be sniffed – it was refused.

At first, I thought there were only the three of us in the room. However,

I became aware that in the deep shadow over against the far wall, were a man – or was it a boy – and a girl in a clinch on a divan littered with dark blankets and cushions. I was the object of curiosity and stood faintly embarrassed. I was to discover that this was the Duvray's daughter and her boyfriend Gilles, or Gilbert, and that he was a real terrorist. He and I became good companions, playing draughts in the evenings. Gilles had two pistols that he kept on the table with the handles towards him. I never quite knew whether to trust him or not. I later heard that both he and poor old Monsieur Duvray were picked up by the Gestapo and eventually shot. Quite how or why I don't know, but Souplicourt was situated under a corridor home for RAF bombers, and I don't for a moment think that I was the first, or last, fugitive that they welcomed in like this. What was clear to me was their belief in what they were doing. Again, I was very aware indeed of the horrendous risks they were taking, and of their selfless generosity. Outside this rural cocoon, which was the height of luxury when compared to reality, the war raged on and on.

On 28 April 1944, my very last night at Jean's house, quite unknown to any of us at that time, a major drama was taking place in Switzerland. It concerned electronic warfare and a diabolical top-secret invention that the Luftwaffe possessed, which had almost certainly played a key role in *Q-Queenie* being shot down. What I would finally discover was that that same night, 830 kilometres to the east-north-east of this rural Picardie bliss, an atmosphere of shock and doom hung over the Berlin Air Ministry as apparently Göring's Luftwaffe had had another security disaster.[8] Obviously, lessons had not been learnt. As the story goes, a second Bf 110 G4 had landed by mistake at Dübendorf–Zürich. However, this time the German pilot's gaff was really serious.

It seems that I hadn't been far wrong in wondering about a new secret German radar but what I couldn't have guessed, and what would make what was left of my hair stand on end when I discovered the truth, was that half their secret new radar system consisted of the Lancaster's top secret 'Monica' tail warning radar transmitter. As we now know, 'Monica' hadn't stayed a secret for any time at all as the Germans had taken the brand new set found in the crashed bomber in Holland and simply designed a Flensburg passive radar receiver to capture our pulses, which they then used with great effect.

It seems that while I was enjoying an excellent meal at the Duvray farmhouse, this radar receiver was part of a new incident at Dübendorf which would provoke a huge diplomatic crisis between Germany and Switzerland, the outcome of which could have had a drastic effect on the war.

A Luftwaffe Pilot, Oberleutnant Wilhelm Johnen, and his crew, radio operator Joachim Kamprath and gunner Paul Mahle, were based at

A fully equipped Messerschmitt Bf 110 G4 was simply too heavy to fly on one engine. (3rdR UOPP, Nimmo Collection)

Hagenau Luftwaffe base (Haguenau in French) on the Franco-German border not far from Switzerland. Strategically placed close to Strasbourg and Stuttgart, they had been scrambled to intercept RAF bombers returning from a raid over southern Bavaria. Having dropped their explosive loads the bombers had banked south-west and had been on their homeward leg – hoping for safety by making an illicit incursion into Swiss airspace.

Three Luftwaffe fighters pursued the Lancasters well over Switzerland where between them two pilots shot down four of the RAF bombers. Earlier in that same operation the third pilot, Wilhelm Johnen, had scored a kill over Germany. Now, in hot pursuit, he was trying to catch up on the wrong side of the Swiss frontier. Hammering his Messerschmitt hard, he pushed its airspeed and engines well beyond the safe limit causing one engine to start dangerously overheating. Losing oil, it had to be shut down. Things were already looking bad when, due to the late snow and icing conditions, the crew found themselves lost in the Alps, which was not a good situation to be in!

Their Messerschmitt was equipped with everything, including the top-secret FuG202 and FuG220 radars, as well as the secret *Schräge-Musik* cannon and a full crew of three. The combined weight of everything on one serviceable engine rendered their fighter unflyable. Johnen simply couldn't hold the weight of full rudder and so a crash seemed inevitable. Joachim Kamprath, who had made the dire error of taking the latest Luftwaffe codes with him, fired distress flares into the night.

Below, at Dübendorf airfield, the Swiss knew exactly what was up there in their air space and switched on the runway lights. Down the grateful crew went to Bavaria – or so they thought. To their considerable dismay they received a frosty Swiss reception. This total disaster was compounded by the fact that gunner Paul Mahle was the very Paul Mahle who had invented *Schräge-Musik*, the deadly, oblique firing gun system. Now he and his vital invention were held captive in porous Switzerland.

When things go wrong, they tend to do so in style and, while Switzerland was neutral, for that very reason it was crawling with agents. Everyone needed Switzerland as a place to reap information, do deals or to make clandestine contact, so news of this new security breach was almost bound to reach the Allies. When the Swiss military attaché to Berlin informed the RLM of the loss of their night-fighter, the air turned blue. This particular aircraft's equipment and the codes could not under any circumstances fall into Allied hands, so that night the phone lines hummed. By dawn, someone plucked up the courage to tell the Führer who went berserk and started ranting about treason and called Himmler, who detailed Waffen-SS chief Ernst Kaltenbrunner to 'do the necessary'.

Göring had already hatched a hare-brained plan to land SS Storm Troopers at Dübendorf and retake the aircraft or blow it up. Despite the likelihood of the Swiss seeing this as an act of war on a neutral nation, the commando team was actually ready to take off when the crazy scheme was vetoed. The new plan was far subtler, but it required instant action.

SS Oberführer Walter Schellenberg[9] the shrewd, slippery and dangerous head of the SS Foreign Intelligence Service (who thought nothing of overriding the Reich's Foreign Minister) had cultivated a 'friendly' relationship with Oberstbrigadier Roger Masson, his Swiss counterpart. Now was the time to use that friendship. Schellenberg and Masson had to meet and thrash this problem out immediately.[10]

As Switzerland couldn't go to war against Germany, the two intelligence chiefs met and hatched a hard-nosed deal in which the Swiss reluctantly agreed to blow up the Bf 110 G4 – in front of a German witness – on the condition that Germany sold the Swiss 12 new Me 109 fighters and parts manufacturing rights at a knock-down price of six million gold Swiss Francs. Plans were going ahead rapidly when the German witness, who had

The Bf 110 G that landed at Dübendorf on 28 April 1944. Note the oil leaks on and under the wing. The Swiss took this photograph just before the aircraft was destroyed. (Swiss Air Force Archives and Museum, Dübendorf)

by now arrived at Zurich, noticed that the SN2 radar had been removed and replaced. It was clear that the Swiss had already taken a good look. The result of their actions was an impasse.

Eventually, the German witness was persuaded that if Hitler wanted the aircraft destroyed he had no option but to sign the agreement – which he did. He also agreed to accept a promissory note drawn on the Swiss government – it being more practical than carting gold bullion about. That night the plane, laden with all its vital equipment, was duly blown up and, as arranged, early the following morning a flight of 12 new Me 109s flew in and the deal was done. The witness returned to report to Göring, apparently taking the Swiss promissory note with him, though this is where the facts begin to fog over. No-one knows what actually happened to the six million Swiss Francs. Both sides agree that there is no trace of the money ever having reached the Reich's coffers. To all appearances, it seems to have stopped at Göring's very spacious back pocket!

That was almost the end of incident, except that all 12 'brand new' Me 109s turned out to have barely serviceable engines – they were worn-out. After the war the Swiss had the last laugh when Germany was obliged to acknowledge this 'error' and had to rectify it.[11]

The Swiss side of the story gives an interesting perspective to the tale.[12] Switzerland was understandably outraged and alarmed by the ongoing abuse of their neutral airspace. When the aircraft landed at Dübendorf-Zürich, the crew were promptly arrested and Swiss engineers and electronic experts did indeed scour the aircraft for anything new. It didn't take long to find 'the goodies', to remove the top-secret radar and Mahle's gun system, or to meticulously study it all, take photographs, make technical plans and then to replace everything. There are also unconfirmed reports that the

Uffz Hans Mäckle's Ju 88 G1 at Woodbridge. (3rdR UOPP, Nimmo Collection)

Allies were made aware of all of this at the time, but if this is the case whoever received the information didn't appreciate its significance or act on it as RAF Bomber Command's crews were not informed that their ground profiling radar system was a death trap. They continued to use it until the next Luftwaffe mishap, which was to come ten weeks later on Thursday 13 July 1944.

That Thursday, Luftwaffe Obergefreiter Mäckle finally gave the game away. He was flying his Ju 88G-1 on a mission over the North Sea when at some point his compass appears to have failed. Disorientated and profoundly lost, Mäckle and his crew (who between them failed to muster even as much understanding of navigation as Louis Blériot) eventually took a bearing on what they assumed to be a Luftwaffe beacon to their east. In fact, they weren't flying north but south, and the signal they had latched onto was being transmitted by an RAF beacon in Suffolk to their west. It led them to unwittingly land at RAF Woodbridge and thus to finally hand-deliver all these vital secrets to the RAF.

British electronics experts and engineers immediately took this unexpected gift apart and finally the awful truth dawned. These Luftwaffe fighters were using RAF tail warning radar emissions as a deadly homing beacon. Within hours this vital information was with the London Air Ministry. This time a warning was quickly circulated and RAF groups took urgent action. The effect was immediate as crews drastically cut the time their ground profile radar was used. This action changed everything. The Luftwaffe was back to the game of pin the tail on the donkey and the RAF losses were much reduced.

New radar-jamming devices were devised and rapidly brought into service. Mäckle's lost Ju 88G-1 turned out to be a major turning point in the war. At that point the Germans lost the electronic war and would never recover.

CHAPTER 6

The Royez
The Simple Pleasures

IN OUR BLISSFUL IGNORANCE, as Switzerland and the 3rd Reich hovered on the brink of war, that Friday evening there was a smell of fresh blood in the air at Souplicourt. Obviously Jeanne Marguery and the Duvrays were expecting something important to happen, though to begin with it seemed a bit of a damp squib to me. Earlier that afternoon there had been great excitement going on. However, it turned out that it was simply over the expected visit of a man called 'Monsieur Baboul' was coming to see them. Eventually, Baboul turned up wearing a shiny black raincoat, Everyone was rattling away in French so fast that I didn't really understand all that was said. Clearly Monsieur Baboul was held in some reverence as every *bon mot* he uttered was laughed at. A bottle of 'paint stripper' Calvados was plonked on the table and things became quite jovial in a hazy sort of a way.

Later that afternoon Baboul went off but, to my great surprise, he came back an hour or so later. His shiny black raincoat was now a shiny red and black and it looked as if he had been in some sort of ghastly road accident. He staggered in with a dead calf slung around his neck like a stole, its throat slit and feet tied together. Blood was coursing down Baboul's shiny black raincoat. They set about cutting up the calf right there on the kitchen floor, blood and guts splattering everywhere. No wonder they had no carpets. In a scene reminiscent of Dante's Inferno, they shared the beast out. Jeanne lovingly cooked the liver in butter and somehow failed to burn it.

The wretched calf hadn't been dead for more than an hour before we were wiping our plates and I can only say that it was delicious, absolutely delicious. Souplicourt was full of simple luxuries like that, so I found that I fitted in rather well. However, it did seem imprudent to ask where this feast had actually come from.

As for communication, there was a French–English dictionary in Jeanne Marguery's bothy. I don't think it had ever been touched. Not surprisingly it was the only thing she had in English, so I read it like a book and found it unputdownable. Before this sortie into France, my French had been non-existent, but by the end of my stay they assured me that I spoke French like a native – one with a terminal speech impediment that is.

On the following day, Saturday 29 April, there was still an air of excitement about the place. Jeanne was unusually rosy cheeked and fussing and titivating as never before. This time, I was introduced to a paunchy little man called Lucien Royez. He was short and round and plump like Mr Pickwick, with a permanent smile on his face and wearing owl-like wire glasses. (I was later to find that when he took the glasses off, as he sometimes did, he looked a different person altogether). I was told that Lucien, who didn't speak a word of English (well, he did, sort of, but he wasn't going to anyway), would take me to Paris that afternoon. I took a great liking to him and from the start we got on like a house on fire. René, his foreman, was with him. He was another of these fearless people in cloth caps – a wonderful man! Thus, all the fuss was explained. I could see that Miss Marguery was smitten by Monsieur Royez and guessed that it was unrequited love; what an odd couple they would have made.

Lucien was a Paris garage owner. He had a petrol pump and workshops in the shadow of Montmartre. René, who had no teeth at all, was tall and thin and Lucien's exact opposite. He clearly worshipped the ground his boss walked on. These two were to teach me just how wonderfully bloody-minded a self-respecting Frenchman can be in the face of authority!

There were lots of fond farewells. Jeanne put on the old Lillian Gish adieu, clamping me in both arms as she wept: 'Don't leave me, don't leave me', at least I think that was what she was saying. Equally, she might have been telling me never to darken her door again. No, that's not fair. She had been very good to me and a pleasure to stay with, if you can take round the clock communist propaganda. She then turned the taps on for Lucien Royez!

I was driven back over the level crossing in Lucien's *fourgonnette* van with René following in another. We almost immediately turned in through a pair of high iron gates and up a long drive. I could just see through a chink in the truck's tarpaulin side screen and was surprised by this big house so close to the level crossing.

We went to the back of the house where I was left waiting while Lucien and René went into the servants' quarters. After a while, Lucien came back out with an attractive young woman who had a body like the Venus de

Two *fourgonnettes* such as the one Lucien would have driven. (3rdR UOPP, Nimmo Collection)

The 'Big House' at
Souplicourt. (Nimmo
Collection)

The house and rebuilt barn, still much the same as it was. (Nimmo
Collection)

A lively moment at one of those places best avoided. (3rdR UOPP, Nimmo Collection)

Milo, only more voluptuous. Standing navel to navel they talked, and all the while he absent-mindedly twiddled one of her breasts, as if fine-tuning a radio! René reappeared, took me round to a barn and left me in the hayloft while, I don't doubt, he and Lucien went off to do something dangerous. They'd come to collect black market eggs and things to take to Paris. Half of this would be for the Germans. I was to discover they had to do this, otherwise they could never afford the petrol or anything else they needed for their Resistance work. An awful lot of that went on but it was a revelation to me. Lucien Royez fascinated me as he had absolutely no fear at all.

While they were gone, looking through a hole in the barn roof I saw a sports car draw up. It was an open-top Delarge, I think, driven by a German officer of considerable rank. He must have been at least a colonel. He was clearly on leave for the weekend and dressed in the most supremely tight fitting jodhpurs. The man looked like an absolute swine, with a fiery red face and a fat backside just built for kicking. I remember wondering how he came to have that car.

This brute of a man lifted a leg onto the fender to dust a spotless riding boot. I was only five yards away and had the uneasy thought that at any moment he must sense my look boring a hole in his back. He didn't, of course, and finally satisfied with the gloss he'd given his swanky footwear, he strutted off to the front of the house.

Eventually we set out on our 60-mile drive to Paris, stopping en route for supper at Beauvais. I knew of Beauvais because of the terrible airship crash there in 1927. During the meal, Lucien and René brought out

Not all Germans 'liberated' quite the car they'd dreamed of. I can't say what this is exactly. A bumper car? A Rosengart? Whatever, it is, some very short French person must have missed this sporty little number terribly. (3rdR UOPP, Nimmo Collection)

personal sharpening stones and proceeded to hone their folding knives to points of incredible sharpness. They cut the meat up into squares and, stabbing it with the points, ate it off the end of their knives. Everything was so different from the British way of doing things.

There was always a meal with plenty to eat for regular customers such as Lucien and René, after all this was farming country where three eggs were easier to find than say a litre of petrol. I was to find that Lucien or René often headed off to Normandy or the Loire for cherries, apricots, or whatever was in season. They carried vehicle parts in the vans as cover. Wherever he went Lucien was a regular customer, so there was no suggestion of eating in a corner. In any case, I imagine that the Germans ate elsewhere but even so one had to beware of collaborators.

After another good meal we set off into glorious weather. It was a wonderful, still evening with lilac skies and my second French full moon was coming up looking absolutely enormous, like a huge soup plate. The air was heavy with evening scent as we drove down a marvellous road lined with apricot trees. By now I had been in France for a month and was really enjoying it.

The road was fairly straight but as we turned a bend there, in the middle-distance, was a railway bridge crossing over the road. It was guarded by what turned out to be a young chap – a lot of the German

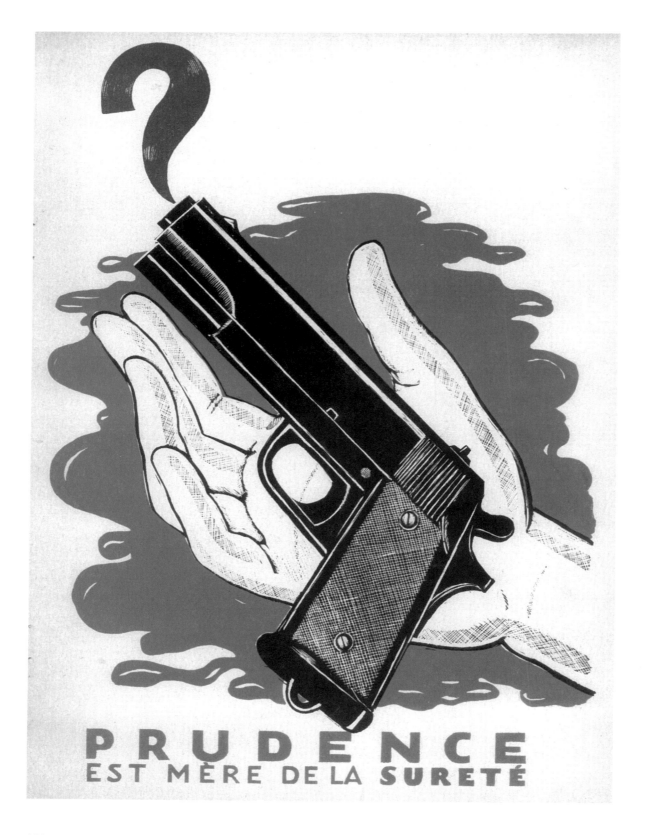

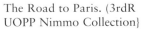

Left: 1934 French political satire, a dire and largely ignored warning. (Paul Iribe, Nimmo collection)

soldiers seemed incredibly young. I wondered what on earth we were going to do, but Lucien showed no concern at all. He pointed to an inn by the bridge and asked if I was thirsty? '*Vous avez soif?*' I nodded; my mouth had dried up. 'Hold tight then!' he said and drove his van straight at the sentry. He just let rip, screeching to a halt barely three inches short of flattening the German against the brickwork, and my head nearly went through the windscreen during the process.

Lucien touched the side of his nose knowingly as the sentry poked his head through the window to yell. He then simply asked 'Would you like a beer officer?' This floored the German private who blustered something about being on duty and . . . 'Oh well,' said Lucien, cutting him dead, 'be a good lad and keep an eye on my van would you.' It wasn't a question; he was simply daring this soldier to have a go. Having put the fear of God into the poor boy, we walked off, strolling over the road to the bar, leaving the shaking German behind us.

Lucien motioned to me not to say a word. They would tell everybody that I was a *réfractaire* and that I was deaf and dumb. Most would suspect, but nobody was to know, that I was a British pilot. A few of the French were actively pro-British but everybody cared about a *réfractaire*, somebody sent off as slave labour. The French resented this and everybody would be on my side. Lucien knew many people at this inn and we had drinks at the bar. It really amazed me how casual it all was.

Apparently René had something to do elsewhere so he left ahead of us

The Road to Paris. (3rdR UOPP Nimmo Collection)

and there was no sign of the sentry when we set out again. After a while we swept into another village, taking a corner at enormous speed. A German Ford lorry was right across the road, filled with soldiers coming back from an exercise. There was a fearful row with their officer. Lucien acted dumb and there was lots of shrugging of shoulders and play-acting. It was a great thing to watch but I did feel as if I was right on the edge of a precipice!

Lucien backed the van into the German quarters pulled back the tarpaulin and proceeded to line the German truck with butter and eggs. He quickly stacked it up in a very practiced sort of way. He looked tremendously efficient – pencil behind the ear and so on. It had the air of a weekly delivery, and maybe it was. It was thoroughly alarming, but I had much to learn about Lucien and what was really going on – I had much to learn about life.

Lucien finally unloaded a rectangular object wrapped in newspapers. He must have seen my doubt. However, he just nodded imperceptibly and lightly touched his nose. I was sitting there in the front of the van really not believing what I was seeing, simply doing as I was told. Thankfully, Lucien was the sort of man who inspired trust. I was soon to find that he was a magnificent actor – a magnificent man really – and definitely a great loss to the stage.

The rest of the trip into Paris was uneventful. Lucien managed to convey that the package was just '*une huile*', an old masterpiece he said 'of Montmartre'. Apparently, an officer had bought it in Paris and asked Lucien to deliver it. Seeing that I was appalled, he winked and patted my knee and said, 'Doon worree *mon ami*, things are goin' on 'ere. You will unnerstan'. I had no idea quite what to expect next. Later, on passing into central Paris close by the Montmartre Cemetery, the van dived into an underground garage, which turned out to be opposite Lucien's apartment. Flat 1, Villa Etex, rue Etex, not far from the Moulin Rouge.

Paris Legend
1. Lucien Royez's apartment.
2. Abwehr HQ (where Neil's fake papers were made).
3. Gare d'Austerlitz.
4. Gestapo building – Avenue Foch.
5. German Paris Kommandantur.
6. Vel d'Hiv stadium.
7. Champs Elysées.
8. Drancy concentration camp (at top right corner of map).
9. Porte de la Chapelle, Montmartre – Allied bombing error.
10. Moulin Rouge, place Pigalle.
11. Arc de Triomphe, place d'Étoile.
(Justus Perthes/Gotha/ Nimmo Collection)

German parade in the place de la Concorde. (3rdR UOPP, Nimmo Collection)

CHAPTER 7
'The City of Light'

YVON AND JACQUELINE – THE Royez's son and daughter – were at the apartment, and while Lucien unloaded the van I was packed off upstairs. A bath was run, pyjamas were produced and I was shown the room that I was to share with 17-year-old Yvon.

Madame Royez was an absolute sweetie. She was a slightly overweight, kindly, concerned woman who would run her hands through her hair a lot and frankly, as I got to know Lucien, I wasn't surprised. She was scared of his lack of fear. He was the most charismatic, admirable man and really they were a tremendously brave family. That night we had a very simple meal, by which time I was ready for bed. The following morning, I was back in the *fourgonnette* and heading for a building on the Left Bank. It was a big, official-looking place and I wondered what was going on. I was taken into a side street and downstairs to a basement where there was a small photographic set-up. There they took my photograph, which would be placed on a fake identity card.

This photographic studio was in the basement of a building adjacent to the Hôtel Lutetia – the Abwehr counter-intelligence headquarters in the boulevard Raspail – where oddly enough the Abwehr themselves forged papers, ran spies and agents, and listened in on clandestine radio traffic. A French Resistance radio transmitter was set up right there. I know this to be a fact as I got it from the horse's mouth. The Resistance felt it was safer to work right next to the Nazi radio receivers and transmitters as it would confuse the Germans and it was also the most unlikely place for them to be located. Besides, they knew that when there was a power cut they would be running on the Lutetia sub-station. All this was going on right under the Abwehr's and the Gestapo's noses – the intrigue and courage shown by the members of the Resistance was amazing!

The next day my nicely used identity card was delivered to the flat with all the right stamps. It was a splendid forgery and looked utterly real – but then, maybe it was! By that time, though I would never know for sure, I suspected that I knew where the blank pass itself had actually come from – the Abwehr offices at the Hôtel Lutetia.[1]

The Hotel Lutetia – the Abwehr and later Gestapo counter-intelligence headquarters. It was a notorious and highly ambiguous place on the Left Bank. (Nimmo Collection)

There were far fewer people out and about in Paris then – many had fled the city in 1940, others had been deported as slave labour or to concentration camps. In all there were only about a tenth of the number of people you might have expected, and the vehicles on the streets were almost exclusively going about German business. (3rdR UOPP, Nimmo Collection)

'Hello Mum, we made it to Paris!' Soldiers from a German police regiment posing in their Ford truck. (3rdR UOPP, Nimmo Collection)

Good German food for the boys. (3rdR UOPP, Nimmo Collection)

A terrible traffic jam in Occupied Paris. (3rdR UOPP, Nimmo Collection)

Place de la Concorde – the change of watch and Paris under a leaden sky.

The Cimetière de Montmartre and, in the background, rue Etex and safety with the Royez family. (Nimmo Collection)

Villa Etex. The Royez's apartment was the one with the balcony, on the 2nd floor. (Nimmo Collection)

Out in the country spot checks were unpredictable. It was safer to hide in a city – in the lion's den itself, so to speak. (3rdR UOPP, Nimmo Collection)

What was always dreaded was an unexpected knock on the door. . . . (3rdR UOPP, Nimmo Collection)

The most interesting characters seemed to pop in and out of the Royez flat. There was one chap, a solicitor called Monsieur Trodzier, who obviously had a hold over the family. He simply knew too much. He looked exactly like Fernandel. And who was Fernandel? He was the famous French actor who looked exactly like Monsieur Trodzier of course. He had a big, loose mouth and an easy smile. He used to bend his knees, ease his crutch and rock on his heels – as I say, just like Fernandel.

Trodzier and his family would arrive on Sundays. He came for his butter, a joint of meat and a good solid meal for them all, which he claimed by right. He didn't have to say a word as the consequences of a failure to deliver really didn't need explaining to any of us. The Royez were fed up with Trodzier and said as much. They genuflected when they mentioned his name, explaining that he was simply too dangerous to upset or to argue with. The impression I got was that, a bit like the Vicar of Bray, Trodzier's loyalties lay with whomever he was with at the time. He most certainly knew who and what I was.

Cities are anonymous places. If you looked unconcerned as if you were on the Champs Elysées for a purpose, you were likely to be left to yourself. (3rdR UOPP, Nimmo Collection)

Whereas in surrounding wooded areas, a group like this would arouse suspicion, someone might talk or denounce them. (3rdR UOPP, Nimmo Collection)

It became clear that outside small circles the French didn't really trust each other, and those that I met certainly didn't trust the police. It seems that you had to assume that they were collaborating. Lucien referred to a sort of prison camp to the north-east of us at a place called Drancy. Apparently, the French police interred people there before they were sent east by train.

Paris was more of a rabbit warren than I had first realized. There were narrow streets and passages, and everywhere there were hidden courts where you least expect them as well as ancient underground passages and quarries. Therefore, in itself, hiding wasn't the problem. Keeping it secret was. It was better not to appear to be hiding or eventually someone would unwittingly, or otherwise, give you away.

The Royez's flat was rather grand – the hall floor was so polished that you could see your face in it. Each member of the family had a pair of felt slippers about the size of snowshoes. They would skate across the floor whenever they went from the dining room to the loo or anywhere else, which is how they kept it all so clean. However, they really had no sense of colour at all. Everything was rather sombre, *brun et on peut le dire*, '*très solide*'. Ironically, they kept their cold meats and festoons of sausages hanging from the loo ceiling, within easy reach of the toilet roll. As a consequence, I really couldn't bring myself to eat them. Even now it makes me wonder about the things that we eat from those sorts of sources!

My time with the Royez family was full of incident. At night we would sit and tune in to the BBC and the crackly 'Free French' broadcasts from London. We even managed to send a real message about me. It was coded and said, '*Le Père Noël dit Bonjour*' – Father Christmas says hello – at this point they called me 'Noël'. They heard this in England and passed it on to the Air Ministry who notified my wife Hilary and the rest of my family. Finally, they knew that I was OK, which must have helped a bit as my father, Dr Duncan Nimmo, had only recently died.

The Air Ministry sent another very careful letter to Neil's father. Neil's older brother, Dr. Alistair Nimmo, opened it to find that at least it contained better news and that Neil was safely hidden in 'occupied territory'. France is not mentioned. (Nimmo Collection)

CHAPTER 8
Revenge and Murder

Blowing with the Wind

A WOMAN IN THE flat opposite the Royez's apartment would send her child out to play in the streets around Villa Etex[1] and the rue Ganneron – just under the walls at the northern corner of the Cimetière de Montmartre. We had the most illustrious neighbours there: Degas, Alexandre Dumas, Jacques Offenbach, Stendhal, Émile Zola, Adolphe Sax . . .? (he invented the saxophone), but one mustn't name drop!

When this woman called her son home at bedtime she unleashed the most strident voice: *'Andréeeee!'* she yelled over and again at the top of her eardrum-bursting voice. Like Jane calling Tarzan, her voice rang through the streets, scattering rooks from the cemetery trees. It happened every night as regularly as a Mullah calls the faithful to prayer, but with rather less effect. It was enough to wake the dead and I wondered what Adolphe Sax would have made of it?

Late one afternoon, Yvon was showing me around Paris. It was another beautiful Parisian spring evening and the sun was still hanging in the sky as the two of us drove down the Champs Elysées in the small Citroën *fourgonnette*. German officers were strolling from office to office or simply heading back to their apartments. Paris really is the most magnificent city, not simply because of its Haussmann planning and architecture, but also because of its very particular luminosity, caused by the light bouncing back up off the abundance of pale limestone. The endless, ancient, half-hidden back streets and passages also added to its wonder. So far, almost the entire city seemed to have escaped any serious damage as, with the invasion of France, very many Parisians had fled and their exiled government had declared the city open (undefended). Basically, they had abandoned the capital, leaving the doors wide open. One could very easily see why Hitler wanted to get his hands on the city – it was quite the most stunning prize.

There seemed to be any number of stunning prizes strolling about Paris as well. Always the capital of fashion, Yvon explained that this warmer spring weather had drawn fashion conscious Parisiennes out in droves. As they were pretty much all fashion conscious, it was quite a sight. He said that while the Occupation had made attractive cloth and materials hard to find, it hadn't changed women's priorities to any great extent – they were

Opposite: A Luftwaffe Bf 110 wing's view of Hitler's great prize – Occupied Paris, So much could, and many argue should, have been fought over. However, had it been the city would have been largely destroyed as it fell. Eventually, thanks largely to the German Governor, General Dietrich von Choltitz who, just before the Liberation, ignored his increasingly mad Führer's orders to reduce Paris to rubble, almost the entire city eventually remained intact. (3rdR UOPP, Nimmo Collection)

German soldiers appreciate the view in Paris. (3rdR UOPP, Nimmo Collection)

Even war could not stop the redoubtable Parisiennes looking glamorous. (3rdR UOPP, Nimmo Collection)

still determined to make every effort.

The average bourgeois Parisienne still had her treasured seamstress or *couturière* who would produce miracles from next to nothing and in many cases from the most unlikely materials. All that was needed was a treadle sewing machine, a pair of curtains or a tablecloth and some upholstery stuffing or seat leather to make rather aggressive shoulder pads and belts, and outfits would appear. Wooden soles were clapped onto worn-out shoes and with the vital stove, over which they could steam out last year's hat before re-blocking and feathering it back to high fashion, there was no stopping them.

I must say, they did really rather well and made Paris very chic and even more of a sight after the austerity back home. I was reminded of Mme Duvray and Jeanne Marguery with their elaborate hats but this was Paris style – rather less upholstery and probably more teeth. Looking at these elegant creatures though, I felt certain that they would not cook as well as Mme Duvray or burn things quite as Jeanne Marguery did. Dear Mme Royez treadled her own sewing machine and once in a while, rather touchingly out of the blue, Lucien produced half a bolt of cloth or a piece of priceless fabric for her and she or Jacqueline would rattle away.

Thus, Paris and her womenfolk were still looking fabulous though the streets were strangely empty. It was like a Parisian August in happier times

Paris. Time for a little glory and another photo opportunity. (3rdR UOPP, Nimmo Collection)

And misery and embarrassment for others. (3rdR UOPP, Nimmo Collection)

when the city's occupants would disappear en masse and, like Monsieur Hulot, Paris would take a holiday. However, these weren't 'happier times' and the apparent peace was wholly deceptive.

Eventually, after wonderful evening Yvon and I drove back to Montmartre. Arriving at rue Etex, Yvon parked the van in Lucien's garage, and said that he had something to attend to so I crossed the road and climbed up the stairs to the flat.

Almost the moment I entered, I heard a strange gurgling shout, and an agonised voice screaming for help, as if someone were near death. I went into the sitting room where Madame Royez was carefully looking across the narrow courtyard. The windows on the other side were close, almost

At the junction between rue Montmartre and boulevard Poissonnière, opposite the Hotel café Brébant even the flic looks surprised! French ingenuity and enterprise surpassed itself as the fuel ran out and all options were tried. Incidentally, the café Brébant has hardly changed – unlike the cobblestones, which were covered by tarmac after the 1968 riots. (3rdR UOPP, Nimmo Collection)

Luftwaffe crew making the most of Parisian tourist attractions. (Nimmo Collection)

looking in on ours. There we saw a man in the opposite flat rushing about, covered with red paint – it was all over him. He was shouting and yelling in a desperate way and I felt a cold chill as I realised that it was not red paint at all. He'd been stabbed many times. I could see his blood splattered on the walls. He was managing to stand at the window and was appealing to anyone for help, which didn't come. I don't think it was the Germans, maybe it was the French doling out another bit of personal revenge. It was a strange, unpredictable time in Paris.

One couldn't be too sure of anything really. About a third of the French were pro-Resistance and pro-de Gaulle and another third were actively pro-German, which left roughly a third who couldn't care less. They simply blew with the wind, like Monsieur Trodzier, and were the really dangerous ones.

In a situation such as this murder, you certainly didn't call the police, especially of course if you were involved with the Resistance and hiding an RAF pilot. The Royez family could do nothing but take note and keep their heads firmly down.

For the Germans, of course, Paris was as good a posting as could be wished for. For troops on leave it was even better. For them the rigours of the Occupation went largely unnoticed. They, like me I suppose, made the most of the hospitality and sights that the capital offered. The difference

being that they were in charge.

Once the trauma of the disastrous Battle for France had eased, many who had made a living by serving tourists cautiously returned to Paris and continued to ply their trades. They learned to coexist with their conquerors. 'Safe' theatres, bars, hotels, burlesque stages and brothels offered the Germans respite, and I saw them tread the tourist path in droves. They gazed at the Eiffel Tower, the Arc de Triumph, Les Invalides and of course Montmartre, where endless groups of Germans were guided around the attractions or sort torrid solace with dubious women. Forgetting their homesickness and the horrors of war, the Germans simply avoided the darker, more dangerous corners – such as public cinemas. Parisians were nothing if not pragmatic and for German troops, the city certainly had the edge on

As soon as they captured Paris Germans troops started taking guided tours of Montmartre, with refreshments at 'Mere Catherine', of course. (*Chicago Post*, Nimmo collection)

I say officer . . . could you direct me to your finest fleshpot? Somehow I doubt that this German was being given a speeding ticket. (3rdR UOPP, Nimmo Collection)

The Parisiana, boulevard Montmartre, A cinema for Germans only, where they could safely sit and watch a film in the dark, or they could head off to somewhere far more exotic.
At Place Blanche – south-east of the Moulin Rouge, close to l'Opéra. Occupied France offered her 'German guests' notable fleshpots and clubs such as le One Two Two, le Sphinx, le Chabanais, Barbarina, and Chez Moune – a '*bar Américain*' where '*Man Spricht Deutsch*' and doubtless the girls did too. . . With luck, they might catch Edith Piaf, who performed for the Nazis, but not always by singing what they expected. It has been suggested, that '*la Môme Piaf*' was with the Resistance. Whatever the case, she regretted nothing. (Nimmo Collection)

Stalingrad. Up until 1944, while RAF bombs rained down on Germany, Paris was in many ways safer for some of them than being at home.

I was later to meet some decent police officers or 'flics' as they were known. Some were actively involved with the Resistance and some even worked the black market to the Allies' advantage. However, it was clear that there were a shocking number of French Nazis about. Lucien talked about Prime Minister Laval and a man called Joseph Darnand and his atrocious 'Milice'.[2] It seemed that Maréchal Pétain had recently awarded Darnand the Légion d'Honneur for his murderous efforts. Lucien told me about the Corps d'Autoprotection Français (the French Gestapo, run by Henri Chamberlain or 'Lafont'). He said that they were the worst.

Given the French government's utter failure to protect France from the misery of the Occupation, I could understand some of what was going on, but not this terrible lot. Lucien warned that these parapolice were 'true fascist zealots, absolute thugs, ready to do anything for their Nazi masters'. As he explained the shame of these people (who were also known as 'Franc-Gardes'), Lucien was for once very

A Suspicious 'Flic'.
(Nimmo Collection)

upset. Apparently, they had been recently formed from the worst of French society and, Lucien explained, 'were low-life criminals and sadists, trained to trace, round up and to kill "undesirables"', which basically meant the Jews, communists and people like me. 'Above all,' he said, 'these brutes are here to trap their own compatriots, *les résistants . . . les salopards*!' Apparently, the Milice had recently tried to wipe out Resistance cells near the Swiss border but this had been a failure so they called on the Germans for help. They were in some ways even more dangerous than the Abwehr or the Gestapo, simply because they were French and so knew the system. Most importantly, of course, they spoke fluent French. Lucien warned that

A German officer's reminder of his French colleagues lounging outside their Paris police station. The third from the left appears to be a '*milicien*' or parapoliceman. The Milice with their highly dubious mandate were utterly ruthless. Many were recruited from among known criminals, and operated openly with complete impunity. However, they didn't last long. By July 1944 these thugs had mostly 'evaporated'. (3rdR UOPP – IR70 SaabrÜcken, Nimmo Collection)

they spotted non-French people where a German couldn't, and that my *réfractaire* cover story would not work with them. If I were caught, he said, they would know at once that I had had help and would 'make quite sure that you talk Neil!' Apparently, they were now operating from rue Lauriston in the 16th Arrondissement. I was instructed 'never to get anywhere near them'. I did not need to be told twice!

When it came to it, of course, one really never knew which of these policemen was with which organisation, especially if they were in plain clothes. I did wonder about that grizzly murder – it taking place right there, overlooking the Royez family flat. Of course, it could have been the Milice, the Resistance, or simply some sort of private account settling going on.

Despite the constant threat of exposure, there were lots of good times in Paris and there were also some moments of pure farce, such as the afternoon I went to the cinema with Yvon and Jacqueline. There were no Germans in public cinemas at that time – they wouldn't have lasted 30 seconds in the dark. Cinemas were segregated but the newsreels were still only showing German propaganda, so usually there was much hissing and yelling. However, on this occasion there was a stony silence as a large Nazi rally came on screen. '*Heil Hitler*!' chanted a fearsome mass of Nazi faithful, and then came the Führer himself! Gloating to his audience, Hitler stepped forward to the microphone and opened his mouth to rant. Just as he did there was a long, loud, resonating fart from four rows in front of us. It was quite something. The whole cinema erupted into contagious laughter. It went on and on, died down and then, as someone tittered, it would break out again. The 'sufferer' must have been bottling it up for weeks. Though exceedingly vulgar, as a comment it was spot on and his – I do trust it was a man – timing was impeccable.

I felt remarkably free with the Royez. I was still in hiding, of course, but it's relatively easy to achieve anonymity in a big city like Paris. I soon learnt that providing one took enough care (without looking furtive), it was safe enough to leave the flat, though I was quite taken aback when, on the first weekend, we boldly took a walk up through the streets of Montmartre. The French turned these walks into a sort of ritual procession. The father, or head of the family, and the first-born son walked ahead and 20 metres

The Brasserie Weber, 21 rue Royale, between la Madeleine and place de la Concorde. This famous restaurant café catered to those who could still afford it and was a favourite with German officers who worked at various nearby HQs. The sports cabriolet parked outside appears to be a Hotchkiss 486. Its 'WH' markings suggests that it was Wehrmacht '*beute*'. Hotchkiss et Cie produced machine guns used against the Germans during WWI and early WWII, by which time Hotchkiss had been nationalised. Following the capitulation, the company and existing weapons fell under Nazi control and Hotchkiss had little choice but to service them. (3rdR UOPP, Nimmo Collection)

behind came *maman* with the smaller children. They walked very, very slowly and would have friends and other family with them. It was a rather a nice habit, very sociable.

Another ritual was taunting the Germans. When they weren't out running errands for their mothers, or getting into trouble, small boys known as *les gavroches* loved nothing better than taking the mickey out of the Germans. They especially enjoyed teasing the Navy officers, who were rather pompously dressed. The children would march directly behind them with bicycle pumps (just the length of the German's sword) tucked into their belts, and small branches on their heads as camouflage. Strutting along fearlessly, they would ape the Germans officers' every move. Understandably, they left men in dark coats and trilby hats well alone, as did I.

Due to the lack of petrol, the few cars that were about ran on gas – huge bags of it were strapped to the roofs of vehicles. There were plenty of horses though, which were used to pull goods about and even to haul a few ancient horse-buses. To be honest, it was a wonderful time in Paris. However, all good things come to an end.

Monday 5 June 1944 began like any other day. It was very nearly two months since I had been shot down and the Royez had been cheerfully looking after me since the end of April. Though we didn't know it at the time, it was the day before D-Day, of course. As usual, Yvon and Lucien were up at 5 a.m. and an hour later I heard the front door close behind them as they crossed the road to work. I dozed until I was called at 10 a.m.

Madame Royez, Jacqueline and I had the most frugal of breakfasts consisting of *ersatz*[3] coffee made of roasted acorns and little else. I spent the rest of the morning composing crossword puzzles as a way of passing the time. Lunch was on the dot of 1 p.m. and, as always, consisted of clear soup, a slice of cold meat from the loo, a lettuce leaf and a chunk of baguette eaten without butter. This was followed by a few cherries or an apricot. The bread was off-white and tasted sour but anything that helped fill the void was more than welcome. Even with the 'country supplies' everyone, including the Royez family, was now going hungry.

Sultan, their excellent dog, was lying on the floor and we had just finished eating and I was helping to clear the table when the doorbell rang. If the Royez had visitors during the week it was always in the evening and I felt a sudden change in the room. A visit at this hour was very unusual. We all froze for a moment and the air seemed charged with panic and Sultan's hackles immediately went up. He had sensed our fear. We leapt into action.

I can quite believe that animals can smell fear, and there was plenty of that about. By this time, if you weren't with the Free French you were almost certainly what an increasing number of French called *Un Colabo* – a Nazi sympathiser. A ring on the doorbell was a moment when something cold hit you in the stomach and in a situation like this it was my job to get out of the way as quickly as possible and into the bedroom. Madame Royez would stall whomever it was to give me time to hide.

In seconds, Jacqueline and Madam Royez had swept away the telltale third place setting, swished the plate under the tap, dried it and lost it on the dresser. Meanwhile, I silently placed my chair against the dining-room wall, tiptoed into the living room, gathered my pencils and paper and skated down the passage, easing the bedroom door shut silently behind me. By now it was an established drill. In 15 seconds I had completely gone to earth (not that it would have given any of us the slightest protection had any visitor been from the Gestapo).

I sat on the bed for about an hour and a half, by which time I had realised that it couldn't be anything bad as I would have known about it before this. Eventually, Madame Royez came in and was all smiles. She told me that a man wanted to see me and that he was 'absolutely all right' and that I could say anything I wanted as he just needed to check up on one or two points that I had made. I went and met this extremely youthful chap who only looked to be about 18 and spoke absolutely perfect English – and so he should, he'd lived in England half his life. This was Patrick, or at least that was his code name. I later came to realise that despite his youth, 'Patrick' was in fact a British spy. He started by asking me questions about where I went to school and anything that would allow him to check up on me. The upshot of it was that they wanted me to get ready to leave the following morning for Bordeaux. From there I would make my way towards the Pyrenees and across a remote mountain pass into Spain.

'There will be an American airman going with you,' Patrick said. 'It is only three days since he landed but he is already being a bit of a nuisance and we need to get him out quickly.' He said that we were to be escorted by one of the Resistance people, a young woman aged about 20. However, he explained very carefully that while she would escort us, she was there only as an observer and to report back quickly if there were serious problems. We were not to make contact with her at all. He went into considerable detail about how we were to conduct ourselves. I was to get on the 6:00 p.m. night train at the Gare d'Orléans-Austerlitz[4] and to make for the end of a corridor in the middle carriages. The American would already be on the platform and would know me by my lack of hair (just like our neighbour'sold dog, I was pretty well bald by the age of 22).

Patrick's news was just what I wanted to hear. Fond as I was of the Royez family by now, starting my journey home was an irresistible thought. I made an effort to sleep early that night but it wasn't to be. I thought through Patrick's instructions again and again and I wondered how different Spain would be? First I'd have to get over the Pyrenees, on foot of course; but off towards Spain on a train . . . how extraordinary! I didn't sleep at all.

CHAPTER 9
6 June 1944

THE FOLLOWING MORNING DRAGGED BY. As usual there were just Madam Royez, Jacqueline, me and, of course, Sultan in the flat. We listened to what we could, which was basically Radio Paris and their Axis biased news, several times that day. However, it was always the same bare statement. The Allies had attempted a landing but it had been repulsed with many casualties. Outside, the street seemed strangely silent. I guessed that most people were staying in, their shutters closed, listening to the radio. We couldn't get the BBC during daylight hours because of atmospheric conditions and the German-controlled French radio was giving the minimum of information, which was highly suspect. A short statement was repeated on the hour. I could understand it quite well and it went something like this: 'In the early hours of this morning an enemy task force made determined attempts to land at one or two places along the Channel coast. These attempts were repelled with heavy losses to the invader.' The Marseillaise and Deutschland Über Alles followed.

We did our share of listening, of course, but in-between I played French draughts with Jacqueline over and over again. I packed and re-packed the much-used satchel-bag that Yvon had given me, checking at least half a dozen times that I had left nothing out and, much more importantly, that I was taking nothing that could be traced back to the Royez. My forged identity card and the precious escape kit were still untouched. The Royez had refused point blank to take any of the money.

On the dot of noon, as agreed the previous afternoon, Patrick arrived for my final briefing. Madam Royez was pottering in the kitchen and Jacqueline and I were playing draughts again in the living room with Sultan snoring quietly at our feet. Long before we were aware of Patrick's approach, Sultan had heard his footstep on the stairs and was wide-awake, his head up and hackles raised. His low growl promised a slow death to any stranger who might come too close. This gave me precious seconds to do my disappearing act. I heard the safety chains being unhitched and in a couple of minutes Jacqueline had come to fetch me. 'He's in a hurry,' she said, 'come quickly.'

I followed her back to the living room where Patrick was standing, legs astride, wearing the same slightly oversized raincoat, his hands deep in his pockets. I wondered if he was carrying a gun. I thought it very likely. Madam Royez and Jacqueline left us to talk and Sultan was banished to the bedroom at the end of the passage. Patrick spoke in English again and I remember still wondering at his perfect accent as he got straight to the point.

'We have arranged everything for you,' he paused momentarily (and my heart stood still), 'You leave this evening, for England.'

'Wonderful! That's wonderful news. Do tell me about *le débarquement*,' I whispered. 'What is happening?'

'There's been a landing in Normandy. I believe it is going well, but that is all I know.'

'Now,' he added, 'you'll travel by train from the Gare d'Austerlitz to Bordeaux where you will change stations and take a second train on to St Jean-de-Luz near the Spanish frontier. For a few days you'll stay well hidden in a safe house there, until a guide is ready and the conditions are right, to take you on the last stage over the Pyrenees into Spain. Once there, you will be escorted to Madrid and fly back to England. It will take about five days in all. OK?'

'Yes!' I replied, 'Very OK indeed.'

I didn't know it at the time but the safe house at St Jean-de-Luz was a hotel owned by the Bonjour family who ran the local Resistance and slipped escapees across into Spain. By pure coincidence the Bonjours were old friends of my family, who had often stayed at this hotel before the war – it is a small world.

French ingenuity at its best. An example of what to do when you run out of petrol, this is the one horsepower taxis! With the extreme shortage of fuel, the front end of a cab would be lopped off, the back adapted and between makeshift shafts, one dejected horse would be put. These could sometimes be seen around the stations of Paris. (WWP, Nimmo Collection)

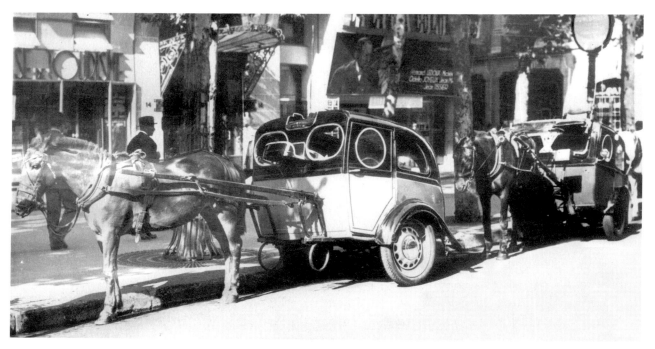

The Gare D'Austerlitz.
(Nimmo Collection)

Yvon arrived at around 4:30 p.m. and, after fond farewells to Mme Royez and Jacqueline, at 5:00 p.m. I set out with Yvon in the Citroën *fourgonnette*, passing Notre Dame and crossing the Seine on the way to the Gare d'Austerlitz. When we arrived at the station, I found, much to my surprise and pleasure, that Lucien Royez was there. He'd come down just to see me off.

Gare d'Austerlitz was like any mainline station in the centre of a city. You'd never have guessed that at that very moment there was the biggest invasion ever going on to the north along the Normandy beaches. D-Day had started, yet here were ordinary people and German soldiers going about their normal business – if anything could be described as normal at that time.

Yvon and Lucien explained that I would have to pass through a barrier manned by two German soldiers and show my identity card. They said that these soldiers would not be concerned with me as they were simply looking for deserters. I honestly didn't know how I differed from a deserter! If I were questioned that would be that, they made it clear that there was no 'Plan B'. There was nothing planned as to what I should do or say as my French simply wasn't good enough. I would just have to 'get the hell out of there', and I wasn't to contact either Patrick or Lucien again. They would stand in the shadows about 40 yards from the barrier and watch me go through. They gave me my ticket to Bordeaux and said that the American would be there on the platform and that I would have no trouble at all spotting him. 'He's obviously an American,' they said, 'The way he walks and moves.' I was stunned. 'And what about me?' I asked. They roared with laughter. 'Oh you're obviously British, every Frenchman can see that; but the Germans can't of course.'

Reeling from this, I said my goodbyes. Though they hadn't said it, I guessed that the D-Day landing was a big advantage as people were far too concerned with their own affairs to pay any attention to a mere British airman in French civvies! They were right. Two hulking great German soldiers (either would have made a good American footballer) with steel helmets and guns slung over their shoulders, were standing on each side of the barrier. However, there was no drama. I got through and, sure enough, there at the far end of the platform was 'Obvious Elmer', as I later came to think of him. Patrick and Lucien had been correct as I recognised him straight away. He seemed so obvious. He was simply a massive great Yank with a brutal crew cut and looking too well fed compared to the French, who were by then very short of food. He was a fright!

It was ages before the train was due to leave and the station was now full of German officers, all waiting for the train. I briefly had that awful feeling again – that they were all aware of me and that I might as well be naked. It was rather alarming. The idea was that we should be there in plenty of time waiting for an unnamed and very attractive woman – probably all part of the ploy. By this time the American had boarded the train and was standing at the end of a corridor pretending to read a book, as was I. It may have seemed obvious, two men pretending to read books, but since it was D-Day the Germans had more than enough to occupy their minds. They weren't interested in us at all.

I had the ghastly feeling of being stared at . . . (3rdR UOPP, Nimmo Collection)

At that point we all waited while absolutely nothing happened. The American became more and more agitated and he began making fearful grimaces and appeared to be unwell. I could see that he hadn't spotted me as our eyes never met. However, by 6:00 p.m. he was in a bad way, almost doubled up. I thought, 'Dear God, this is dangerous, either the man is seriously ill or he's crazy'.

When at 7:30 p.m. we had long passed the advertised departure time, I felt that I had better go up and talk to him. I squeezed along the corridor past the compartment where the girl was sitting and caught her eye. She immediately knew that something was up.

Carefully sidling up to the American, it was clear that he was in all sorts of trouble. Looking up and breaking the vows he had made to Patrick, he whispered, 'Yer must be Pierre . . .'

'Ssshh!' I responded.

'I'm in terrible trouble bud. I just godda go to the john!'

France had been invaded and he had celebrated. However, the wine and the stress had not mixed well. I pushed my way back past the girl's compartment, where again I caught her eye. She stepped out onto the platform where I quietly joined her. We walked along casually and out of the corner of my mouth I told her what the trouble was. She shrugged as only the French can: 'Couldn't he find a corner round the back of the train by the buffers?'

However, by that time he had already climbed down onto the rails and lowered his trousers. Two SS officers strolling along the platform had spotted him on the track and turned away, snorting their disapproval. What can you say? They were hardly likely to ask him for his papers. It was a ridiculous situation!

The train still didn't leave. Eventually, the sun began to set leaving the station in deepening shadow. It was getting uncomfortably close to curfew hour when there was no question of being out on the streets. The young Resistance woman came up to me in some distress. 'What'll we do, what will I do?', she whispered. Clearly, we were somehow going to have to find somewhere to hide and fast but first we had to leave the train and get away from the station as best we could, and not as a group. I asked her if she knew of anywhere at all that we could go? She thought for a moment and said, 'Well . . . yes, I think so. It's not ideal and it's quite a walk'. She made the decision. 'We'd better go quickly,' she said, 'I'll give you five minutes and then I'll go ahead. I'll head left out of the station. Be very careful Monsieur.' She then explained, 'It will not be safe to look back as that's the sort of gesture the Gestapo notice and you can be quite sure that they will be watching what happens now, so keep relaxed but don't lose sight of me. Go tell the American. Five minutes, no more'. She smiled nervously, 'Good luck *Monsieur*'.

'Thank you *Mademoiselle*, you too.' I said and headed back up the train to Elmer. Poor man, I really felt sorry for him, he must have felt terrible. Rejoining him I rapidly explained the situation and told him much the same thing – to follow me at a distance, and not to lose sight of me. I wished him luck too. He had not yet met the girl, which was just as well really as he was far too obvious and far from used to Paris, let alone this sort dangerous game. As people were beginning to pour off the train, I stepped down onto the platform and spotted the girl as a bit of a stampede started. The tannoys were announcing contradictory messages stating that trains would be leaving and then that there would be no trains. All the while, the light was fading which added to the growing air of panic. To a certain extent this favoured us as the German soldiers seemed to be doing little more than watching as people streamed out of the station.

Patrick and Lucien had left ages ago, and in any case they lived on the other side of Paris. It was a real worry. Here I was with two people I didn't know and, as far as I could tell, nowhere safe we could actually get to before the curfew started. Now we absolutely had to make the non-existent 'Plan B' work.

To the left a Catholic church, to the right, Joseph Darnand and Xavier Vallat's 'Jewish Question' Milice Headquarters. (Nimmo Collection)

Once past the curfew hour, Paris was dark and deadly. (Nimmo Collection)

CHAPTER 10
'Plan B'

Refuge

O N LEAVING THE STATION we ran with the crowd. The curfew meant that it would be dark before long and of course 'dark' meant just that as there would be no street lamps, not a light showing anywhere and simply nobody about. The young woman was obviously taking it all very, very seriously indeed and scurried across a main road to the opposite pavement, trying to get us safely off the streets before we were challenged. Clearly, we were in grave danger.

As we kept heading west along the Left Bank and into a warren of side streets, it grew steadily darker, obliging us to run and get closer to one another. Eventually, of course, I heard a car coming and my heart sank. At that hour it could only be the Germans. Beams from its hooded lights started to play low on the narrow side road as we dived across to a walled pavement on the other side. Surely that was madness? We were trapped. However, just as the car was turning the corner and the beams were bound to catch us, we dodged into an opening in the wall. It was the very place we were aiming for. Luck was still with us, just! Breathless with the danger, I glanced back as an ominous black shape gathered speed and passed the open doorway.

Gulping in breath, the girl explained that the house belonged to family friends and that she felt sure they would be OK. Whatever, the choice had been made. We went up a short flight of steps and crossed a patio. We were soon introduced to the family and there was much excitement and talking in whispers with everyone shushing and so on. It was clear that these people weren't part of the Resistance, and that it had all come as quite a surprise to them. However, they were good enough to take us in and while they feed us onion soup and fresh bread, we talked. They were a university couple and spoke a little English. However, I had enough French by then to hold a conversation. It was rather exciting and there was a great feeling of conspiracy there in the candlelight. Elmer and I slept on their floor that night and at dawn 'Pierre', another Resistance contact, arrived. He tore into the girl, saying that she had done everything wrong and that they must never involve outsiders as they had to be cleared. She was near to tears and under the circumstances I thought Pierre was unfairly tough.

The Monod family (right to left): Samuel Monod (Maximilen Vox), Liane Monod and their son Richard. (Archives Sylvère Monod)

That morning we moved to a house close by, in the rather chic rue Visconti and very close indeed to Saint-Germain-des-Prés. It belonged to an artist and his wife. His materials were everywhere and I was amazed to find that I recognised his distinctive style of thin line drawing. This was the work of Maximilien Vox, a book illustrator whose work I had admired before the war. 'Vox' was actually Samuel Monod, a short and dapper little man with a greying goatee beard who seemed old to me – in reality he was about 50. He, his wife Liane and their 14-year-old son Richard turned out to be interesting company and seemed pleased that an unexpected fan had arrived! Vox was interested in history, the state of the war and how the British saw things from the other side of the Channel. However, unlike his very capable wife Liane, he was not an enthusiastic *résistant*.

He saw history from another angle and, alarmingly, he spoke up for Hitler quite a bit. He claimed that when Paris fell, the 3rd Reich had sent in their finest troops and that, generally speaking, their behaviour was impeccable. I had to admit this was, to a limited extent, true.

He talked of 1940 when Norway, Denmark, Holland, Belgium, Luxembourg and finally France had fallen, and how the. German machine had been unstoppable. He spoke of how Germany had

Vox *bois*, '*Le Livre*' Vox. (Archives Sylvère Monod)

taken Czechoslovakia – a move that had largely been sanctioned by the Allies – and the invasion of Poland (which of course had not). However, Vox said, by then it was all too late. When the invasion of France had come, the French government had simply been complacent and weak, just like the British, he said, and hopelessly unprepared for the overwhelming blitzkrieg – the Germans were simply too efficient.

He spoke of how France and Germany had been at loggerheads throughout recent history and how, after The Great War, the Allies had handled Germany disastrously. In 1923, France had invaded the Ruhr, so Germany had been bound to wreak revenge. He said that Vichy politics had spared France the Polish fate, and I suppose this was true. What was really alarming was that when I foolishly compared Hitler with Napoleon, (the British always saw Napoleon as the great ogre), Vox was truly indignant and deeply offended as he greatly admired Napoleon. *Nul point* for democracy! It was a crass and tactless thing for me to say. However, it demonstrated how very differently nations perceive history. I learned a good deal about life (and tact) during those few days.[1]

Though the atmosphere at the Monod's was not as relaxed as being with the Royez, I got to know this family a little. Maximilien Vox was well known, outspoken and in the public eye and betrayal clearly concerned him, as it should. However, whatever his politics, Vox was a great artist and he did hide us so we were very lucky to have his help and that of his family.

I also got to know Elmer during our time with the Monods. You had to like him. He was a straightforward young man of farming stock from one of the mid-western American states. At 20, he was six foot one and aggressively fit with his hair shaved into a vicious crew-cut. He looked precisely what he was – a sergeant air-gunner with the USAF. Elmer had been tipped directly into the deadly air war. Running the gauntlet of daylight raids deep over occupied territory, American aircrews risked all. Elmer had only been in England for ten days when his fifth mission had been directed at an unspecified target – probably one of the V1 launching ramps near Calais. His B-17 bomber had been one of 100 or more taking part in this mass raid, and when it was shot down, he was one of the lucky few to get out. Like us, one wing had been on fire and as the order came to jump, he 'sure did jump'. His parachute opened, but only just in time and he landed very heavily, within feet of a remote farmhouse somewhere north of Paris. This was just three days before D-Day.

He was momentarily stunned by the impact and when he came to he found himself confronted by a pair of bleary-eyed bandits, one was aged about 50 and the other nearer to 80 years old, each with a murderous looking pitchfork at the ready. When they saw, from the badges and insignia on his leather flying-jacket, that he was not German but American, they were all handshakes, nods and smiles. Between them, they unlocked his parachute harness and lead him, still reeling and staggering, into the farmhouse like a trophy.

Elmer was very funny in a self-deprecating way. He told of how he was shepherded into a big kitchen. 'Anyone,' he said, 'would have thought the war was over.' He found himself sitting in the kitchen with the farmer, his wife, his ancient father and, it seemed, the whole family seated round the room staring at him, 'As though I was an ape or s'm'n'. A tumbler of red wine was thrust into his hand and topped up. As he caught their eyes, they would nod and smile encouragingly, raising their glass to him.

The wine flowed freely, and the air was thick with *entente cordiale*, 'but,' he said, 'mighty thin in conversation', for the family spoke no English at all and Elmer's French was limited to '*Vive le French*'. This was the first time Elmer had tasted wine and, although he wasn't sure he liked it, he was determined to keep pace with them. Soon he'd 'reached the plimsoll line', probably accelerated by a degree of shock. Leaning unsteadily towards the farmer he hissed, 'Where's the John, bud?' This drew a complete blank. '*Quoi?*' asked Papa. Elmer tried again. 'Where's the John, bud?' he asked, a bit louder this time. After the best part of a bottle of wine each, this seemed remarkably funny to the farmer and set him laughing uncontrollably, and then the whole family then joined in. This didn't help Elmer's problem, so he tried again: 'Where's the WC?' However, the pronunciation of 'W' and 'C' is so entirely different in French so this too drew a blank. 'Where can I splash my boots?' Then finally, in desperation, 'Where can I have a piss?'

Papa let out a great sigh of comprehension and announced to the gathering, '*Il veut pisser*'. The whole family let out an '*ah-ah!*' of comprehension and Papa, seizing on an excellent opportunity to give Elmer a much needed French lesson, rose to his feet, placed his hand on his buttons and announced, '*Moi, je piss*'. Then, warming to his task, he pointed to mother. '*Maman*,' he said, '*elle piss*', and mother, smiling and nodding said, '*Oui, je piss*'. To which Elmer replied enthusiastically, 'Yes, *je piss* too bud! Now please!' '*Oui! Oui, il comprend!*' shouted grandfather – who evidently didn't – and worse came next: '*Grandpère, il piss.*' '*Oui, je piss.*' Sage nods of encouragement. This was followed by performances by *grandmère* and so on. Finally, it was the turn of *le petit*, a child of about ten, who did his piece, so to speak. I guess Elmer was finally shown the bathroom. However, I was laughing so much that I forgot to ask. He was a cheerful soul that huge American, great fun.

On the third morning a most unexpected thing happened. Patrick arrived and there, behind him in his *fourgonnette*, with a great beam on his face, was dear Lucien. I was delighted. The proposition was that I should leave and go and knock some sense into three RAF airmen at an address they were vague about – the Resistance never revealed that sort of thing too soon.

'While they wouldn't insist,' they said, they would be 'very grateful' if I could try to tame these three bandits. I really couldn't say no, so while Elmer stayed on, I left the Vox home dressed in a grey grocer's coat, carrying a basket of rather sorry-looking potatoes. Mme Liane Monod squeezed my hand as Vox said 'Well, goodbye old chap!' in rather pointed English. I replied (in my execrable French), 'Oh no, no sir, it's *au revoir*'. Doubtless, poor Vox rather hoped it wouldn't be *au revoir* at all. I think he forgave me everything but my dire Napoleon gaff. I still blush when I remember that.

Patrick and I walked right across Paris, four or five miles over the cobbles up to Montmartre and as I had had no real exercise for weeks, by the time we got there my feet were bleeding. Patrick led the way, wearing a bright-coloured pullover and pushing a bicycle. He just kept on going at a purposeful stride and never at any time looked back over his shoulder to see if the 'grocer' was still there. We walked west beside the Seine and, taking a side street behind Notre Dame, skirted around the island and the dangerous administrative centre before crossing to the Right Bank by way of Pont d'Arcole to head north-west. The few German staff cars, BMWs and so on that we saw generally had a camouflage of branches lashed to the roof. Towards Châtelet there were more soldiers and officials out on the streets, which should be avoided by two civilian men together, hence we gave no sign that we aware of each other.

At the top of the rue Montmartre, Pigalle and the 'Moulin Rouge'. (3rdR UOPP, Nimmo Collection)

Yet another masterpiece of the Sacré Cœur. (3rdR UOPP, Nimmo Collection)

A 1943 German soldier's naughty memento of the Moulin Rouge. At Pigalle, when it came to 'horizontal collaboration' it was business as usual – and it still is. (3rdR UOPP, Nimmo Collection)

We passed a horse bus, its three horses harnessed abreast with nose bags on, looking positively Dickensian. Old fashioned even in those days, it must have come out of mothballs at some museum. Still, it was practical enough in the wide, mostly empty boulevards. Quite a large proportion of the people that were about, were Germans on leave, or German staff in Paris. It was June with its gloriously hot weather and lilac blossoms. The smells of garlic and horse chestnuts were everywhere and there was a seductive peacefulness to the occupied capital. Keeping to side streets, continuing north-west, we passed Les Halles and then pushed endlessly on up the rue Montmartre. Eventually, we came to Place Blanche at Pigalle and the Moulin Rouge – we didn't stop.

On one Sunday walk I had climbed up to the Sacré Cœur with the Royez family to take a look and it's true that once you see it close-up, the basilica isn't old, or of much interest. Like a studio set it's clearly designed to be seen from a distance. Lucien detested it, saying that its construction had only started 70 years ago and that in 1897 the poor of Paris were still trying to halt it. Lucien described it as 'a nasty, *bourgeois*, and *nationaliste* rightwing *effronterie*!' that dominated one of the poorest *quartiers* simply to celebrate crushing the 1871 Paris Commune. He added, 'The odious pile has one saving grace, it gives artists something to daub and flog to our cultured German friends!' Finally, I understood what he'd delivered en route to Paris. Lucien was having a ball and he didn't miss a trick!

That same afternoon Lucien had taken me to the back of the basilica to look down over the north-east of Montmartre. It was a sobering sight. Down

German soldiers banter with the locals at Montmartre. (3rdR UOPP, Nimmo Collection)

German police patrols regularly searched and trained in the Bois de Boulogne and took their canteen wagon – shades of the Wild West. (3rdR UOPP, Nimmo Collection)

at the bottom of the hill there was a huge, devastated, burned out area and not far beyond it, as Lucien pointed out, the SNCF La Chapelle marshalling yard to the north of the Gare du Nord, both of which appeared to have survived almost intact. I thought of Souplicourt and asked. 'The RAF?'

'Yes, I'm afraid so,' said Lucien 'and then the Yanks the following morning – they managed to bomb the same area.'

The devastation was no distance at all from the Royezs' own apartment. It *had* been Lucien that Jeanne had been so worried about, and no wonder. 'It was on the 21 April, just before I picked you up.' He continued, 'at least 650 dead and there were so many injured – and so many funerals'. Lucien seemed philosophical about it, however. 'When we get you home Neil,' he half joked, 'see if can get the RAF to bomb more accurately. It might have been better to have left it to the Resistance – the RAF can't afford to make mistakes like that'.

'Could the Resistance have handled it?' I asked, even though I wasn't supposed to.

'Who knows?' said Lucien, 'We couldn't have done much worse could we?' He dropped the matter.

He was right.[2] I had seen the dire results of residential bombing back in London, but that was Hitler and I expected that of the Nazis. To see first-hand what we were capable of doing was a salutary experience.[3] I thought back to the pathfinder's crackly chatter on the night of our fateful Aulnoye-Aymeries raid:

'How's that one old man?' . . . 'Looks bloody miles away to me.'

Then they had given the green light to bomb. I winced at the thought. Lucien had been right, we couldn't afford to lose friends. However, I was

Whenever the Allies made a mistake, the Nazi propaganda machine went into top gear overdrive and capitalised on it. (3rdR UOPP, Nimmo Collection)

La Chapelle, north-east of Montmartre, after the 21 April RAF raid that went so wrong. Neil and Lucien would have looked down from a vantage point up at the back of the Sacré Cœur above the ruins. (3rdR UOPP, Nimmo Collection)

What would explain this? Who was really working with whom? Who was friend, and who foe? This very odd photograph sums it up. What had already seemed an unfathomable mess – a blur – had become seriously bizarre. (3rdR UOPP, Nimmo Collection)

learning that in stocking armaments in city centre rail yards, the Nazis knew exactly what they were doing and that they capitalised on any Allied blunder.

Deep in these thoughts, and keeping well back, I followed Patrick up through Montmartre. I was beginning to recognise places. As usual, there were German soldier milling about but they seemed to be off-duty and more interested in sightseeing and chatting up women than in a man pushing bicycle and a grocer's boy with his basket. Nevertheless, we passed on the opposite side of the street.

Outrageous propaganda posters were best ignored. Did the Germans really hope to persuade people to have confidence in them? Everyone now knew that having invaded France they were capturing *réfractaires*, Jews and whomever the Nazis deemed to be 'undesirables' and shipping them east. (3rdR UOPP, Nimmo Collection)

Random cycle patrols such as this one were dangerous. (3rdR UOPP, Nimmo Collection)

Trudging down off the 'Mont', my feet were killing me. Cobbles had never felt so hard and never in my life had I been so glad to see a cemetery. I got a big welcome from Madame Royez, Jacqueline, Yvon and especially from Sultan, all of who must have thought I was safely out of the door. However, they were to have me for another week as there was the problem of getting enough petrol, and then there were the roadblocks and spot checks. Also, the van had to be going in the right direction in order to justify the trip.

During this time, I met Lucien's cousin. He, like Trodzier the shifty solicitor, would come on Sundays for his share of the black market goods. He spoke a different French from the Royez and described them disparagingly as 'les Parigots', the Parisian equivalent of Cockneys. God bless Cockneys, is all I can say! I noticed that neither of them objected to taking Lucien's increasingly scarce food. However, I could hardly criticise that.

Lucien made it clear that German or French spot checks were far more dangerous than major roadblocks as the latter tended to be substantial and erected in predictable places, which meant that with a bit of care they could generally be avoided. However, the Germans often carried out rapid spot checks, particularly after a denunciation or tip-off or, for example, if the Gestapo had tortured and 'cracked' a Resistance worker. Obviously, these checks came out of the blue and one could never be sure to avoid them. If I were stopped, great calm would be required.

Looking outraged, even vaguely furtive or simply cautious would be to court trouble. This is where that experience of walking directly through the SS tank regiment breakfast parade soon after jumping into occupied France actually helped. It may have been heart stopping, but in the end it had proved to be a useful lesson in self-control and that allowed me some freedom of movement in Paris.

CHAPTER 11
Three Men in a Cellar
The Mad Hatter's Tea Party

Eventually, I was driven about 30 kilometres south of Paris to a town called Montlhéry. Here, while staying in a house with a grandstand view of the world-famous Montlhéry race circuit – which was by now a Luftwaffe base – I was to learn the full meaning of the word anarchy.

Paul Gaultier, the head of the local Resistance cell, owned the house and various others besides. In fact, he seemed to own rather a lot. He himself lived in a grand sort of way in another district. He was a fearsome alcoholic but at least you could say that he had a tight grip on things. He was certainly ready to help a good number of Allied airmen – which was very much appreciated – but quite what else he was up to one didn't really like to think about. The first great surprise of the day was that I was bundled into a local police car and driven to Gaultier's house to collect our black market meat ration for the week. Having helped load the police car, I was led upstairs to a long refectory table where we were served a sumptuous meal complete with wine and liqueurs, and all the while Paul Gaultier was shaking with the DTs.

Apparently, the three errant airmen were living in another of Gaultier's houses and had been making a total pain of themselves. They had managed to find their way into the wine cellar and get drunk out of their minds. Consequently, they were singing at full volume and causing mayhem. Paul Gaultier wanted me, as an officer, to go to the house and sort them out. It was quite funny really. When I got there, I found they were a Welshman, an Australian and a quiet Englishman and they were definitely on the edge of mutiny. The plan was to split the Welshman and Englishman away from the Australian and put me with him in yet another of Paul Gaultier's houses. The silly thing was that they had been told that I was a captain and had thought that meant a group captain, about three ranks higher than I actually was. I wasn't wearing uniform, of course, so they were very subdued at first. However, the moment they found out I was 'only a bloody flight lieutenant' they changed completely, in a nice sort of way, and they were extremely relieved.

It turned out that the Gaultier family would leave the three men babysitting while they went out and the wine cellar was never locked. I could see straight away what the problem was.

Meeting these three, and listening to their stories, made me realise that I had been behaving with great caution and had gone to great lengths to make contact with the Resistance. Looking back on it, I needn't have tried so hard. However, at least I hadn't been captured, I suppose.

Caution really wasn't Taffy's strong point (you won't be surprised to hear that he was the Welshman). He had been in a Pathfinder Lancaster whose crew, as they dropped their marker flares on a target somewhere near Paris, had managed to set light to their own aircraft. Taffy hadn't waited to be told to get out. He had just jumped and floated down into farmland. Going to the farmhouse, he banged on the door, shouting that he was a friend, 'a Comrade from Cardiff', or something like that, and they set the dogs on him. He decided that the French were definitely 'on the other side' and so took his bright yellow 'Mae West' life jacket and waved it at traffic passing nearby on the main road heading out of Paris. What was remarkable was that so many of them seemed to be German staff cars and troop trucks – doubtless some on their way to his crashed Lancaster. No-one took any notice, so he blew his rescue whistle and flapped his Mae West at them again. However, nobody stopped.

Annoyed by such brazen rudeness, Taffy went for comfort eating instead. He opened his escape kit and ate all the chocolate and the Kendal Mint Cake. Then, spotting the money in the kit, he felt the urge to celebrate his parachute jump. Dawn was now breaking and he somehow found an open workman's *café*. Plonking his escape wad on the counter he asked for a beer, in Welsh-flavoured English. At that point a very hairy arm shot across the counter, grabbed him by the collar, yanked him over and shoved him down some steps into a back room. This was his introduction to the local Resistance.

Taffy had another claim to fame. He chain-smoked anything that looked vaguely like a leaf and flicked countless smouldering fag ends out of the window. One day a glowing butt landed in the baby's pram below and set it on fire. Fortunately for us all, and most especially for the baby, a passing neighbour put the fire out before Paul Gaultier's grandson was fried.[1]

The Australian was a man called Rolley Nurse. He was a navigator, I think. He had red hair and a truly splendid beer stomach. He was a hell of a nice guy but went completely wild from time to time. All he needed was talking to and calming down a bit, as he was simply frustrated and worried. Rolley was a sheep farmer with something like five million acres in Western Australia. The land had belonged to his father before him and he was concerned that it wasn't being well managed. He and I would do the washing up and play draughts, which helped calm him a bit.

The third chap was a nice man but I don't remember him too well. What I do know is that he was an expert fly trapper and could catch flies in handfuls – he was even better at it than I was. We would put a small pile of sugar on the table and wait until all the flies had settled, then he would flick an open hand across the top of them and throw them onto the table to stun them. He once caught 17 in one go.

We all helped with the gardening and rapidly became green-fingered experts. There was some ghastly grub that would burrow into the roots of the lettuces, destroying them. We would pull the lettuce up, gouge around for a grub, stamp on it and stuff the lettuce roots back into the soil. It never worked. All the while the local police car would deliver black market meat and produce to our door. The service at Montlhéry was remarkably good, so apart from getting home we really had everything covered.

Paul Gaultier seemed to own or run everything in the vicinity. His daughter and her husband rented the ground floor. The son-in-law had been a French submariner until 1940 when, in order to stop the French Navy falling into German hands, the British sank most of it at Mers-el-Kébir in Algeria, which, if you'll pardon a dreadful pun, didn't go down too well with the French. However, I don't think he cared much. He hadn't liked being a submariner.

His wife, who made the most delicious rice puddings, owned a dog, which was a cross between a Blood Hound and a Rottweiler. This dog would jump up and snap wasps in half, spitting them out on the floor. It was a tremendously hot summer and wasps and flies were everywhere in those balmy conditions, giving all of us – including the dog – something concrete to do.

I stayed at Montlhéry until 20 August, when General de Gaulle and his mob finally drove into Paris. We were becoming blasé and started spending afternoons in town, visiting the local bars. One in particular was a nice place called l'Hôtel du Cheval-Blanc (The White Horse). As the Resistance began to scent victory, some of them became less careful. It could be quite alarming really. One afternoon we were all sitting in a semicircle outside The White Horse enjoying the evening sun. I was sandwiched between two Frenchmen and next to them were several German soldiers drinking and admiring the sunset, oblivious of whom they were sharing the view with. One Frenchmen became a bit excited and over talkative. Turning to the soldiers began taunting the them: 'We know something you don't know. Not so far from here is someone you would like to meet!' I leant forward, took a sip of his beer and kicked him hard under the table.

The news was that there was an endless battle going on in Normandy, where the Allies were trying to break out from the beachheads. Every night at dusk, Ju 88 fighter-bombers would take off from the airfield just a few hundred metres from the house. We overlooked it, so we had quite a good view of them lifting off. They would return about an hour after take-off, having dropped their bombs.

Neil's favourite watering hole The White Horse. Allied airmen and *résistants* would meet here for a drink, rubbing shoulders with German soldiers, who didn't seem to notice anything odd about who was sitting next to them! It was like something from the post-war BBC comedy series *Allo, Allo*, except that this reality would almost certainly be considered 'too far fetched' as script material. However, even more bizarre events were to follow at Mrs White's inn. (Marie de Montlhéry)

I kept wondering how I could steal one of these aircraft and fly it back home. However, it would have been totally against my orders, the main one being that once with the Resistance, stay put. In any case, it would have taken rather more courage than I possessed to sit in an strange aeroplane cockpit, labelled in German, and to take a chance on whether the tanks and sumps held enough fuel and oil to fly it back to England. I believe one pilot did manage it, but you'd be lucky not to be shot down by the British, or by the Germans for that matter.

CHAPTER 12
Der Nachtjäger Helmut Bergmann
The Blind Fog of Battle

Life in Montlhéry was not without its hilarious moments, in fact both sides had their eccentrics. Nevertheless, life was slipping by. Neil had been married for just seven months, most of which had been spent away from his wife with the last four being spent hiding from the Gestapo.

In the first week of August, Neil noticed that German air traffic was becoming more frantic. At the same time, he was dwelling more and more on life back in Britain. On 8 August 1944 it would be his wife Hilary's 20th birthday so it was no wonder that he was eyeing Luftwaffe fighters and longing to escape. However, what was about to happen 175 miles to the north of Montlhéry on 7 August 1944, just the day before Hilary's birthday, would have had Neil transfixed and would certainly have stopped any thought of flying a Luftwaffe aeroplane north towards Britain.

Major American B-17 daylight attacks had already taken place on all the Luftwaffe airfields in the Reims/Laon area and there were further raids on 23 June when 113 American B-17 bombers descended on Laon/Athies. Seventy-one attacked what was still Helmut Bergmann's base at Juvincourt, 43 bombed Laon/Couvron and ten went for Lille/Vendeville. They succeeded in doing immense damage to the Luftwaffe infrastructure and added countless craters to an already pockmarked landscape, which was now peppered with unexploded bombs adding to a mass of lethal, unstable live munitions, a fair bit of which dated back to WWI.[1]

It is very likely that these attacks on the airfields around Reims occurred because of vital information that had been passed to London stating that there were strange goings on at Juvincourt. For some time there had been unexplained building work, with more equipment transporters coming and going than usual. There had been odd noises too – a strange sort of rushing sound, a long, high-pitched whistling wind that the Juvincourt locals found alarming. Helmut Bergmann's wish for better aircraft was coming true and he, and other NJG 4

The Ar 234 V1 on an early flight. Note its trolley with a parachute. This image may have been cropped and printed from a film frame. Film was certainly taken of a similar event.

Staffelkapitän, were helping to bring their dream to fruition. A wholly new type of aeroplane had come to Juvincourt, the single-seater Arado 234. It was jet powered and so new that it was un-flyable. The plane was not complete as the undercarriage had yet to be decided on. A retractable undercarriage would be too heavy and take up too much airframe space and a fixed undercarriage would cause too much drag. A rapid compromise was reached. The plane would be fitted with lightweight retractable skids, enabling this new jet to land on a grass runway. With that problem solved, there was the small matter of how to take off in the first place.

In fact, the Arado 234 never did take off. Its Jumo 004 jets proved so unreliable that it was simply used as a taxiing test-bed. This was done using a crude-looking, three-wheeled, grand piano-style trolley or stretcher. By spring 1943, the first flight-cleared engines were fitted to the Ar 234 V1, and on 15 June it made its first test flight by trundling down the runway and, as it lifted off, simply abandoning its trolley. Within three months there were four of these flying prototypes, but they were still underpowered. Two more Ar 234s were built, each fitted with two twinned pairs of BMW 003 jet engines. They flew using the 'brick principle', i.e. the harder you throw something, the more likely it will be to fly. Finally, under the control of specialist test pilot Erich Sommer, the Ar 234 V7 variant was ready to be 'thrown' very hard indeed. It was expected to reach some 900kph at 12,000 metres where it should prove unstoppable.

By the beginning of August, the Germans were desperate for up-to-date reconnaissance photographs of the Normandy beachheads (the Allies were streets ahead of the 3rd Reich at photographic reconnaissance). Therefore, on 2 August 1944 fine weather at last offered the necessary window. Bergmann and his colleagues took off to provide a massive fighter escort and, now fitted with reconnaissance cameras but still using its disposable 'piano stretcher' in lieu of an undercarriage, the Ar 234 V7 trundled down the runway like a Steinway concert grand piano in a hurry. As Erich Sommer took off from Juvincourt and headed west, he was making what's often claimed to be the world's first true jet-powered operational flight.

Erich Sommer rapidly outstripped his admiring escort and at 16:32 the jet streaked over Asnelles-sur-Mer and Arromanches, where Sommer photographed the floating docks and the Allied invasion armada at the Omaha beachhead. The flight was a great success but the photographs proved to be highly alarming – the activity along the Normandy coast said everything. Returning to a 'pancake landing' at Juvincourt, it seemed clear to Sommer that jet power was the future. However, an undercarriage would help (it was being designed) but unless the RLM was quick, and unusually decisive, it might arrive too late to help stop the Allied invasion.[2.]

Increasingly often, Luftwaffe aircraft abandoned their airfields at dawn and hid from American bombers during the daylight hours in woodland at

Luftwaffe pilots – safety in numbers. (3rdR UOPP, Nimmo Collection)

the edge of nearby fields. Helmut Bergmann, Günther Hauthal and Wilhelm Schopp found this quite pleasant, as on fine days they could rest or work in the woods. However, any venturing off base was only done in groups as anything else could prove deadly. The three were a good *Kameradschaft*. They had survived the American raids on Juvincourt, so it would be folly to amble off alone and get themselves murdered.

Bergmann's own demanding air battles continued throughout Operation *Goodwood* (an Allied break-out from the Normandy beachheads on 18–20 July 1944). The Allied advance had been successful, bloody and crushing. Their stark air supremacy and logistical supremacy were obvious. The Wehrmacht wavered and was whipped. Hitler, who was by now ordering non-existent troops into battle, responded by ordering a counter-attack and promised to send 300 Luftwaffe fighters into the fray – quite where from, or how he would get them there, the Führer didn't explain.

Back in London, endless caustic memos, letters, meetings and verbal battles went on to try to persuade Air Vice-Marshal 'Butch' Harris to bomb the synthetic fuel plants scattered across Germany at places like Duisberg, Molbis, Munich, and the plants in the Ruhr coal fields. However, that task was largely left to the Americans. According to British journalist and

author Leo McKinstry, Harris was loath to do it, claiming that it was a waste of Bomber Command's effort and that the only way to demoralise Axis troops and airmen was by targeting civilians and bombing the heart out of their home cities – 'dehousing' was the euphemism. Such soul-searching and doubt would cast a long post-war shadow over Bomber Command to such an extent that it would take until the end of June 2012, fully 65 years after the event, for a fine and fitting memorial to be erected. This memorial is dedicated to the 55,573 Bomber Command aircrew, Bergmann's victims among them, who lost their lives in the attempt to stop Hitler's Nazi scourge. Whether the continued RAF bombing of city centres worked, or simply inflamed German hatred for the British *Terrorfliegers* was a moot point. In the meantime, the French Resistance was growing ever bolder, which made tootling down to a local bar in some car or other a foolhardy thing to do, especially on a regular, predictable basis.

It was tempting to be lulled into bucolic French ways but to develop predictable habits or timetables was always dangerous. (3rdR UOPP, Nimmo Collection)

For the occupying forces obtaining or pooling *beute* cars in Belgium and France appears not to have been much of a problem. However, finding petrol for them was difficult. Fuel of any sort was becoming scarce, though even the Germans felt that had the RAF got its act together, things could have been very much worse. (3rdR UOPP, Nimmo Collection)

A jerry can of petrol, a box of apricots and a few eggs. All sorts of useful and vital things could be delivered by, or fell off the back of a lorry. (3rdR UOPP, Nimmo Collection)

Above: Careless talk could lead to a bumpy ride home. (3rdR UOPP, Nimmo Collection)

Left: Grübler, the Vienese chef at the Hôtel de Commerce, leaning on a purloined Citroën 11CV. By now Grübler had probably shaved his moustache off and had a haircut as there was definitely that sort of change in the air. (3rdR UOPP, Nimmo Collection)

below: Just the place to pause and talk about nothing remotely important – who was listening to, and who was watching, whom? (3rdR UOPP, Nimmo Collection)

One of Erich Sommer's reconnaisance photographs. (US National Archives)

During a depressing pre-flight briefing on the evening of 6/7 August, Helmut Bergmann saw Sommer's reconnaissance photographs again. They were stark evidence of the gravity of the situation. The Reich had not expected an invasion so far to the west and since June had been rapidly moving their defences to Normandy. However, it seemed to be too little, too late.

Bergmann, Hauthal and Schopp were to join Hitler's phantom, 300-strong fighter force and help the Wehrmacht and crack SS troops on the Cotentin (Cherbourg) peninsula. The German troops had been cornered and were about to launch Operation *Lüttich*, Hitler's top-secret counter-attack around Mortain. To Bergmann it looked as if they needed all the help they could get; '*Ist das wirklich ein echter Himmelfahrtskommando?*'[3] he wondered.

Refuelled, rearmed and exhausted, they nevertheless had to wait as the fog over Normandy was still dense. However, by the very early hours of 7 August air power was so urgently needed that they were unable to delay

Fake aircraft like this wooden Me 109 were often placed as decoys. (3rdR UOPP, Nimmo Collection)

Bodenpersonel on a couple of liberated chairs admire the wildlife. (3rdR UOPP, Nimmo Collection)

By 1944 many Bf 110 pilots were fledglings. It was with these nose cannon that Bergmann destroyed *Q-Queenie*. (3rdR UOPP, Nimmo Collection)

A Bf 110 being loaded with a belt of nose cannon shells. (3rdR UOPP, Nimmo Collection)

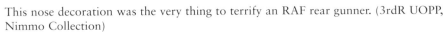

This nose decoration was the very thing to terrify an RAF rear gunner. (3rdR UOPP, Nimmo Collection)

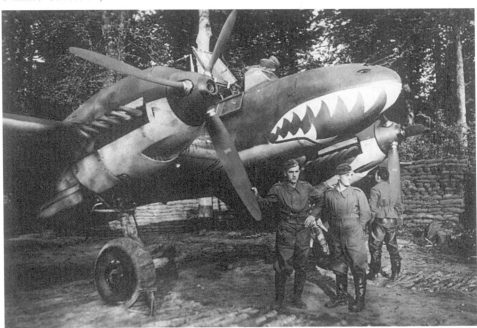

Milk, beef, bacon, *würste* and eggs. What a find!

further and were scrambled. Their Messerschmitt[4] lifted off and headed west. As they flew, Bergmann felt increasingly alone. Briefed to expect a heavy allied fighter presence he studiously avoided other Luftwaffe airfields as the Allies would be waiting to pounce and the elderly, basic design of his fighter was no match at all for the Allies' Mosquito, Typhoon and Thunderbolt fighters. Nevertheless, he couldn't help thinking 'where is everybody?' To Bergmann it seemed ominously quiet.[5] What he didn't know was that at his destination Operation *Lüttich* had started early. The Normandy weather had been poor for days, with heavy, dank fog cloaking everything. It hadn't been suitable flying weather – and it still wasn't!

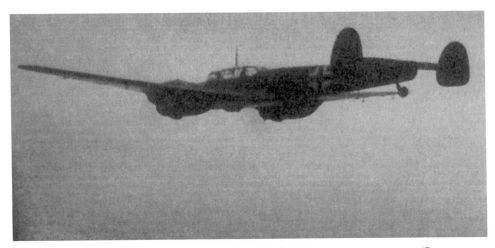

Shown in this photograph from his own album, Helmut Bergmann goes west. (Bergmann Weitz Nimmo)

Suspecting that the Allies were already on the move, Generalfeldmarshall Von Kluge and SS General Paul Hausser correctly guessed the vulnerability of the Reich's radio and landline traffic and so, against Hitler's explicit and increasingly fantastical orders, they had launched the attack early at midnight on 6/7 August. Feeling that stealth under the cover of fog was their only hope, Von Kluge kept very quiet about the plan, but by 11 a.m. on 7 August the fog had burnt off, deserting and revealing the German Army. General Hans Freiherr von Funck and his SS Panzer divisions were now horribly exposed and facing a multitude of Allied forces from a bewildering number of countries. In those early hours, heading into the thick of it, Bergmann and his crew would very clearly have to watch their tail.

Watching his tail was simply not enough and early on 7 August Helmut Bergmann's luck ran out. Exactly how or why is not known. Bergmann, Schopp and Hauthal simply disappeared into the fog of battle – exactitude was a very rare commodity on that frantic day. There is no doubt that they were shot down, but

Günther 'Hans' Von Kluge, *der kluger Hans*. They all had their nicknames and Von Kluge's was 'Clever Hans' – a play on 'clever hands'. (Bundesarchiv, 146-1973-139-14)

by whom? Also, in the end, is the answer that important? It has been claimed that Flt Lt Surman of RAF 604 Squadron made the 'kill', which is likely, but not certain. It was also claimed that Flt Lt Edward Richard Hedgecoe of 85 Squadron shot down Helmut Bergmann but as Hedgecoe was over Bavaria on the night of 6/7 December 1944, that wasn't possible – he was in the wrong place at the right time.

Over a matter of months Helmut Bergmann had visibly aged. (Bergmann Weitz Nimmo)

There is a third possibility. As much as a battle can degenerate and 'get out of hand', the one around Mortain did. In fact, both sides made dire tactical mistakes. The skies were simply overcrowded, mid-air collisions and misidentification were inevitable and the hopeless misery of 'friendly fire' was rife.[6] The British bombed the Canadians; the Luftwaffe fired at each other, the Wehrmacht and the SS; and the SS 1 Leibstandarte 'Adolf Hitler' Panzer division, who so excelled at brute barbarity, fired on the Luftwaffe, among others.

One disastrous SS error seems to open the door to an alternative end scenario for Bergmann, Hauthal and Schopp. It is possible that Helmut Bergmann arrived close to Mortain and dived into the fray. Below him, in the undoubted mayhem of ground battle, a crack SS Grenadier became aware (probably by radar) of twin-engined fighters banking and diving towards his position and, swinging his cannon, he let them have it! Thus, a disastrous pair of SS 'own goals' – a pair because, while the Grenadier hit just one aircraft, it is also likely to have been Bergmann's twin-engined Messerschmitt that spiralled down in flames, crashing onto and destroying the lead Waffen SS 1 Leibstandarte tank.

'Der Blond Helm'. (Bergmann Weitz Nimmo)

This theory, though it could be considered far-fetched, is actually very likely. Helmut Bergmann was certainly at the right place, at right the time as he was shot down on 7 August. An SS Grenadier did shoot down a fighter, which did crash onto the lead Waffen SS 1 Leibstandarte Panther tank, halting Operation *Lüttich* for several crucial hours. Though it has been claimed that the fighter was Bergmann's, the fact is that we can't be sure. There were other claims, both about the tank and about Bergmann, and in the ferocity of the fighting on that particular day it simply isn't possible to state very much with complete certainty.

The German counter-attack at Mortain failed, ending in what can only be described as a bloody massacre. It was quite simply a slaughterhouse at which 'Der Blonde Helm' was one of very few Luftwaffe pilots to arrive. Once the battle was over, there was the ghastly task of clearing up. American GIs and their *Knochensammlung*[7] SS prisoners found remains and Bergmann and his crew's 'dog tags'. These were temporarily buried. Statistically speaking they were simply three more bodies in a sea of German remains.

Well into September casualty records still hadn't properly started and the International Red Cross certainly thought it likely that Bergmann and the

MÜNSTER (WESTF.), **den 14.7.44.**
Schlossplatz Nr. 2.

ALFRED MEYER
GAULEITER UND REICHSSTATTHALTER
OBERPRÄSIDENT DER PROVINZ WESTFALEN

Dr.M./Krs.

An den

Ritterkreuzträger
Herrn Hauptmann Hellmut B e r g m a n n

H a n d o r f b. Münster.
=============================

Sehr geehrter Herr Hauptmann !

    Zur Verleihung des Ritterkreuzes zum Eisernen Kreuz
durch den Führer spreche ich Ihnen persönlich, wie auch im
Namen der Bevölkerung des Gaues Westfalen-Nord meine herz-
lichen Glückwünsche aus.

    Der Heimatgau ist stolz auf Sie.

    Zu Ihrem Kampfeinsatz für die Freiheit des Grossdeut-
schen Reiches wünsche ich Ihnen weiterhin alles Soldatenglück.

Heil Hitler !

[signature]

Gauleiter.

On 14 July 1944 the Westfalen Gauleiter
Alfred Mayer wrote to Helmut Bergmann
giving his congratulations for the award of
the Knight's Cross – and to wish Bergmann
'All soldier's luck'. It's unlikely that
Bergmann ever saw this ill-timed letter, as
three weeks later he, Günther Hauthal and
Wilhelm Schopp were dead. (Bergmann
Weitz Nimmo)

crew were prisoners of war and was hunting for them. Eventually, Bergmann's family received the dreaded letter saying that their son's remains had been found. Much later, his remains were reburied as Helmut Bergmann in the German military graveyard at Marigny, Block 3, Row 31, Grave 1182.

Thankfully, my father Neil Nimmo survived Bergmann's attack on the night of 10/11 April. However, that night alone 38 of his victims did not. It is not for Neil's children to forgive, that gift belongs to the many victims' families. What can be said is that when Helmut Bergmann and his crew

Vorläufiges Besitzzeugnis

Der Führer
und Oberste Befehlshaber
der Wehrmacht

hat

dem Hauptmann Helmut B e r g m a n n

das Ritterkreuz
des Eisernen Kreuzes

am _____ 9.Juni 1944 _____ verliehen

_____Berlin_____, den ___27.September 1944___

O.K.L.Chef f. Ausz.u. Diszpl.

J.a.

[signature]

Oberst

Helmut Bergmann's Knight's Cross of the Iron Cross, was awarded on 9 June 1944 but not signed and delivered until 27 September 1944, while Helmut Bergmann, Günther Hauthal and Wilhelm Schopp were still officially still 'missing'. In fact, they had died weeks earlier on 7 August and by the time this was signed Paris had been liberated for over a month. (Bergmann Weitz Nimmo)

died, Bergmann was only just 24, Günther Hauthal 23 and Wilhelm Schopp was the old man at 25. In the interests of reconciliation it must be right to recognise that they and very many young men serving the 3rd Reich were also victims of Hitler's barbaric regime.

As the three died, the Battle for Europe didn't even catch its breath and Allied forces were now flooding in. General Patton and the Americans broke out at Falaise,[8] rapidly sweeping down to the south of Paris where, not far from Montlhéry, they swung back north to liberate the capital. They were a wild bunch, the Americans, and it was to be a bit like the arrival of the 7th Cavalry.

It seems likely that this haunting photograph of Bergmann was taken earlier in the war specifically in case of disaster and, if the worst happened, was to be included on his *Sterbebild* (death notice). Many had these portraits taken, and many were used.
For a good number of weeks Bergmann and his crew were simply reported as 'missing' and by then it was all too late for *Sterbebilds*, so this page is as close as it gets. To die at 24, fighting for such a despot, is a terrible tragedy. (Bergmann Weitz Nimmo)

CHAPTER 13
Cricket on the Front Line

Flying Shells and Butterflies

BY MID-AUGUST WE were going very much where we pleased around Montlhéry. While everyone was looking after their own skin, all pretence at hiding had gone. It looked then as if the war was over, which it wasn't of course, not by any stretch of the imagination.

On the morning of 18 August, I was in the middle of Montlhéry with Taffy and Rolley, not far from the Pont des Belles Dames, where a great commotion was going on. We knew that American forces were very close, but a rumour was going about that a German Tiger tank had broken down in the middle of the town and we were determined to take a look. Then, as we turned onto the road to Marcoussis, there it was! It was true, the SS crew were clambering over the defunct tank desperately trying to mend it, as if the devil himself was on their tails, without success. Their situation was fraught with danger as their hostile audience was growing by the minute. I could see that all deference towards the Germans, pretended or otherwise, had evaporated. When the crowd actually began trying to capture them, the SS crew took advantage of a passing Wehrmacht truck, leapt on and rattled off, simply abandoning the tank.

Word was that the Americans could appear at any moment, so we started off to the west of Montlhéry. Sure enough, as we approached a small rise, an armoured Jeep crept cautiously over the brow towards us. It was an American Jeep! This was it, an advance guard of the Allied forces and quite clearly Taffy, Rolley and I were standing right in the front line! Spotting the tank, the Americans came to an abrupt halt and then reversed at high speed. As they weren't fired at, and encouraged by our waving, they very cautiously came forward to a point where they could take a look through binoculars. The tank was clearly worrying them so, waving a white handkerchief, we ran to meet them. We told them that the tank had been abandoned and warned them, as best we could, of what they could expect to find in Montlhéry.

They had obviously been scared stiff, as the dreaded Tiger tank was quite the most deadly piece of fighting equipment known to either side during the war. Had it been operational it would certainly have made mincemeat of both them, and their armoured Jeep. These Americans were

180

The SS Tank captured in Montlhery on 18 August 1944. (Roger Michelet FFI/Patrimoine et de la Culture Mairie de Montlhery)

fully occupied with their advance on Paris, so we left them to it and rushed back to the house to report our wonderful news.

That was a memorable day! We started lunch at about 11:00 a.m. and finished it at 2:00 a.m. the next day. There was wine on the table the whole time during this great alfresco meal. People arrived filled with excitement, re-telling stories and rumours about Hitler being dead, and so on. We finished the marathon meal with onion soup, which seemed to be something the French always did. There was a donkey in the garden and a small box hedge maze – a child's one. In my 'euphoria', I tried to ride the donkey around the maze which it seemed to quite enjoy. I never felt so high as I did then. It was like being at 40,000ft without oxygen. A rare and magnificent swallow tail butterfly fluttered with us in the garden, adding to the celebration. We played a form of cricket that I've never seen before or since. You take a lozenge-shaped piece of wood and other sticks, plus your own bat. The lozenge is placed on the ground. You hit it, it bounces up and you hit it and score runs. While we were playing, shells started flying overhead. I had no idea that they travelled so slowly. The sound preceded them but despite this I still didn't manage to spot one. They sounded as if they were about 50–100ft above us. I have no idea if they were American or German. It was the most incredible day, sort of Alice in Wonderland Mad Hatter's tea party! At one point a posse of FFI[1] in an open-backed lorry appeared. They were still intent on hunting down the truck and Tiger

181

tank crew, who seemed to have got away in the confusion.

The Americans came as far as Montlhéry that day but the joy soon soured. They got desperately drunk that night and were knocking on women's doors and being sick in the gutter. It really was a disgrace. This lack of control surprised the French who had probably been expecting something more heroic than an army resembling a Viking horde. Despite producing the finest wines and alcohols available, the French tended not to drink it in nearly the same quantities as Anglo-Saxons, so this behaviour came as quite a shock. Of course, there are plenty of French alcoholics. Paul Gaultier was hardly alone in his affliction, but by and large the French don't go out en mass simply in order to get legless.

I suppose that conquering armies have always tended to let off steam after a battle, and liberating the town had certainly been that. Also, the local French were more than pleased to see them and welcomed them as heroes while plying them with drink. Doubtless, some of the young women were particularly enthusiastic in their welcome, but even so some GIs were just like over-excited children who didn't know how to behave. It was all a bit depressing. I felt that if there was one time that they should have behaved well then it was that night. I tried to explain this to my French friends but found that my mouth wasn't working properly. It began to dawn on me that these friends were very drunk too and, come to think of it, so was I.

Despite the Americans' antics, I don't think there were any serious incidents. In fact, most people were simply celebrating. Most, but not all of course. There were plenty for whom 'The Liberation' was anything but welcome. Those who had been collaborating with the Germans were now in real trouble. In the turmoil and political vacuum, acts of violent

The game ended in a massacre with countless thousands of German casualties. They were fortunate if they simply survived the Normandy breakout. Exhausted, those who were left went into full retreat. (3rdR UOPP, Nimmo Collection)

Confusion, retreat and another near miss! (3rdR UOPP, Nimmo Collection)

Within days of the Falaise pocket surrender, the Ocupation was all but over as the Allied Normandy breakthrough very soon proved decisive. (3rdR UOPP, Nimmo Collection)

retribution were increasingly common.

A lethal jockeying for power was under way, mostly between the communists and conservatives. Both had their armed factions of course and quite a few simply spilled over from the Resistance. These were dangerous times and whole families were riven – some collaborators, some actively pro-Ally and, in some terrible cases, some children who had denounced a parent or a sibling.

Old scores were being settled. French women, who were known to have slept with Boche soldiers, were being ruthlessly routed out and these *collaborateurs horizontales* had their heads shaved to the scalp publicly. Some took it well enough, treating it as a sort of joke. However, there were women who were destroyed by such treatment. Affairs happen in war, and as their own Vichy government was in bed with the Nazis and collaborating, it may have proven difficult to say no. The types who so publicly attacked these women were often enough desperate to demonstrate that they had never been *collabos*, that they had been *résistants* all along. Whatever the reason, it was not a pretty sight.[2]

An unbelievable thing happened next. Unbelievable, that is, unless the circumstances are fully understood. No matter what the actual truth was,

1944: French *résistants* and *collabos* settling scores. (US ARMY Signals, Nimmo Collection)

the current Mayor of Montlhéry was being accused of being a collaborator and his days were numbered. In the rising tide of patriotism the townspeople were going to kick him out of office. Monsieur Gaultier's Resistance cell urgently wanted a non-communist, or even better, a Conservative to take the Mayor's place. I suspect that in those double-dealing, bet hedging times they also needed irrefutable public evidence that they had been exclusively fighting with the Allies. 'Anyway, it's just a matter of how we appoint a successor,' said Paul Gaultier, hesitantly. 'We would like it to be you.'

Me? An RAF pilot! I thought he had completely lost the plot. He had to be joking! But no, he really was serious. He wanted me to stand on the pub balcony in the centre of Montlhéry and lay claim to the most important office of Mayor 'as a *fait accompli*' he said, thus pre-empting the other factions.

I didn't see it like that at all. I think that Paul Gaultier wanted someone to shield him and to come between him, as head of the local Gaullist Resistance, and the communists and their bullets. Neither of us, I think, were in any doubt that either side would have killed either of us had they felt we were getting in their way. I think he might have been offering me up as a sort of sacrificial Gaultier, if you see what I mean. I wouldn't have anything to do with this, it wasn't me at all.

What nearly mucked things up though was that there were dozens of war correspondents around by now, and someone blurted the story out to the British press. We were invited to supper at Le Cheval Blanc, the hotel at the Montlhéry crossroads. Throughout the Occupation Mrs White, an English woman, owned and ran it. She had survived by never putting a foot wrong, although in fact she was working with the Resistance. Mrs White threw what was a lavish reception for those lean times, at which we were presented to the British Press as people who had been hidden by the local Resistance. It was at that reception that someone told the journalists what had happened.

Noel Monks, an Australian war reporter for the Daily Mail, claimed it as his exclusive. It seems that, in those days, the press had some sort of honour amongst themselves. He was a nice chap until he started to grill me. Given my immediate background, and as he wasn't likely to pull my fingernails or water board me, I didn't give the poor man an inch. I said my story was nothing of interest at all, boring. I didn't tell him a thing. I'm not sure what my motives for that were, except that by then secrecy was ingrained in me. I kept remembering that the war wasn't over and instinct told me to keep a low profile.

There were lots of Allied airmen around by this time and they were getting up to some pretty strange things. Four Americans who had been shot down were out on the loose, free-booting around Montlhéry. They managed to capture a young SS officer and wanted proof that they had done this, just in case he escaped. They asked if I would go and look at him, which I did. I found him trussed up, sitting in a corner of an attic. It was fascinating as he looked like a horribly cold fish, yet I shouldn't think he was much more than 19. I don't know what happened to this soldier, as we were moved the next day, the 19 August[3]. I think the Resistance wanted to get us home quickly, before we started causing real trouble.

Repatriation was rather extraordinary. I didn't expect the Resistance to be nearly as well organised as they were. The following morning we were rounded up, stuffed into cars and bundled off to the centre of Paris. A lot of the members of the Resistance had been up all night drinking, placing bombs and blowing up Germans, so in order to keep the driver awake I gave him a Benzedrine tablet from my escape kit. Perhaps this was not the best idea as his driving became erratic and he had no judgement whatsoever.

Entering Paris there were queues of cars. People who had fled to the provinces were now pouring back into the capital, doubtless wondering what they would find. They were hooting and waving flags. Then who should I see being driven in an open car, with a woman on each arm, but my American friend Elmer! He was absolutely enormous and had gained at

Liberation of Paris – Place de la Concorde. (Roger-Viollet/Topfoto)

least three stone. Clearly, living with the French and eating their food had agreed with him!

We were taken to no less a place than the Hotel George V, just off the Champs Elysées, one of the finest hotels in Paris. The Royez were there and it was the most wonderful reunion. We went back to their flat that evening and sat and listened to the radio by candlelight, drinking a glorious Nuit St George and soaking up the news, intercut with interviews.

There was a German air raid on Paris that night and in our tipsy state we all staggered up to the roof to have a good look. The streetlights were on and Paris was alight in every sense and had an air of Christmas about it. After all we had been through, it would have been ironic had we been hit. But then it was a night to live dangerously.

The following morning, I was invited to the Paris apartment of a man I'd known in Montlhéry. He had clearly been a collaborator and had simply swapped sides when he saw who would win. His place was a sort of underground bunker and extraordinarily luxurious; all plants and running water. It was almost like being in an aquarium with every kind of device imaginable. A door opened and a little old lady came in, dressed in black lace and carrying a stick. He kept calling her *grandmère*, but she clearly disapproved of him. He was trying to persuade her that people like me were his main work, helping the Resistance – which was absolute rubbish. I think that everybody who had been working on both sides (and many had had to in order to operate at all) were now in trouble and desperately trying to justify themselves. I had been produced as evidence, but *grandmère* wasn't having it. She seemed almost totally dismissive.

Paris was undergoing a chameleon-like change and it was not the place I'd left in June. An air of chic normality was reappearing as if it had always been bubbling below the surface. The city had indeed survived and life continued, with a few more pavement chairs and a singular lack of Germans. However, although on the surface there was normality, it covered deep-lying problems. The French would have serious trouble repairing their shattered Republic.

The next morning I went down stairs to breakfast at the George V. Maurice Buckmaster, the head of the French section of the SOE was there,[4] with a twit of a Lieutenant in the slickest uniform you ever saw in your life and with an equally slick French accent. Anyway, I didn't have long to think about him as we were bundled into an open lorry and driven out to Versailles, where there was an American POW camp. The authorities had to vet us to be sure we weren't German spies. We were there for three of the longest days of my life. We weren't actually kept behind wire, but we were next to the camp where a few hundred Germans were cooped up, looking miserable. It felt odd to have been so comparatively free in Paris under German occupation only to find myself, to all intense and purposes, imprisoned by the British. It had to be done of course, but it wasn't a pleasant experience.

We were interrogated separately two or three times by a joint team of British and Americans. Who was this person? Who was that? Where had we stayed? And so on. I was still coming to terms with the fact that I could safely tell anyone these things. Eventually, we were driven to Bayeaux, loaded into a DC3 and flown across the Channel. Landing at Northolt on the outskirts of London. I was home at last, but not for long . . .

CHAPTER 14
Pathfinders

Going 'Hedgehopping'

DESPITE THAT HARD-WON Normandy invasion and the Liberation of Paris, Nazi Germany was far from capitulating and all surviving Allied aircrew were badly needed. After further debriefings and the shortest of leaves, Neil was back doing his part in fighting Hitler's seemingly endless madness. Although pleased to be back in Britain, Neil felt pangs of anti-climax. He missed Lucien Royez in particular and hadn't forgotten the view over the ruins of north-eastern Montmartre, or what Lucien had said about accurate bombing.

Friday 13 October 1944 was a good day for Neil as he was posted to 'A' Flight 142 Squadron, part of Air Vice Marshal Donald Bennett's Pathfinder group. He would now be based at Gransden Lodge near Cambridge. He had wanted to join the Pathfinders group as, with a keen navigator and his own interest in navigation, he felt that he might be able to do his small bit to improving accuracy. If not, then at least he'd have tried.[1]

Neil started with de Havilland Mosquito familiarisation flights and by

Pathfinders. The De Havilland Mosquito. (RAF)

Sadly, this grainy image of Neil and Hilary Nimmo, with Hilary's always cheerful mother Una Sharp in the foreground, is the only period photograph of them that exists. (Nimmo Collection)

16 October he had passed his various medical tests and met an excellent navigator, Flight Sergeant Jack Craddock. They were to regularly crew a legendary Mosquito XXV Pathfinder.[2] The two began raiding Germany almost immediately and, as whatever they did was done to perfection, I do rather pity those on the receiving end. After the war there was to be endless public soul searching about the raids on German city centres where civilian casualties had been very high. By no means all Germans supported the Nazis but they paid a terrible price for those neighbours who did – firebombing wasn't a picky business. I did once ask Neil if he had had doubts about those raids. He said that Hitler's fascism had been a desperate threat that in the end left no choice. He felt that whatever the cost, Hitler and the Nazis simply had to be stopped.

Neil and Jack's first Mosquito raid was to Hannover on Monday 20 November 1944. They didn't get far and it very nearly proved fatal. Just after take-off, they suffered serious technical problems and had to abort. Fully loaded with fuel, flares and bombs, they turned back.

Neil's logbook wryly notes: 'I bent the bleeder on landing – bombs up'. To the initiated this terse comment says everything. They had returned to base awash with fuel, incendiary flares and a full payload of high explosives. A heavy impact with the runway had damaged their Mosquito[3] and nearly ended it all – many didn't survive that sort of incident. That night Neil's strikingly beautiful wife Hilary Nimmo, a WRAF, was on duty in the Pathfinder Operations Control Room and aware of it all. Her only option was to keep quiet and to get on with her work, as one or other of them shouldn't have been stationed there. In fact, they were both so shocked and so determined not to make a fuss that they didn't make contact until Neil had returned from a successful operation, which wasn't to be long.

Around this time a rumour started doing the rounds at Pathfinder Operations Control stating that one of their pilots, Flt Lt Neil Nimmo, had not only already been shot down over occupied territory, evaded capture, made it back and, rather than being taken off operations, was now with Pathfinders, but also that, against all the rules, his young wife, 'that blond girl Hilary Sharp', was also with Pathfinders and she was, in fact, Mrs Nimmo.

This was bad news as being married and both operational in the same RAF Group was strictly against Air Ministry regulations, as was Neil having evaded capture in occupied Europe and coming back onto operational duty. Worse still, Hilary had already flouted the rules by telling lies and joining up at just 16, when she had been underage. A lifetime seemed to have passed since then and now that Neil Nimmo was back, they were spending illicit weekends together huddled up at Mrs Hibbins' guesthouse in Huntingdon. However, someone had spilled the beans. As they were married, it was hardly immoral, but it was considered a serious

Year 19.4.4. Month / Date	AIRCRAFT Type	No.	Pilot, or 1st Pilot	2nd Pilot, Pupil or Passenger	DUTY (Including Results and Remarks)
—	—	—	—	—	— Totals Brought Forward
Nov 20	Mosquito XXV	KB 430	Self	F/Sgt Craddock	N.F.T.
20	Mosquito XXV	KB 430	Self	F/Sgt Craddock	Abortive Op' to Hannover (I bent the bleeder on landing. Bombs up)
21	Mosquito XXV	V	Self	Sgt Logie	From Wyton.
21	Mosquito XXV	KB 444	Self	F/Sgt Craddock	Operations Stuttgart (completely clueless, but got there + back somehow.)
22	Oxford		Self	F/Sgt Craddock	Base - Hendon - Tangmere - Base
23	Mosquito XXV	O	Self	F/Sgt Craddock	Air Test
23	Mosquito XXV	O	Self	F/Sgt Craddock	Operations Hannover (Still clueless, but better 2nd time)
25	Mosquito XXV	F	Self	F/Sgt Craddock	N.F.T.
25	Mosquito XXV	R	Self	F/Sgt Craddock	Operations Nuremberg (Navigator passed out over A. 2nd time Better.
27	Mosquito XXV	R	Self	F/Sgt Craddock	Operations Berlin (Good trip, but lousy marking) 2nd time
28	Mosquito XXV	KB 473 D	Self	F/Sgt Craddock	N.F.T.
28	Mosquito	D	Self	F/Sgt Craddock	Operations Nuremberg (Really good trip, top of it 1st time!)
			GRAND TOTAL [Cols. (1) to (10)] ....Hrs. ....Mins.		Totals Carried Forward

breach of government rules. Hilary was instructed to report to the operations base Commander, who just happened to be 'The Man Himself', Air Vice Marshal Donald Bennett.

Donald Bennett was a remarkably talented, 'loved or loathed' character. Generally speaking, his crews admired him a great deal but his outspoken contempt for bureaucracy meant that the British Establishment would have gladly dropped him on Berlin and preferably without a parachute. Expecting the worst, Hilary was marched in and found herself in the presence of this surprisingly young and rather good looking air vice marshal. She was mightily relieved to find that, rather than severely disciplining her, Donald Bennett was very attentive as well as very attractive. When she admitted these breaches of regulations Bennett gently asked, 'Why did you do this?' He seemed to accept Hilary's reply as somewhat unorthodox, but perfectly reasonable. Hilary had explained that

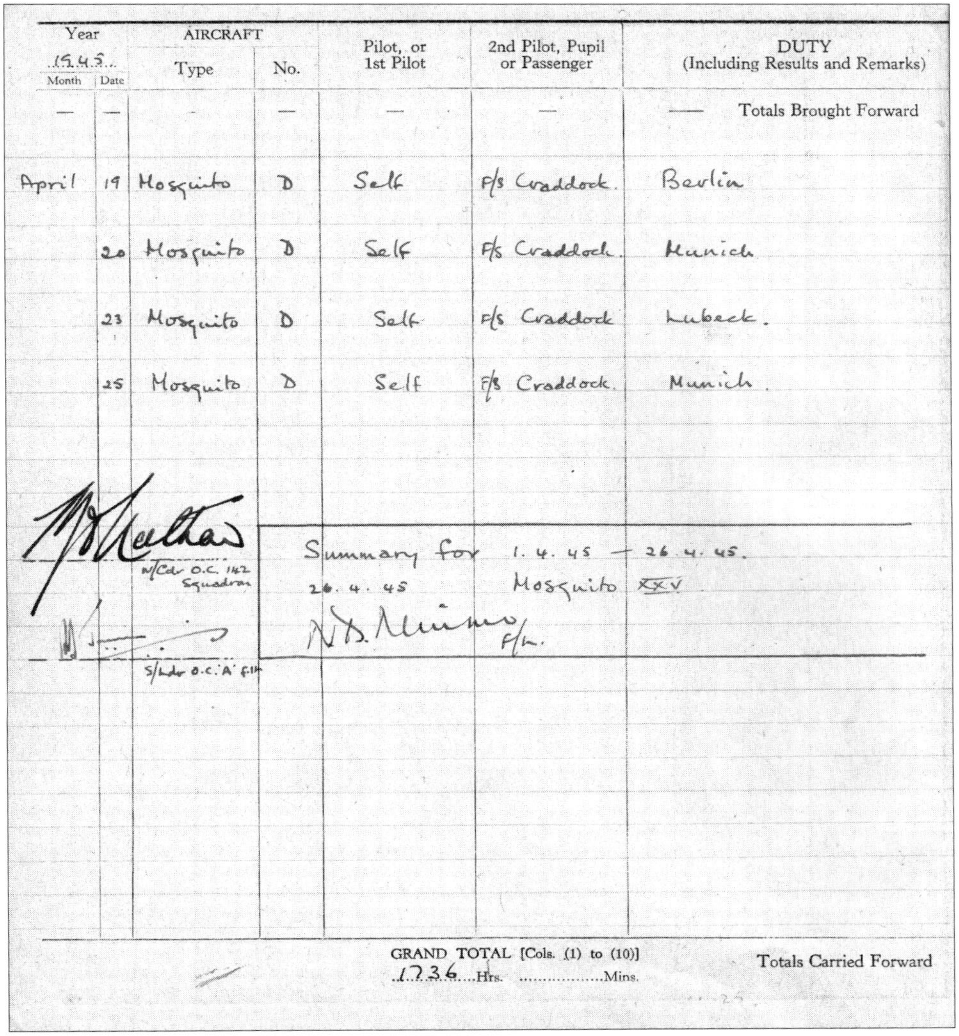

Year 1945		AIRCRAFT		Pilot, or 1st Pilot	2nd Pilot, Pupil or Passenger	DUTY (Including Results and Remarks)
Month	Date	Type	No.			
—	—		—		—	— Totals Brought Forward
April	19	Mosquito	D	Self	F/S Craddock.	Berlin
	20	Mosquito	D	Self	F/S Craddock.	Munich
	23	Mosquito	D	Self	F/S Craddock	Lubeck.
	25	Mosquito	D	Self	F/S Craddock.	Munich.
						Summary for 1.4.45 — 26.4.45.
						26.4.45 Mosquito XXV

W/Cdr O.C. 142 Squadron

S/Ldr O.C. 'A' Flt

N.D. Minns F/L.

GRAND TOTAL [Cols. (1) to (10)]
1736 Hrs. ....Mins.   Totals Carried Forward

since her husband Neil had come back from Occupied France and had been posted to the Pathfinders, being in the Operations Room herself, she knew when he had returned from a night's raid and she found that for the first time in months she could sleep.

It was quite clear that they understood each other and without actually spelling it out, it was implied that as far as Bennett was concerned the rules 'could go hang'. The matter was closed. Hilary and Neil were to continue as they were and remain in the Pathfinder Group under Bennett's protection, though it was very clear that Bennett expected them to be discreet at Mrs Hibbins' guesthouse. The unspoken agreement was that if things went badly for Neil, there was to be no fuss in the Operations Room. It was a tall order, but having confidence in them both, Donald Bennett simply put a lid on the matter.

The next day Neil and Jack bombed Stuttgart. Neil's log notes read:

21st November, Stuttgart, completely clueless, but got there and back somehow.
23rd November, Hannover. Still clueless, but better. 2nd home.
25th. November, Nuremberg. Navigator [Jack] passed out over target. 2nd home. Better.

. . .

They were soon confirmed as a Pathfinder master-bomber crew. These crews flew lone aeroplanes with no defensive armament. They raced ahead of the main flight of bombers and, at the given hour, pinpointed the target by dropping the first flares and bombs to guide the heavy bomber force onto the night's chosen victims. Pathfinders played a vital role and much had changed since the disastrous RAF failure over Nuremberg.

Jack Craddock was now Neil Nimmo's regular navigator. They became good friends and worked well together. On one operation to Berlin, as they reached the German coast flying outbound above cloud cover, they were astonished to see a 'pool of back-lit cloud' on the port wing. It started to glow brightly and then, to their astonishment, from out of this cloud poked a huge cigar-shaped thing, which streaked off towards Britain. They had heard tell of such weapons but this was their first V2 rocket sighting.

Neil and Jack's favourite aircraft was an extremely fast Mosquito XXV code named *D-Dog*. They really enjoyed this Canadian-built de Havilland timber and canvas racing machine. Basically, it was 'a kite' and like *Q-Queenie* was fitted with two massively powerful Detroit-made Packard-Rolls Royce Merlin engines. Mosquito and aero engine production had become truly international.

In the early hours of the morning of 16 December 1944, the Germans launched a massive counter-attack in the Ardennes. Sepp Dietrich and his 6th SS Panzer division made a frenzied attempt to break through to Liège and to Luxembourg. This was the beginning of the ferocious Battle of the Bulge, which went on through Christmas 1944 and into the New Year. It came to an end in failure for the Germans on 7 January 1945. Hitler agreed to withdraw but not to surrender and as a direct consequence bombing was intensified.

Neil Nimmo was determined not to be shot down again and so he and Jack Craddock worked out their own rather unorthodox methods. Even though *D-Dog* was fast, her crew managed to do accurate work and return safely back in Britain quite astonishingly fast – much quicker than should have been possible. At the time neither of them chose to explain how they managed it, as they would certainly have been 'carpeted'.

They would fly *D-Dog* flat out across the North Sea and on over occupied territory and Germany keeping to the specified altitude. However, their survival depended on faultless navigation and piloting. Arriving early, they would locate and verify the target and then, strictly against all accepted

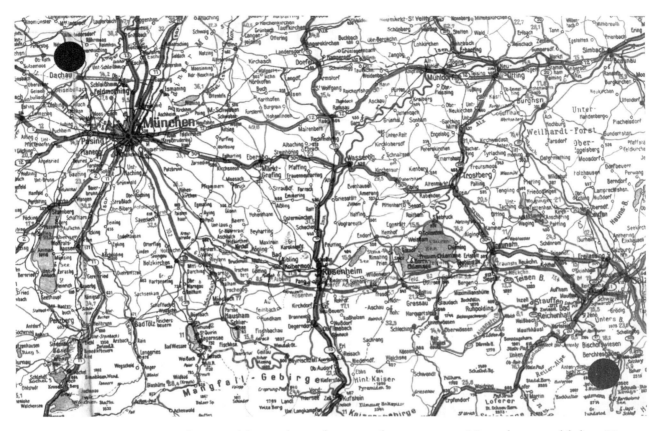

Top left, Dachau extermination camp; bottom right, Berchtesgaden. (War Office 1944 Gen Staff 448 AF 5924 1st ed, Nimmo Collection)

rules, would overshoot the target by some way. Next they would do a U-turn and, heading home allowing for wind speed and direction and their reverse route, at the specified altitude and time would drop their marker flares and bombs on the target and promptly dive down to 'hedge height'. They would then head directly home and, keeping low enough to avoid German radar detection and possible fighter attack from below, they'd race for the Channel. It was a tactic that worked. However, it called for a great deal of nerve as it meant flying back straight at the incoming bombers and diving directly under the Lancasters, which were of course about to drop their destructive loads. They had to count on their fellow pilots avoiding 'creep-back' (bombing early), as they could well be directly underneath. As a method it was a success and they often arrived back way ahead of the others. As Pathfinder Mosquitoes carried no armaments, the Mosquito's speed and handling were vital and *D-Dog* had all that in good measure.

Neil Nimmo piloted many Mosquito raids on Germany this way, including ones to Bremen, Kassel, Frankfurt, Hanau, Hannover, Nuremberg, Hamburg, Stuttgart and Berlin itself 17 times. When Göring realized that Mosquitoes escorted and took part in the Berlin raids, he announced, 'The war is over'. For once, he was right but it didn't stop Hitler.

Thankfully, Neil was not involved in the infamous Operation *Thunderclap* and in particular the ruthless Dresden firebombing on the night of 13/14 February 1945. During that night's second wave 1,800 tons of high-explosive and incendiary bombs blew apart and incinerated nearly 40 square kilometres of the old city centre, and possibly as many as 50,000 people – many of them civilians. Neil flew the following night as one of 12 Mosquitoes on a diversionary raid on Duisburg, just 25 kilometres from Bochum, Helmut Bergmann's home city.

As with many RAF European theatre aircrews, Neil and Jack's last operation was on 25 April 1945 and it was spectacular. Neil flew *D-Dog* as a pathfinder/master-bomber on a vaguely identified operation to Munich. In fact, it was an attack to the south-east on the SS barracks, the Berghof complex and Hitler's 'Eagle's Nest' at Berchtesgaden.

While the curvature of the Earth and the Bavarian Alps rendered their 'Oboe' navigation equipment all but useless, it was a beautiful day and Berchtesgaden stood out well against the grandeur and absolute beauty of the snow-covered German-Austrian alpine border. Hitler's complex was hit and badly damaged. Surviving SS troops demolished the rest to avoid the Allies turning it into a tourist attraction. Turning for home the Allied frontier was now very close and there was a general feeling of 'job done and we have survived!'

Berchtesgaden 'Munich Op', 25 April 1945. (© Imperial War Museums, C5247)

CHAPTER 15
A Sticky End

It was long after Neil Nimmo had returned from France that he began to discover what had happened to his fellow *Q-Queenie* crew members. In fact on that fateful night of 10/11 April 1944, the very worst happened to Jim Tooley, Eric Munslow and Geoff Stansfield, who now lie in the Saint Pierre Great War Cemetery at Amiens. To compound this tragedy, one stark reminder of what this violence really meant is that Eric Munslow's wife was expecting a child. Eric Munslow and his daughter Hilary would now never meet.

The four other crewmembers: Neil Nimmo, Jock Alexander, Ernest Berchell and Peter Johnson, not only survived but escaped capture. They couldn't have done this without help from the French.

That night on the Aulnoye-Aymeries raid alone, while 38 crewmembers were killed (all shot down by Bergmann), two further Allied crewmen escaped capture. In all, six were to find the help they needed on their escape

Consequences and retribution. (3rdR UOPP, Nimmo Collection)

routes home. Just four other crewmen were captured.

Any French person knew that if they were caught helping Allied airmen they faced a certain and dreadful end at the hands of the Gestapo. These *résistants* knew that along with the direct threat from the Germans, they also ran the very great risk of being denounced by less sympathetic, or simply frightened, French neighbours. It only took one careless person to seal their fate. However, these remarkable families took the risk and were ready to pay the price. Too many brave souls, such as Monsieur Duvray and his daughter's boyfriend Gilles, were captured, tortured by the Gestapo and finally shot. Neil's story, along with those of the other Allied airmen whom he met while evading capture, give a good indication of just how many selfless and generous French Allies there were in beleaguered and occupied France.

While Neil Nimmo rejoined the RAF raids on Germany, after the Liberation of France people returned home and many true *résistants* quietly faded into the background as secrecy about what they had been doing had become ingrained. However, things were not as they had been as, while the Vichy government had been ousted, much trust had been lost. With the Liberation an inevitable rendering of accounts had come and for a while pro-Axis collaborators were identified, routed out and roundly dealt with. Paris took on a very tense and fragile sort of normality.

After the war, Helmut Bergmann's shattered father had his son's remains disinterred and finally buried at Marigny, France. He gathered Bergmann's papers and albums and retrieved family photographs, making a collection which finally found peace in an attic somewhere. Eventually, the immediate Bergmann family died out and the collection was sold to Hamburg Military Antiquarian Helmut Weitze. It remains as a wonderful, yet sobering, insight into the life of a young Nazi pilot and as a reminder of the tragedy of the many lives cut short by war.[1]

The return to Paris. Some things would never be the same . . .

. . . and some would never change. Meanwhile, the war continued . . . (3rdR UOPP, Nimmo Collection)

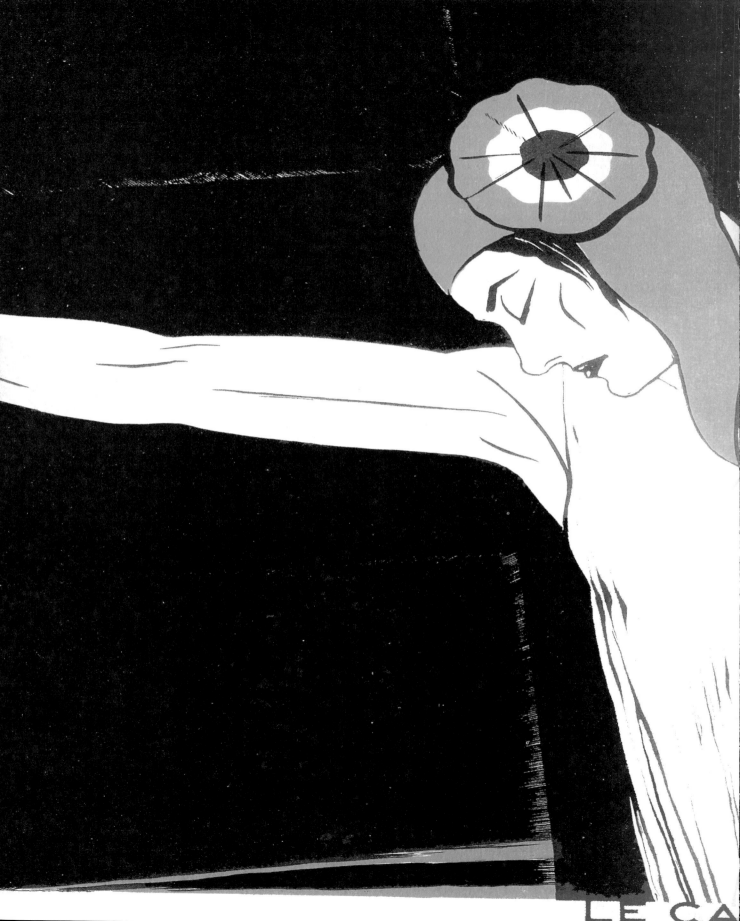

Afterword

La Belle France – La Loi du Silence

As my father Neil witnessed for himself during the last days of the Occupation, the French have a pragmatic way with facts and politics. With enough effort the unalterable can be altered and the done undone; it is quite simply the French way of doing things. That said, of course, at times other governments have admitted to being economical with the truth, so the French are not alone.

When de Gaulle returned in 1944, France was in turmoil, rudderless and highly flammable. The problem was the sheer number of factions at each other's throats: there were 'goodies' and 'baddies'; Nazis and *résistants*; the far left and the far right. There were also those who had all too often acted out of self-interest, the dangerous third that Neil described as having blown with the wind, the slippery, dangerous *résistance de dernière minute*. They were hell-bent on proving that they had always been 'good guys'. Add to that Vichy officials, undiluted Nazis such as René Bousquet and traitors such as Pierre Laval, who would not escape death and was hanged. All in all, what the Germans left behind was a seething mess. One obvious problem is that there was, and still is, no French word for 'bully'. Oddly, a bully doesn't seem to exist in France, and yet there were plenty of utterly ruthless bullies about rapidly reshaping their pasts. Often enough, the French knew it but another problem was fear which was exacerbated, amplified and even generated by power. Even among the powerful there was fear; fear of other people who simply 'knew too much'.

Thus, what Neil saw was General de Gaulle coming back to a country on the brink of anarchic civil war. De Gaulle understood this and 'did the necessary' by immediately, and somewhat outrageously, claiming to have liberated France – not only from the 3rd Reich but from the USSR, the USA, and the British. What he couldn't say, but clearly intended to do, was to liberate France from the French themselves. In his 25 August 1944 speech, de Gaulle shamelessly rewrote history. With little mention of the Allies he claimed that they! *La Résistance*! The Free French! had liberated Paris. He stated that Maréchal Pétain's Vichy state had simply been an aberration, a thing of no great importance and that it had held no legitimacy and had never actually been France. Above all, de Gaulle had

Published by Iribe in 1934 and positively prophetic. 'Is politics nothing other than the art of deliberately lying?' Voltaire (1694–1778). (Paul Iribe, Nimmo Collection)

rather optimistically reclaimed France as 'One Nation'.

'*Vive La France Libre*!' He yelled . . . and the crowds roared.

The Allies didn't much trust de Gaulle to hold things together and de Gaulle was suspicious of his allies' expansionist policies (with good reason). His heroic oratory and talk of 'One France!' were the seductive shot in the arm that the war-sickened French so craved. Following a spurt of murders

and a reasonably short period of official trials, both the hunt for collaborators and the executions stopped. By September 1944, de Gaulle's provisional government was in place and by October 1946 the fourth Republic was formed, at which point de Gaulle stepped aside.

However, the Fourth Republic was an ill-conceived thing and while various unstable governments came and went, deepening mists shrouded France's actual role during the Occupation. Vichy police and Milice records of denunciations and deportations still existed but they were suppressed and even today are kept secret, strictly locked away in French state archives. They cover horrors and treachery that were not to be discussed and not to be taught in schools in any great detail. Books and films dealing with the Occupation years were banned for decades. The French refused to expose many of the horrific wartime acts and so, very obviously, could not come to terms with them. Acts of collaboration were 'un-committed' and

Vichy Prime Minister Pierre Laval was one traitor who would not survive. Here at Compiegne station he was greeted with Nazi salutes, as he was sending three people into German forced labour camps for each liberated French military prisoner of war. (Nimmo Collection)

Laval's swap – one French POW coming off the train on the left, three deportee slaves being loaded onto the train to Germany on the right. There was never any doubt about Laval's guilt. However, he was given a highly dubious, politically expedient trial, then rapidly executed before the 1945 elections. (Nimmo Collection)

quietly swept under an increasingly lumpy carpet. However, while treacherous anti-Semites such as Capitaine Paul Sézille[1] may have conveniently died many others, such as the French Nazi René Bousquet, were to live on without penalty.

In truth, de Gaulle was probably right to do what he did; it is very difficult to see what else he could have done to stop France descending into total chaos. Everything was now '*POUR LA FRANCE*! . . . Shhh! Don't mention the rest. . . .' The danger and dire price to be paid for this state-inspired amnesia was that it offered serious war criminals vital cover, enabling some to keep their grip on positions of fearsome power, and for some to start their murderous ways again. Fearsome is the right word, and fear permeated to the very top.

As with World War I, World War II bled on into a refocused fear of communism and, for the French, a continued fear of losing their colonies

and so came the war in Indochina and deep trouble in Algeria. By 1958 France was in a state of emergency again and de Gaulle was recalled. He was to stay in power for a further, very stressed decade. Turbulence and trouble were never far off. The communists and extreme right were still vying for power and de Gaulle used repressive measures to keep dissents in check. Another favourite tool of his was the appeal to patriotism, using the Resistance. A good demonstration of this is the 'death' of the legendary French *résistant* and ex-Chartres Prefect, Jean Moulin. To try to understand this controversial subject, we have to return to the war years.

Throughout World War II and on into the 1950s, 26 rue des Plantes in the Parisian 14th arrondissement had been a hotbed of far left intrigue. Some very surprising people gathered, lived in, or passed through that building. During the German Occupation, Jean Moulin had a flat there. Then in June 1943, near Lyon the Gestapo were tipped off and raided a Resistance meeting at a doctor's surgery at Caluire. Among others, Jean Moulin was apparently arrested and tortured, and is said to have died. However, it all happened a bit oddly and his remains were never convincingly produced or found. Jean Moulin, French war hero, may also have been an active member of the Communist International (Comintern), some of his close friends certainly were. Directed from Moscow, the French Comintern often used 26 rue des

1950. A protester, injured during a battle with the police outside the offices of *Le Figaro*. There had been violent objections to the publication of a clandestine photograph of the now fugitive Waffen SS Officer Otto Skorzeny calmly sitting outside at a *café* on the Champs Elysees. (Nimmo Collection)

Above: 1951. The protests and violence continued and police tactics were highly questionable. Beatings and kicking were commonplace. Eventually, under the control of Maurice Papon, the yet to be exposed and tried Vichy War Criminal, they would turn to murder which would, in turn, lead on to the 1968 student revolution. (Nimmo Collection)

Above right: Saturday 19 May 1958. A workman at Nanterre looks at World War II-style posters as General de Gaulle bids for power. The posters are blatantly aimed at reminding the French of de Gaulle's patriotic 'One France' Free French past. He won the election, heading off revolution but he was to become very tough indeed. (*Chicago News*)

Plantes for their Paris meetings. With entrances on two different streets, the building was ideal for such comings and goings. According to British historian Patrick Marnham[2] one has to at least ask if the excessively secretive Jean Moulin was involved?

Moving on to late 1964, when his long reign was already heading for a trouble, de Gaulle felt the need to whip up a patriotic, Resistance-inspired fervour. To this end, he decided to publicly honour his World War II version of Jean d'Arc. On the icy, hushed day of 19 December 1964, bristling with sombre pomp and endless high-pitched speeches about '*La Résistance*' and '*La France Libre!*', under the reverential gaze of French (state) television cameras, de Gaulle had an imposing coffin transferred from somewhere or other and laid to rest in the Panthéon (the Paris equivalent of Westminster Abbey). De Gaulle was very publicly honouring war hero Jean Moulin with himself, de Gaulle, unusually wearing his Free French uniform, in the foreground. In doing this, de Gaulle might have been interring Jean Moulin but he was also resurrecting his own heroic, Free French past.

Historians suggest that the one dignitary who may not have been present at Jean Moulin's internment ceremony was Jean Moulin himself. There was no body in that imposing coffin as none had ever been found. It has been said that it contained a mound of SS-identified ash. However, it is highly unlikely that having captured, tortured and, it is claimed, slaughtered Moulin (who possibly took his own life en route to Germany), Klaus Barbie, 'the Butcher of Lyon', and his fellow members of the Gestapo would then save his ashes to give to post-war France. It has also been suggested that during his Panthéon ceremony, Jean Moulin was also alive and safely exiled in Moscow and even that he denounced the Caluire meeting. That hardly seems likely but there is no certainty in these matters and the allegations and questions rumble on.

Given the volatility of the situation in France at the time, de Gaulle was almost bound to call on patriotism again – as Neil saw, that is the French way of things. However, it was not enough. De Gaulle may have been papering over the cracks and optimistically presenting France as a unified nation again, but he wasn't fooled, and he certainly wasn't 'Mr Nice Guy'. In keeping with French tradition, he used the police, gendarmerie and the CRS (French para-military riot police) to hammer protesters and communists. Police brutality was rife and that combined with an under-funded education system led to the 1968 student riots and de Gaulle was finally ousted. De Gaulle might have gone, but during his time in power some of the nastier 'lumps under the carpet' had become increasingly active. These included Maurice Papon, the conspicuously guilty ex-head of the Vichy Bordeaux Police and author of many Jewish deportation orders. Papon had, within days of de Gaulle's 1944 return, made sure that he was photographed close to the conquering hero. By then, of course, Papon had rewritten his own history becoming an ardent Gaullist Free French supporter and *résistant*. Those who knew otherwise also knew better than to say anything. Papon was a truly dangerous man with no scruples.

In the 1960s, he had become de Gaulle's Paris Police Prefect and, turning his gaze on Algerian and communist protestors, used his powers to kill and maim in large numbers. Many protesters were clubbed and drowned in the Seine, there was a police-led massacre at the Paris police headquarters and people 'disappeared'. Nevertheless, de Gaulle decorated Papon, who was soon to become the French Finance Minister. That was one move too far

Blue Fear. Paul Iribe's 1934 prediction remained relevant for decades to come. (Paul Iribe, Nimmo Collection)

and his arrogance undid him. Nazi hunter Serge Klarsfeld stepped in and Papon was arrested for war crimes and brought to trial, French style.

The Prosecutor's investigation remained 'in progress' for an astounding 17 years, at which point it turned out that all the necessary evidence had always been available in those French state archives. It seemed that rather than open up embarrassing, incriminating old wounds, the State would much prefer that the old man just die . . . but he didn't. In the meantime in 1992, after years of procrastination, Paul Touvier, Lyon Milice chief and deeply racist mass murderer was also brought to trial and condemned to life in prison. Fifty years on, things were improving.

The question to be answered is, just who was responsible for letting these trials grind on so slowly? Papon's amassed inside-knowledge was deadly and he simply knew far too much. He had no remorse and defied gravity and justice by living on. Eventually, of course, his trial had to happen and in 1998 he was found guilty on several counts of Crimes Against Humanity. Characteristically, he refused to accept the verdict or to be stripped of his Légion d'Honneur. Before sentencing he fled to

In the meantime, in Spring 1958 the government fell again. The now heavily armed police protected emergency negotiations leading to General de Gaulle's return to power. The aim was to rally the French with patriotism. (*Chicago News*)

Switzerland but the Swiss immediately extradited him back to Paris by helicopter. Back in Paris he was sentenced to a remarkably short term in prison and then, on account of his old age, was released. As a defiant rude salute, Papon made sure that he was seen on national television eating at star-clad restaurants and telling the world how well he was. By the time Papon finally died he was 96 years old and had somehow persuaded the State that he should be interred with his Légion d'Honneur. Reminding me of Guy de Maupassant's ruthless, greedy antihero Georges Duroy, Papon too displayed his red Légion d'Honneur rosette 'like a splash of blood on his collar'. As one of Papon's holocaust victims said, 'As well as being a remorseless dead man, [Papon] intends to remain a vengeful corpse'.

Paris police break up a group of communists. (Richard Dale, Nimmo Collection)

Papon was not the only one to have his deeds swept under the carpet. Hardened racists such as Bousquet, the ex-head of the Vichy Police, were still at large during this time and in his case too there seemed little state appetite to do a great deal about him either. Eventually, years on, even the much-respected statesman President François Mitterrand turned out to be René Bousquet's 'personal friend'. Depressingly, on his deathbed, Mitterrand finally admitted to his own Vichy past and to having protected Bousquet from prosecution. Bousquet, and others like him who escaped attention, were party to Interior Ministry inside information – in other words, they too knew far too much.

This is not the only odd French happening in recent years. Ex-president Nicholas Sarkozy visibly involved himself with anything heroic, *la résistance* possibly being his favourite cause. He regularly turned up at anniversaries and publicly honoured French wartime heroes – much as president de Gaulle would do. It was one of his more visible political pastimes – all to the good of course. However, one did sometimes wonder if there wasn't a further agenda.

In 2009, to the distress of surviving World War II French Resistance workers, and apparently against official advice, President Sarkozy awarded the Légion d'Honneur to the founder of a large European retail chain. What distressed the Resistance families was that following the Liberation in 1944 a young man from their area, with the same name and remarkably similar credentials, was identified and sentenced to death, in particular for denouncing a group of Finistérien FTP *résistants* to Gestapo officer Herbert Schaad. However, before his execution his family produced a medical

Papon fled to Switzerland before sentencing but was promptly extradited. (Reuters/Xavier Lhospice)

certificate claiming that he was mentally unfit and so not responsible for his actions. He was released and went successfully on into big business.

The French newspaper *L'Express* published a facsimile of the post-war interrogation. However, when interviewed by them the retailer in question claimed that the affair was closed, that the dossier was empty, or that people had been confused and that it hadn't been him who denounced Resistance workers to the Gestapo.

In the meantime, relations of one of the denounced (who was shot by the Nazis) say that they always knew who that particular suspect was and who he had remained. The matter has been covered by respected French journalists (who have been pursued for their pains) and it has been widely reported by a number of top French newspapers and news agencies – among them *Le Figaro*, AFP, and *L'Express* – and broadcast in detail by *Envoyé Spécial* the much-respected France 2 documentary magazine programme.

If what has been reported is true, then this man's Legion d'Honneur sat oddly with Sarkosy's respect for *la résistance* but not at all oddly with Maurice Papon or Joseph Darnand's debased national trinkets. Whatever the truth, ensuing protest has been met with legal action and a reportedly staunch reluctance to open the French archives which cover the relevant period and which, it is claimed, would elucidate the matter. Meanwhile, the latest Court hearing on the matter would not be heard until after 2012 and any

In the fur coat, surrounded by SS and Gestapo, collaborator, René Bousquet. (Bundesarchiv, 1011-027-1475-37/ Wolfgang Vennemann)

ramifications from that event that took place in Occupied France were postponed and far from over. Then in Autumn 2012 he died and so the publicity of a court hearing and possible exposure of the state files wafted away.

The French don't claim to be paragons of civic responsibility, and generally speaking they are not, it's more a matter of *Vive La France . . . et chacun pour soi!* — every man for himself. It cannot be claimed that other nations paragons of virtue either. For example, British history involves all sorts of nastiness such as the Highland clearances and the behaviour of British authorities and troops during the Irish Potato Famine, which can both be reasonably seen as ethnic cleansing.

However, until recently, France still seemed governed by a secretive hand and the French appear so used to political obfuscation, to leaders rubbing up against 'old heroes', to VIP trials collapsing, to uncomfortable threats, and to strangely botched assassination attempts[3], that they have become very cynical and scornful of politicians.[4]

In July 1992, François Mitterrand refused to apologise for Vichy France. However, in July 1995 President Jacques Chirac bravely stuck his head above the parapet. He was the first French president to apologise for the help that the Vichy government had given the Nazis in deporting 320,000 Jews to the death camps. It seemed as if there was progress. However, it wasn't long before Jean-Marie le Pen was repeating his nationalist dogma.

Finally, On 22 July 2012 president Hollande marked an awful 70th anniversary at the memorial at *Vel' d'Hiv'*[5] (the old Paris winter velodrome close by the Eiffel Tower in the Paris 15th arrondissement).[6] He stepped up to the cameras and unequivocally described the horrendous round-up and eventual deportation to the Nazi death camps (mainly Auschwitz) as '*Un crime commis en France par la France*' – a crime committed in France by France. He went on 'the truth is hard, it is cruel . . . as with this roundup not one German soldier was mobilised . . . Not one . . . It was a [French] crime against France and her French values.'

He then went on to gracefully applaud Chirac for having been the first of seven post World War II presidents to apologise for France's roll during World War II. François Hollande may not be every Frenchman's *verre de vin*, but he seemed to be playing things refreshingly differently, one detected a whiff of honesty in the air . . . well one hopes so any way. This speech was, to those in France, almost like the Liberation all over again. Old men were close to tears, which shows how bad the denial has been, and how promising those late July 2012 public statements seem.

That said, thinking on French attitudes under Occupation, it is all too easy to criticise while conveniently forgetting that there were many others who, given the same conditions, would most probably have behaved in the same manner. One can only hope that most would have been as brave as many French people were.[7]

Many well-educated French were taught little about the inter-war and Vichy years. What they were taught – what was rammed home – was to avoid the subject. '*La Loi Du Silence*' reigned and most still don't wish to discuss it. The result is that many still seem to be ignorant or in denial and far too many toy easily with what French historian Michel Winock describes as 'Closed Nationalism'. In the 2012 French presidential election, during the first round very nearly a quarter of the French electorate voted for the Front Nationale, the National Front, something we all should think about for our own sakes as history all to easily repeats itself. Europe in particular is going through very dangerous times and when you look at financial scandals such as the Barmat brothers and the Weimar collapse the greater seem the parallels that can be drawn between those pre-war times and the scandals and dangers of related extremism today.

The World War II historian Ian Ousby sums up French post-war shame very well:

Even from the start, however, the myth could not completely stifle the sense of shame and despair to which Sartre testified. Alongside the official commemorations, an act of collective forgetting was also required. It was written quite literally into the title of André Mornet's[8] book published in 1949, *Quatre années à rayer de notre histoire (Four Years to Strike from Our History)* . . . What had to be forgotten was what the French had done to the French. . . .[9]

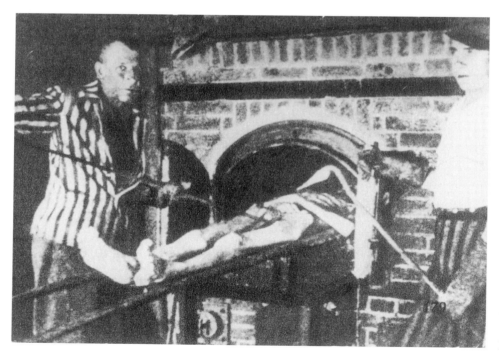

Dachau, early 1945. These three victims say it all. Their heinous crimes could have been one of many: to be Jewish, Polish, a *résistant*, a homosexual, an Armenian, a Roma or a Sinti. Alternatively, they could have been Jehovah's Witnesses, communists, unwell or disabled or, in some other awful way, simply been seen as surplus to requirements.
'To the living we owe respect, but to the dead we owe nothing but the truth.' Voltaire (1694–1778). (Bundesarchiv, 183-H26996)

Bibliography

Adders, Gebhard. *History of the German Night Fighter Force 1917–1945.* Jane's, London 1979.

Babington Smith, C. *Evidence in Camera.* Penguin, England 1961.

Beevor, Antony. *Stalingrad.* BCA, London 2005.

Beevor, Antony. *D-DAY.* Viking, New York 2009.

Bennett, Donald. *Pathfinder.* Frederick Muller, London 1958.

Boiten, Dr Theo. *Nachtjagd War Diaries.* Red Kite, 2008.

Brustein, William. *The Logic of Evil: Social Origins of Nazi Party 1925–33.* Yale University Press, New Haven, CT 1996.

Carell, Paul (Paul Karl Schmidt). *D-Day Invasion. They're Coming.* Corgi Books, England 1974.

Chamberlain, Austen. *Austen Chamberlain Diary Letters.* Cambridge University Press, England 1995.

Chorley, Bill. *Royal Air Force Bomber Command Losses 1944.* Ian Allan Midland Counties Publishing, Leicester 1997.

Deutsch, Harold. *The Conspiracy Against Hitler in the Twilight War.* University of Minnesota Press, Minneapolis 1968.

Deutsch, Harold. *Hitler and His Generals: The Hidden Crisis, January–June, 1938.* University of Minnesota Press, Minneapolis 1974.

Dreyfus, François-Georges. *Histoire de Vichy.* Librairie Académique Perrin, Paris 1990.

Foreman, John. *Fighter Command War Diaries, July 1944 to May 1945.* Air Research Publications, Walton-on-Thames 2003.

Gooderson, Ian. *Air Power at the Battlefront: Allied Close Air Support in Europe 1943–45.* Routledge, Westport, CT 1998

Hallion, Richard P. *Air Power Over the Normandy Beaches and Beyond.* US Air Force and Museums Program, 1994.

Lewis, Bruce. *Aircrew: The story of the men who flew the Bombers.* Leo Cooper, London 1991.

Marnham, Patrick. *The Death of Jean Moulin, Biography of a Ghost.* Pimlico, London 2001.

McKinstry, Leo. *Lancaster: The Second World War's Greatest Bomber.* John Murray, London 2010.

Middlebrook, Martin. *The Nuremberg Raid*. Morrow, New York 1974.

Ousby, Ian. *Occupation: The ordeal of France 1940-1944*. John Murray, London 1997.

Parssinen, Terry. *The Oster Conspiracy of 1938: The Unknown Story of the Military Plot to Kill Hitler*. Pimlico, London 2004.

Paxton, Robert and Michael Marrus. *Vichy France and the Jews*. Stanford University Press, 1981.

Robb, Graham. *Parisians: An Adventure History of Paris*. Picador, India 2010

Sereny, Gitta. *Albert Speer: His Battle with the Truth*. Picador, London 1996.

Sharp, C. Martin. *D.H. A History of de Havilland*. Airlife, 1982.

Sharp, C. Martin. & Michael J. F. Bowyer. *Mosquito*. Faber and Faber, London 1971

Sternhell, Zeev. *Neither Right nor Left: Fascist Ideology in France*. Princeton University Press, Princeton, NJ 1996

Webster, Paul. *Pétain's Crime: The full Story Of French Collaboration In The Holocaust*. Dee, Lanham, MD 1999.

Winock, Michel. *Nationalism, Anti-Semitism, and Fascism in France*. Stanford University Press, Palo Alto, CA 1998.

Other Sources

Der Angriff, 19 April 1944

Jewsbury, Wallbank. Article on inter war reparations: http://history-world.org/ww3.htm

Judt, Tony. 'France Without Glory, New York Review of Books'. Online 23 May 1996

RAF 315 Squadron Pilot List

RAF 245 Squadron. *The battle of Mortain*

Soucy, Robert J. New York Review of Books (in an online exchange). 8 August 1996

http://www.pilotfriend.com/photo_albums/timeline/ww2/Avro%20Lancaster.htm – Avro Lancaster technical details.

http://aerostories.free.fr/events/juvin/page2.html – information about the Arado 234 at Juvincourt

http://www.vectorsite.net/ttwiz_09.html – radar information.

Appendices

Appendix One

Q-Queenie Avro **Lancaster DV288 SR-Q**[1]

Current location: remains of *Q-Queenie* found at Vignacourt, Picardy, France by Dany Dhelly and Steve Gater

Type	Lancaster MKIII
Serial Number	DV288
Squadron	101
X1D	SR-D then SR-Q
Operation	Aulnoye
Departed	10 April 1944
Lost	11 April 1944

One of Serial Range DV155–DV407, DV288 was one of 200 Lancasters ordered from Metropolitan-Vickers (Metrovick) in 1941. It was probably built in Manchester during the summer and autumn of 1943 and transported to Woodford for final assembly and flight testing. This particular Avro Lancaster was a Mk III fitted with American Packard-built Rolls Royce Merlin engines. Otherwise, it was identical to the Mk I.

DV288 was delivered to 101 Sqn ABC equipped on 31 Oct 1943 as DV288 SR-D and re-registered as SR-Q. DV288 took part in the following key operations: Berlin 18/19 Nov 1943; Berlin 22/23 Nov 1943; Berlin 23/24 Nov 1943 – aborted; Berlin 26/27 Nov 1943; Berlin 2/3 Dec 1943; Berlin 16/17 Dec 1943; Berlin 29/30 Dec 1943; Nuremberg 31 March 1944 – damaged; Aulnoye 10/11 Apr 1944 – Lost. By the time the aircraft was lost, it had flown a total of approximately 150 hours.

'Airborne 23:20 10 Apr '44 from Ludford Magna to bomb the railway yards. Homebound, at 22,000 feet [sic]. Claimed by a night-fighter.'

Those of the crew who did not survive are buried in St Pierre Cemetery at Amiens.

The first five named are shown as being on their 17th sortie [sic], but both Air Gunners had each flown 34 operations. Flt Lt N. D. Nimmo, Evd; Sgt J. Alexander, Evd; PO E. J. Burchell RCAF, Evd; FO R. N. Johnson RAAF, Evd; Sgt J.A. Tooley, KIA; FS E. Munslow, KIA; Sgt G.E. Stansfield, KIA.

Appendix Two

<u>S</u>gt Jock Alexander – RAF debriefing report
Secret* (exp)

Regional RESEARCH SECTION (S.C?)   Report NO: K196   Copy No. 15

REPORT ON LOSS OF AIRCRAFT ON OPERATIONS

Aircraft: Lancaster III No. DV.288   "Q" of 101 Squadron
Date of Loss: 10/11th April, 1944   Target: Aulnoye Marshalling Yard
Position of Loss: North of Amiens – Vilancourt (Vignacourt?), homebound.
Cause of Loss: Fire caused by unseen fighter
Information from: Sgt Alexander, J. McK., Flight Engineer, on first operation
Remainder of Crew:

                Captain/Pilot: F/Lt. Nimmo, N.D. DFC,   ) On first operation
                Navigator: F/O Berchell, E. J.,   ) " "
                W/Operator: Sgt. Tooley, J.A.,   ) " "
                Air Bomber: F/O Johnson, R.N.,   ) " "
                M/U Gunner: F/Sgt. Munslow, E.J.,) On 35th operation
                Rear Gunner: Sgt Stansfield, G.,   ) " "

Route: Base – Newbury – Selsey Bill, 4942N 0100E – 4923N 0317E Target
                5018N 0353E – turn wide left – 4953N 0048E – Shoreham – Reading – Base

Narrative:

1. The Lancaster took off from Ludford Magna at 2200hrs. The outward trip was uneventful.

2. About 4 mins. Before zero hour an aircraft was seen to go down in flames at the target. Then green markers were seen and the Master Bomber gave instructions to bomb (them?) Lancaster "Q" made its run in to bomb, at about 9/ / 10,000 ft, fighter flares were sighted.

3. Informant was putting out "Window" and, after bombing the Captain ordered him to check that bombs had gone. He saw 6 x 1000lb. bombs hung up in the bomb bay. So the Pilot altered course and made a second run over the target. This time the bombs released satisfactorily, bomb doors were closed and course set on the homeward route.

4. Some time before reaching the Channel coast a defended area was sighted ahead, on track. A Lancaster was coned in searchlights, then two more Lancasters directly ahead were coned and seen to go down at intervals of a few minutes. No flack was seen.

5. About a minute–and–a–half after leaving the searchlight-area, informant saw a burst of flame in the starboard wing. Informant was beside Captain at the time watching for fighters, the Air-

Bomber was watching in the nose, but neither saw any flack or tracer, or felt or heard any explosion or shrapnel hitting the aircraft; and the gunners reported nothing. (Informant was on the intercom nearly all the time). There were no searchlights either. Informant concluded they had been attacked by an unseen fighter.

6. Informant reported the fire to the Captain, at first believing it to be in an engine. Before feathering the propeller he saw that the flames were too far aft, and burning on top of the wing, from which blobs of blazing petrol were dropping off as if coming from a fuel tank. When the Captain was satisfied of this he at once ordered the crew to bail out. Height was about 9,000 ft.

7. While informant went for Captain's chute he saw the air bomber opening the front hatch. The air-bomber jumped first, followed by the navigator and informant. The latter saw their parachutes open as he bailed out, but saw no one else leave the aircraft. He watched the Lancaster curve downwards, the fire spreading right along the wing, and finally exploding on impact with the ground. There was no explosion before that. About 2 mins. later informant landed in fields on the edge of a forest about 25 kilometres north of Amiens at a place given as Vilancourt, evidently Vignacourt.

8. Local informants stated that one member of the crew had been taken prisoner, and that 4 bodies had been found in the wrecked aircraft and were buried at Amiens???

24644/6   BC/S.30270/ORS   26th July 1944.

Notes

Introduction

[1]There is very little photographic evidence of the Occupation years in France, which is not so strange as it was hardly advisable to point a camera at the occupying Nazis. Of those photographs that were taken, few seem to have survived. Fortunately for history, the Germans themselves seemed keen to record their every move. However, despite this the dearth of available evidence in France is marked.

'3rdR UOPP' stands for '3rd Reich unidentified, original, privately taken photographs'. All such captioned photographs included in this book are reproduced from original WWII photographic prints, negatives or diapositives held in the Nimmo Collection. Found in the UK, France, Austria, Russia, Australia, Poland and Germany, they were taken by Axis soldiers or airmen of scenes they felt worth recording. Every reasonable effort has been made to identify copyright holders of the included images, but almost all were disposed of anonymously, one by one. They provide unexpected atmosphere and unique insight into events. For that reason alone they are of public interest and worth saving from oblivion.

It is believed that none of these particular photographs have been previously published and that no further negative or original example is likely to exist. Nevertheless, they are being treated with due respect and any notice of error as to their provenance will be gratefully received and fully investigated. Many of these photographs have been carefully restored. However, none have been factually altered and all are hallmarked for identification.

[2]The Allies did not completely lose their foresight as in the House of Commons there were those who spoke out very forcefully against Hitler. For example, on Thursday 13 April 1933, Nobel Peace Prize winner Sir Austen Chamberlain (Neville Chamberlain's illustrious half-brother) made a stinging attack on 'the new spirit of German nationalism'. However, it did little good. Sir Henry 'Chips' Channon, an arch Conservative, vehemently attacked Chamberlain saying: 'He [Chamberlain] is ossified, tedious, and hopelessly out of date'. Unfortunately, on 17 March 1937, the farsighted Sir Austen Chamberlain died of apoplexy leaving his very short-sighted brother Neville running the ship.

Chapter 1 – The Reluctant Hippopotamus

[1]There just might have been an eighth secret crewmember that night. 101 Squadron Ludford Magna was deeply involved in electronic war, and was the only squadron fitted with Airborne Cigar (ABC) – *Q-Queenie* was fitted with this. It consisted of radio equipment tuned to Luftwaffe frequencies, which would be used by an eighth, fluent German-speaking crewmember. It had notable success in confusing the Luftwaffe by feeding disinformation. On one occasion they were even convinced to break-off and return to base. For a long time the Luftwaffe thought these signals were broadcast from Britain. We don't know if there was an eighth crewman on this operation.

[2]Most of the bombers that were shot down in that phase of the war were victims of one of a few Luftwaffe Aces who had worked out a hideously effective technique (known to Luftwaffe pilots of the 'Von Hinten Unten' approach). One of their very experienced pilots would home in on a shoal of bombers and position himself 1,000ft or so below them, so that he could look up and see his prey silhouetted against the night sky. He would close in and, matching his speed with that of his victim, fly directly underneath, out of sight. He would then pull the fighter up vertically, raking the bomber from nose to tail with cannon fire.

[3]These aircraft may have been returning from other RAF raids on Laon or Tours.

[4]These were the facts as perceived by my father. They do not equate with the story told much later by Ernest Berchell; but then Ernest Berchell's account doesn't fit well with Sgt Jock Alexander's account either. However, the situation they were in was as desperate as it gets. When he attacked, Helmut Bergmann had doubtless killed, or badly maimed, some of the crew. My father had a stricken Lancaster to keep airborne, so to be fair, Neil could have been mistaken. It is possible that Ernest Berchell was lifting, helping or moving a badly wounded and struggling airman and not fighting him in order to get out first.

[5]This scene would haunt Neil for the rest of his life.

Chapter 2 – The Night Hunter

[1]'The Blond Helmet' was a nickname for Helmut Bergmann, who was indeed blond.

[2]*Fasan* means pheasant – the code for an expected Allied attack.

[3]Both the Luftwaffe and the RAF had a version of Window but neither side wanted to use it first and thus give the game away. A 'penny weapon', it was simply aluminium-backed

black paper strips jettisoned in their hundreds of thousands simulating a large number of aircraft. Window rendered current radar sets all but useless.

[4]In fact, fearsome inter-Ally battles were going on between Eisenhower, Churchill, and ACM Harris of RAF Bomber Command. Harris was determined to continue bombing German cities, Eisenhower wanted to bomb German logistics in occupied territories and Churchill was loath to cause more French casualties. Eisenhower eventually won and by April 1944 RAF and USAF raids concentrated on German rail networks.

[5]The Allies had their own versions of these rail/road vehicles as well.

[6]That, of course, was equally true for the Allies and the coming invasion of Occupied Europe. As far as Eisenhower was concerned, Occupied Europe's rail infrastructure and the German supply routes must be cut. However, once Operation *Overlord* had broken out from the beachheads the roles would immediately reverse – as they retreated, the German forces would be blowing up the bridges and marshalling yards and the Allies would repair them as fast as they could. However, that was a headache for the future, for the moment it was 'attack and destroy'.

[7]In fact, as it turned out, the RAF attacked all three and Tours that night.

[8]This is how Bergmann referred to RAF aircrew in his papers.

[9]When it worked, the Liechtenstein FuG202 radar with its wasp-like nose antenna was very useful, as long as it wasn't jammed by Window.

[10]A code name, *Schräge Musik* is what the German's call Jazz.

[11]Dadart's group of five comprised Antoinette Croix, her son Serge (who had infiltrated the Luftwaffe base at Courcy), Germaine Brémont, Mols Verachten a German-speaking Belgian, who worked at the German Kommandatur at Cormicy and Alfred Gaunel who was inside Juvincourt itself.

[12]*Steuerknüppel* means literally a wheel on a knobbly stick (known as the 'joystick' in the RAF).

[13]Lit. – 'You two hunters.'

[14]Lit. – 'You're joking captain, let's get it in the bag.'

[15]'Window' was first used with great effect between 24 July and 2 August 1943 during the fearsome and devastating mass raids on Hamburg. During Operation *Gomorrah* it had rendered the German radar systems all but useless.

Chapter 3 – Day One
[1]We now know that this was the N1. In those days it was the main trunk road to Paris. When I visited the spot 40 years later the road had widened and all the trees were gone. I believe that Napoleon first lined the roads with trees to give shade to his armies on the march.

[2]They were probably speaking 'Picard' or 'Steig', both heavy local dialects.

[3]After a long wait due to heavy snow cloud cover and at the last minute, on 18 February 1944 the RAF had successfully bombed Amiens prison and, in a diversion, the train station. It allowed key Resistance prisoners of the Gestapo to escape. One of them was known to have been involved in the plans for Operation *Overlord* – the coming D-Day invasion. The very low-level, mid-day attack worked and while many died, a great many escaped, including many Resistance workers scheduled for execution the following day.

[4]Under the circumstances, if caught we could and would be interrogated by the Gestapo, with all that that meant. The Geneva Convention relative to the treatment of prisoners of war was drawn up in 1929 and was grossly abused by some countries during WWII. It was rewritten in 1949. The relevant clause now reads 'Belligerents are forbidden to use pressure on a P.O.W. to supply more than the minimum information' (Encyclopaedia Britannica).

[5]I had always imagined the Somme to be a major river but when I went back with my son Keith some 45 years later, the point where I'd crossed was just a sort of watercress bed!

[6]Camps-en-Amiénois.

[7]Tap o' Noth is a very strange place in Scotland. It is a huge, conical hill that looks very like an enormous slag-heap, which is surely too vast to have been constructed by man. It is topped to this day by a walled Pictish hill fort of vitrified stone. The Picts somehow fired the stones until they fused together. It lies close to a wild, high-level plateau called the Cabrach. It was quite densely populated by the poorest of Scots families and was viable until about 1914 when the young men were called up into the Gordon Highlanders and basically wiped out during World War I. Without that generation the area was doomed and soon died off. It was largely abandoned or taken by the Lairds to add to their shooting estates.

Chapter 4 – *Die 1930er und So hoch die Erwartungen!*
[1]With its arms and motor manufacturing, Czechoslovakia was of considerable value to the 3rd Reich, and once Czech dissenters, Czech Jews and even the German Jewish Sudetendeutsche were quelled, transported or frightened into applying for exit visas, Nazi Germany took over. Before long, by brute Gestapo force the, Stellvertretender Reichsprotektor SS Obergruppenführer Reinhard Heydrich eliminated the unwanted. Happily, the French were spared Heydrich, who was tipped to move to greater things in France. However, before that could happen, on 27 May 1942 'The Butcher of Prague' was fatally attacked by SAS-trained Czech partisans and he died of septicaemia on 4 June 1942.

[2]The Allies also had planes nicknamed 'flying coffins' – the unloved American Martin B-26 and the British A. W. Whitley and Fairey Battle.

[3]Lit. – 'blind flying school'. It was used to train pilots to fly at night using instruments.

[4]Schnaufer, two years younger than Bergmann, finally claimed 50 kills.

Chapter 5 – Trapped

[1]An Old Epsomium word for coming close to unloading in your underwear.

[2]'Lyon' was in fact a common Resistance code name. It's clear that Neil had stumbled on a Resistance meeting, which must indeed have terrified M. Lyon's group as Helmut Bergmann's 7th Lancaster victim had crashed close by at Guignemicourt. Ironically, this was much closer to the signal box than *Q-Queenie*. Monsieur Lyon would have been very aware of these crashes and that due to the RAF bombing and Resistance escapes at Amiens, the Germans were out in force scouring the area. To take Neil in and hide him at a time like that was very brave indeed.

[3]China seemed to enjoy serving as a hot water bottle on cold nights in the Nissen hut at the airfield back in England. Sadly, China died while Neil was in hiding in France – he just gave up the ghost.

[4]These were the Ascq reprisals. In fact 86 villagers were massacred during the first two days of April 1944.

[5]Neil was mistaken about this. There were many communist *résistants*.

[6]From April 1944 through to the final liberation of France, the RAF increasingly bombed the French rail infrastructure. French areas held by the Germans were often wrecked with many civilian casualties. Montmartre/la Chapelle was far from being a lone tragic mistake. Caen in Normandy is just another example. The Vichy French used the RAF bombardments to their advantage. See: http://www.ina.fr/economie-et-societe/vie-sociale/video/AFE85000752/obseques-des-victimes-du-bombardement-de-la-region-parisienne.fr.html

[7]Horsemeat isn't taboo in France. In fact it's considered to be healthy, delicate, and good for children and invalids, as it's very lean.

[8]The earlier, similar security disaster had occurred on 15 March 1944, when Oberfeldwebel Helmut Treynogga and radio operator Heinz Schwarz had somehow managed to land their Messerschmitt Bf 110G at Zürich-Dübendorf in neutral Switzerland. The plane had landed intact, complete with the new secret Lichtenstein FuG202 radar. That time, it seems, Swiss neutrality had held as the tail radar units on RAF planes were still being used a month later, giving them away in droves.

[9]Unlike SS chief Ernst Kaltenbrunner, Walter Schellenberg escaped execution by convincing the Allies that he knew too much to be shot. In 1939 he had helped capture British agents and to plan an invasion of Britain. In Portugal he only just failed to trap the Duke and Duchess of Windsor. He gave evidence against his Nazi colleagues at Nuremberg, and while in Paris he was said to have been Coco Chanel's lover.

[10]There is no chance that Oberstbrigadier Masson was

fooled – he was almost certainly playing the 3rd Reich at their own game. His Swiss Security Service was indeed running like a precision cuckoo clock – bang on time and full of surprises.

[11]Gebhard Aders tells this story well in his *The History of The German Night Fighter Force*. Further research confirms the incident.

[12]The Swiss documents relating to this the top-secret German night-fighter were classified as 'secret' until 1 August 1985! The Swiss plans and photographs are still held in their Air Force Archives at Dübendorf. The diplomatic dispute between Germany and Switzerland triggered by the emergency landing did go on a bit. See: Hans H. Jucker, *Beiträge zur Schweizerischen und Deutschen Radargeschichte*; Elisabeth Bengzon and Max Kägi, The Air Force Museum Dübendorf, *Geheimer Nachtjäger in der Schweiz (Secret Night-Fighter in Switzerland)*; and Divisional Commander Ernst Wetter, *Allgemeine Schweizerische Militär-Zeitschrift 1989*.

Chapter 7 – 'The City of Light'

[1]Unfortunately, I handed this over to the RAF de-briefing officers when I arrived back in England. I wish I hadn't given it up now.

Chapter 8 – Revenge and Murder

[1]If you type Villa Etex, Paris, France into Google Earth, the camera stops at 5 rue Etex, right between what was the Royez's apartment on the second floor above the epicerie, and the modern building facing it on the other side of rue Etex. Sadly, in the late 1980s this ugly modern building replaced Lucien Royez's garage workshop.

[2]Joseph Darnand formed the Milice in early 1943. Among the first to try to play both ends at once, he was made a Waffen SS Obersturmführer for his loyalty to Hitler. He then tried to become a *résistant* and, when this failed, he finally fled to Germany where, in October 1945, he was caught and shot by the French.

[3]*Ersatz* coffee was the German term for fake coffee. *Ersatz* came into common English usage for many years.

[4]It has since been re-named simply Gare d'Austerlitz.

Chapter 10 – 'Plan B'

[1]In his unpublished memoirs, Vox notes that by early 1944 he had upset the great and the good, and while referring to himself as *le pontife de la collaboration*, swears that he held little remorse. However, he describes how his wife Liane was with the highly active '31 rue du Louvre' Resistance cell and protests that just after D-Day he 'couldn't come home without finding an American in his bed, or an RAF pilot in the bathroom' . . . Elmer and Neil!

[2]In a frightful, ironic twist, at 2:20 a.m. on 21 April one stricken Lancaster returning from the ill-fated raid, attempted to land at Croydon airfield. Overshooting the runway, it crashed into and demolished two houses at Wallington killing three of its crew and at least three civilians.

[3]On the night of 9/10 April 1944 (the night before Neil was

shot down), the RAF bombed the Lille-Déliverance marshalling yards destroying a residential area causing a major loss of life. It's said that just 24 hours later the RCAF bombed rail yards at Ghent, badly hitting a Belgian residential area.

Chapter 11 – Three Men in a Cellar

[1]'Taffy' was in fact Sergeant Arthur Pritchard, and apparently as eccentric as Neil says. His story can be found at www.BBC/Home/WW2 People's War, where I'm certain that he has referred to Neil as 'Peter' ('Pierre' was one of Neil's code names). Taffy says that after walking into the bar he'd ordered champagne, not beer!

Chapter 12 – *Der Nachrjäger Helmut Bergmann*

[1]The quantity of munitions left abandoned after the two world wars is colossal as, with all wars, a very high percentage had failed to explode. In the 1930s the French *démineurs* (bomb disposal squads) started clearing live munitions left on WWI battlefields. In 2011 they are still clearing these same WWI areas and finding an average of 1,500 kilos of live munitions every day. There is so much to find and defuse that, 90 years on, whole areas around Metz and Verdun are still closed to the public. However, if you think that's dire, Germany is reportedly clearing an average of 5,400 kilos of WWI and WWII munitions a day. (Spiegel Online)

[2]Eventually, with the liberation of Norway, an Ar 234 with an undercarriage would be captured at Stavanger. Mercifully, by that time the Luftwaffe's 'new' jet had arrived too late to save the 3rd Reich, though it had been a very close call. The captured Arado was considered booty, and so given RAF markings!

[3]Lit. – 'Is this really a go to heaven mission.'

[4]Bf 110 G4, serial number: 140320 3C + CS.

[5]The vast majority of the 300 fighters Hitler had promised for Operation *Lüttich* couldn't get there. American fighters had them pinned down to airfields around northern France. It has been claimed that no Luftwaffe fighters came within 40 miles of Mortain, and also that there were many – neither is correct. Bergmann and at least one other NJG 4 pilot certainly arrived, but they were among the very few that did.

[6]It has been claimed that Flt Lt Surman, piloting an aging RAF 604 Squadron Halifax bomber, shot Helmut Bergmann down, which is highly unlikely as 604 Squadron had already converted to de Havilland Mosquitoes. However, during August 1944, 604 briefly used a forward base in Normandy. John Surman did claim a Bf 110 kill and this claim relates to one of at least two Bf 110s the Luftwaffe lost in the area that night. It's at most a 50% possibility that his kill was Helmut Bergmann so it is likely, but it can't be stated as fact.
Paul Carell, born Paul Karl Schmidt (ex SS chief Press spokesman for von Ribbentrop) has written about the operation. However, his statements have to be seen as generally unreliable. Carell is adamant that no Luftwaffe fighters arrived, whereas at least two Bf 110s did reach Mortain that night and Helmut Bergmann piloted one of them. When Carell says 'an enemy fighter-bomber' was shot down and landed on the lead 1st SS Panzer Division tank, thus blocking the entire division for some hours, others corroborate the statement. However, it could have been Helmut Bergmann' plane. Given his position, the weather and the hour, it seems to be a strong possibility. If so, given Hitler's state of mind it would certainly be something the SS would have wished to cover-up.
There are two unverified German research sources. Translated from German, the following, as yet unverified research is apparently quoting from Otto Weidinger's *Das Reich*, vol V, Munin-Verlag, 1944 (banned in France):

> On the night of 6/7 August 1944, Helmut Bergmann with his crew, sergeant Günther Hauthal and sergeant Wilhelm Schopp, in their Me-110 (G4, factory number: 140320 3C+CS) did not return from a sortie into the Allied invasion area in Normandy. Bergman's ME 110 was shot down four kilometres north-eastwards of Mortain and fell (crashed) on a Panzer of the 1st SS-Pz.Div. Leibstandarte. This Panzer was the lead vehicle of the mass German forces at the beginning of operation "Lüttich", a large-scale attack against the Americans. There is a mention of this aeroplane falling on the Panzer. [As reported] In the LAH and the 2nd SS-Pz.Div. document "Das Reich".

Another source is SS Obersturmführer Georg Preuss' often quoted, but elusive text, 10.Kp./SS-Panzergrenadierregiment:

> It is true that one fighter bomber we shot down landed on a Panzer and destroyed it. Most other Panzer and Schützenpanzerwagen, however, fell victim to this intensive air bombardment, which lasted hours. Those Grenadiers still able to fight had spread themselves out to the left and right through the terrain's many hedges. They were happy to see that the bombers swarming like bees over our heads were finding more rewarding targets than individual men. I agreed with them. . . . After that it was over with the campaign in Normandy.

[7]*Knochensammlung* literarily means 'bone collecting'.

[8]Not so far to the north, on the other side of the Channel, Air Vice Marshal Donald Bennett was becoming increasingly frustrated. He had no time at all for British bureaucracy and saw that as far as Allied army communications were concerned, Pathfinders and Bomber Command were simply 'not in the loop'. If the results of that hadn't been so dire, the failure to communicate might have been laughable.
'Friendly fire' was depressingly common but at Falaise 'friendly bombing' reached a terrible climax. One British pilot bombed a spot held by Canadian troops who rapidly identified themselves as Allies by firing the Allied army colour code of the day, and then the carnage really began,
Pathfinders had been told nothing about the army flare system and, tragically, the Army flare colour of the day was the same as the colour chosen by Pathfinders for marking targets. The inevitable happened and the Canadians were heavily bombed taking many casualties. As the battle

moved on, so friendly fire and mid-air collisions took a dreadful toll on both sides. A lack of coordination and cooperation between Montgomery's forces and RAF Bomber Command added yet another thorn in Bennett's side and inevitably one of his lunchtime lobbying appointments ensued. This time, it was with De Guingand, Montgomery's much-respected chief of staff. Unusually, Bennett had time for this soldier and explained that in his view, the Allied armies were missing a vital trick by not keeping the RAF informed of little things such as the daily army colour codes and by not calling for Bomber Command's help even at very short notice if necessary. Bennett explained (probably not very tactfully) that they were actually there to help, not to bomb the army. It turned out to be a timely luncheon.

On the ground, the allied pincer was closing in and so Air Marshal 'Butch' Harris' loyal assistant Senior Air Staff Officer Robert Saundby passed Bennett a request. He was very sorry, but could Pathfinders help the army? Under the cover of fog the Germans appeared to be retreating towards Argentan and Grace. The bomber force was fully deployed, so could he please destroy the Germans' east–west escape road? Bennett's answer was of course 'Yes'.

Using the very dangerous H2S ground profile radar to 'see' through the fog, Pathfinders blind-marked the Germans' only escape route. A small force of spare bombers then 'plough-bombed' the area. The SS found themselves trapped in what was already a slaughterhouse. The battle loss rate was 40% though, in fact, 60% had already escaped.

Chapter 13 – Cricket on the Front Line
[1]FFI – Forces françaises de l'intérieur, or French Interior Forces, who were Resistance fighters in a more open form.

[2]The people who committed this sort of very public humiliation were often what the French still derisively call la résistance de dernière minute. They had usually been collaborators themselves and now needed to be seen to have been résistants! This behaviour was going on all over the place and they left their traces. Many of the 'souvenir photographs' of 'brave Resistance cell groups' are fakes, showing dubious people attempting to rapidly rewrite history. The last thing a genuine cell would have done was to pose for a photograph.

[3]On 23 August, Leclerc's French army arrived and the SS officer was handed over. That day Montlhéry was officially liberated by l'Armée Leclerc.

[4]SOE was short for Special Operations Executive, the British service responsible for picking and sending British agents or spies into France and other occupied territories. He had a nice reputation (secret at the time of course) of giving a personal present to all his agents before 'he sent them in'. Most oddly, he seems to have been involved with The Beatles in the 1960s.

Chapter 14 – Pathfinders
[1]Thankfully by late 1944 great improvements in accuracy were achieved.

[2]The Mosquito had become a legend and yet Donald Bennett had put up a terrific fight to have Pathfinders equipped with Mosquitoes at all. To begin with, Bennett's

absolute bête noire, The Air Ministry, declared the de Havilland Mosquito 'unfit for purpose' and 'impossible to fly at night'. At a typically feisty meeting, Bennett told them he was surprised to hear this, as he personally had been flying them at night for weeks and had found them 'excellent, no problem at all, just what we need'. He added, 'It's just a matter of knowing what you are doing . . .' The armchair brigade had no immediate answer to that so Donald Bennett got not only his Mosquitoes but also yet another furious black bureaucratic mark against his name.

[3]Mosquito Nº KB 430.

Chapter 15 – A Sticky End
[1]By the purest fluke, I found that Helmut Weitz had the Bergmann collection. To my delight, and that of my brothers, on hearing that I was writing this story, Helmut very generously invited me to his Hamburg gallery and allowed me access to all the original Bergmann documents and to select, photograph and use what I needed to tell this wider story.

Afterword
[1]Until just before the Germans invaded Paris, 21 rue de la Boétie housed Paul Rosenberg's famous art gallery. Rosenberg had connections all over Europe and knew what was happening to the east and that, as a wealthy Jewish art dealer, he and his gallery were in imminent danger. He could see what was coming and knew that he was on Nazi and Vichy lists. Therefore, he was busy moving his own and friends' art works (including works by Van Gogh and Picasso) to secret locations in France, London and New York, where he had already been invited to take refuge and to open a new gallery. At the 12th hour, Rosenberg left for America.

When the French government declared Paris an 'open city' and fled, the German and French fascists arrived. Rosenberg was proved right as one of the early addresses to be sacked was his gallery at 21 rue de la Boétie. It was seized by the violently anti-Semite Institut d'études des Questions Juives (the Institute of studies for the Jewish Question), which was one of those dire SS Nazi and French Nazi euphemisms for a group of thugs who hunted down, rounded up and deported Jews. Capitaine Paul Sézille soon became the director of this murderous organisation and he worked closely with the Gestapo in the nearby avenue Foch. (Sézille died on 20 April 1944 thus escaping execution).

Paul Rosenberg wrote to Maréchal Pétain from New York protesting at the way he, his business and his art works had been treated, saying that he knew with certainty that such a brutal, criminal regime couldn't last and that when the inevitable liberation he would take legal action against the Vichy government and those who had stolen his property. When the liberation finally came he kept his promise. However, even after the French Liberation, the French legal defence team argued that as the Vichy Government had confiscated the property and his remaining works of art, they were not his to fight for. Paul Rosenberg took his case before the Swiss Courts and won.

[2]Patrick Marnham. The Death of Jean Moulin, Biography of a Ghost.

[3]There were several very strange botched attempts on the

life of Charles de Gaulle and one on François Mitterrand, which was sadly uncovered as a bid for a sympathy vote.

[4]Every now and then (often following some pressing event), a French service, department, function or other has apologised for the roll they played during the Occupation. For example, in January 2011, it was the turn of the French Railways (SNCF). Chairman Guillaume Pepy gave Bobigny station near Paris to be converted into a memorial to the 20,000 people who were transported by the SNCF to the German border, and on from there by Deutchen Reichsbahn to Nazi extermination camps.

This was a good, if remarkably late, gesture. However, there are several doubts hanging over this contrition. SNCF seems to have been pushed into making it by, at best, ill-informed American lobbyists who had blocked SNCF from bidding for lucrative contracts to build networks across California, Maryland and Florida because of their involvement in transporting World War II prisoners east.

It should be remembered, however, that when the Vichy government had taken over in France, the SNCF had come under Vichy and German control. There were significant numbers of wartime SNCF *cheminot* who were with the Resistance and who paid with their lives. Even now, quiet heroes such as the SNCF *cheminot* 'Monsieur Lyon de St Segrée' should not be dishonoured by a convenient money-related apology.

American lobbyists may have overlooked this and also the fact that when in 1939–40 the Nazis invaded Poland, the Low Countries and France, they had long been ill-treating racial minorities. As logic would suggest, reports of camps being built and of barbaric racist behaviour had regularly leaked out to the Allies. In fact, as far back as March 1933 protest rallies were held in New York about such Nazi behaviour, and the growing influx of Jewish refugees had plenty to say. Even so, America dragged its heels, didn't want to get involved, and didn't wish to increase its incoming refugee quota. America's reticence may have been fuelled by the fact that by 1934, due to the financial crash, almost all European allies had stopped paying America World War I reparations. Also, one has to remember that while there is no doubt that American intervention would eventually enable Hitler's defeat, at that stage the USA had dire financial problems of its own.

Even so, American journalists had long been reporting on Hitler and National Socialism. From 1926, the Berlin based *Chicago Tribune* Central Europe Bureau Chief Sigrid Schultz was mixing with the Nazi elite. Schultz reported back with considerable inside knowledge. Göring suspected and threatened her but by living very bravely, and using the by-line 'John Dickson', she filed critical dispatches with false datelines from Scandinavia to *The Chicago Tribune*. As he recounts in *Berlin Diary 1934–1941* and *The Rise and Fall of the Third Reich*, William Shirer (*Chicago Tribune* and CBS) also warned of the dangers of the 3rd Reich.

In July 1938 President Roosevelt held his Évian Conference to discuss the huge influx of refugees fleeing Nazi brutality. This conference involved some 31 nations, but it failed to reach any consensus about taking the refugees in. Then, Polish resistant worker Witold Pilecki allowed himself to be captured and sent to Auschwitz. Here he organized a resistance group and by October 1940 they had smuggled camp plans and reports about an extermination programme to the outside world. However, these reports seem to have been taken as exaggerated.

The USA did not declare war on Germany in those early years of World War II. It was not until 7 December 1941, when the Japanese attacked Pearl Harbour, and 11 December 1941, when the Axis nations declared war on the USA that the declaration was accepted and the USA finally joined the war against Hitler and his allies.

In other words, it seems that it was neither for American lobbyists, nor the French government to expect the SNCF to give a simple blanket apology for transporting humans east on their way to the death camps as the issue was a vastly more complex than that.

[5]Vel d'Hiv was an infamous French-run internment camp. At the Vel d'Hiv, as with other such camps, the Vichy police requisitioned the location and then rounded up Jewish families and pack them into the hall, which had almost no facilities at all. So, steeped with misery, it rapidly turned into a human cesspit. Drancy, another such camp, was worse in that it was the railhead for the cattle trains heading east to Auschwitz. Drancy became known as *l'antichambre de la mort*, and so it was. Pitiful, shocking stories and scribbled notes filtered out of the Drancy camp – they still turn up occasionally. I found three chilling and distressing ones recently. The first was a registered envelope addressed to the French 'Capitaine [Paul] Sézille' at 'l'Institut d'études des questions Juives'. It would almost certainly have been a denunciation.

The second is a card sent from Drancy about a mother and child in Paris. I don't know if this was an informer or an inmate trying to make contact. What seems tragically sure is that a Drancy inmate had, probably fatally, given away their address at 36 rue Amelot, a house very close to the Bastille and to the Marais, in what was a predominantly Jewish area. The French sensors will have read the card. Some informed in the hope that having done so they personally were less likely to be aboard the next cattle train heading east to Poland. The third envelope was from the Paris Police Prefecture to SS Officer Heinz Röthke. It rather exposes the Paris Police Prefecture, particularly as we now know who went on to run it and how the police acted in post-war France.

Although Drancy was run by the French police, it was under the control of the SS, firstly supervised by Theodor Dannecker, then Heinz Röthke and finally Alois Brunner. All three were SS officers and extreme anti-Semites. When the war was over, all three should have stood trial. However, while in prison in Germany Dannecker committed suicide, and was found 'guilty in his absence'.

Oddly, after the war Heinz Röthke (once a barrister) worked in Lower Saxony as a legal advisor. Equally oddly, while he was sentenced to death in absentia, a succession of post war French governments failed to pursue him for Crimes Against Humanity. Heinz Röthke died with his secrets on Bastille Day July 1966. At that time Maurice Papon was the Paris prefect of police. Had Röthke been conveniently 'forgotten' simply because he knew far too much for political comfort?

Alois Brunner is said to still be alive and living in Syria. It is claimed that at about the time that East Germany collapsed, during the confusion and euphoria as The Wall came down and state archives changed hands, key papers that would have incriminated Brunner quietly disappeared, thus confounding Interpol.

Originally founded in 1923 as the Vienna-based International Criminal Police or ICP, with the Anschluss the SS took control of what would become Interpol and moved it to Berlin. Reinhard Heydrich and Ernst Kaltenbrunner were among its presidents. What the SS must have learned about international policing, criminal contacts and traffic and escape routes, and then used up to 1945 (and probably beyond) is deeply thought provoking.

[6]On 16 and 17 July 1942, 13,152 men, women and children – mainly Jewish – were rounded up in a massive *rafle* (swoop) by the French police and stuffed into the velodrome. Without facilities, food or water, the conditions became inhuman. The Swedish Ambassador tried to intervene, but in vain. These people were sent on to Drancy concentration camp and from there they were transported east to Poland and the death camps. Very few survived. It was this event that Lucien Royez had discussed with Neil.

[7]It is important to note that France was not the only nation to have opened its doors to the Germans. Following the BEF disaster, the strategically unimportant Channel Islands (which were part of the British Commonwealth) were 'demilitarised' (abandoned). Jersey and Guernsey were unnecessarily bombed and the islands were invaded on 30 June 1940. Four camps including Larger Sylt (a concentration camp, which held the island's Jewish population) were built on Alderney. Run by the SS and Organisation Todt, hundreds died. The remaining islanders had a very difficult time. Sadly, there were also accusations of collaboration and of fraternisation by women who became known locally as 'Jerry-bags'. After D-Day the islands were cut off and not liberated until early May 1945.

[8]André Mornet was the Procureur Général de la République française, (French Attorney General). Among others, Mornet condemned Mata Hari, le Maréchal Pétain and Pierre Laval to death (Pétain's sentence was commuted to life imprisonment). Mornet died in July 1955.

[9]*Quatre années à rayer de notre histoire*. Editions SELF, 1949

Appendix One
[1]Compiled and directly quoted from various sources and has not been fully verified.

Top: Letter to Vichy Jewish Question office. Capitaine Paul Sézille, was one of Vichy France's very worst. A registered letter would avoid a decent person working at *La Poste* 'losing' it. (Nimmo Collection)

Centre: Letter to Vichy Jewish Question office.
If he did actually send this letter, Hugo Brumlis had given the mother and child away. The French police censors at Drancy now had their address. A question to be asked is, who was Hugo Brumlis? It seems very likely that his name is of Bohemian-Jewish origin. Many there spoke French, so it seems probable that Hugo Brumlis fled north to Paris from Nazi persecution, only to be overtaken when Paris fell and, like many refugees, was captured and sent to Drancy. (Nimmo Collection)

Bottom: Letter to SS Officer Heinz Röthke from the Paris Police Prefecture. (Nimmo Collection)